$650

Unrelenting Readers

Unrelenting Readers:
The New Poet-Critics

PAUL M. HEDEEN
AND D. G. MYERS
EDITORS

Story Line Press
Ashland, Oregon

Published by Story Line Press, Three Oaks Farm, PO Box 1240,
Ashland, OR 97520-0055, www.storylinepress.com.

This publication was made possible thanks to the
Nicholas Roerich Museum and our individual contributors.

Book design by Sharon McCann
Cover art by George Hitchcock

Library of Congress Cataloging-in-Publication Data

Unrelenting readers : the new poet-critics /
edited by Paul M. Hedeen and D. G. Myers.
p. cm.
ISBN 1-58654-029-7
1. American poetry—20th century—History and criticism—
Theory, etc.
2. American poetry—20th century—History and criticism.
3. Criticism—United States—History—20th century.
I. Hedeen, Paul M.,1953-
II. Myers, D. G. (David Gershom)
PS323.5 .U57 2004
811'.5409—dc22
2 0 0 3 0 1 7 4 8 7

ACKNOWLEDGMENTS

In addition to the poet-critics featured here, a number of people made indispensable contributions to this anthology. After reading an essay on poet-critics by one of the editors, Dana Gioia first suggested the project. He has urged it to completion every step of the way, as has Robert McDowell of Story Line Press, who commissioned the book. Their inclusion in this anthology is a testament to the same spirit in which they have supported it all along—their utter devotion to poetry and criticism. Also owed thanks is Mark Royden Winchell, former editor of the *South Carolina Review* (and biographer of critic Cleanth Brooks) who first proposed the essay upon which this anthology is based. Others at Wartburg College and Texas A&M University who have helped include Janet McCann, Ferol Menzel, and J. Lawrence Mitchell. Olivia Coil, Linda Engel, Erin Ries, Katie McCann, Bethany Snyder, Shellie Lienhard, and Alyssa Connell offered the kind of clerical assistance that too often goes unrecognized. Kel Hocker and Ellie Miller deserve our appreciation for their brilliant eleventh-hour editing. Kate, Marian, and Sarah Hedeen and Naomi Myers have been loving, patient, and encouraging. But the ones who made possible not only this anthology but the commitments it represents—and here the editors speak for the contributors as well—are those to whom the book is dedicated.

To our parents

Contents

✻

Introduction

PAUL M. HEDEEN AND D. G. MYERS

W hat you hold in your hands is an anthology, not a manifesto. And yet this book advances the claim that a new movement of poets has arrived on the literary scene. This movement is neither geographical nor generational, though all of these poets began their careers since the late Sixties. It is united neither by gender nor race; not by its practice of "form" and not by its conviction that the poem is a "field." Simply and sheerly, it can be known by its devotion to critical intelligence. The poets in this anthology have one thing in common, which distinguishes them from their contemporaries: each of them is also a serious critic of poetry. Heirs of Sidney and Jonson, Dryden and Shelley, Stevens and Eliot, they subscribe to the Renaissance ideal of the literary career, believing that great poets are obliged to try their hands at *all* of the literary genres. For them one of the most important genres is criticism. Their allegiance, however, is not merely to an ideal of the career. Criticism is important to them because poetry is important to them. Criticism is another means for engaging in the labor of poetry. Despite the expansion and professionalization of creative writing workshops since the Second World War, and despite the fact that most of the poets in this anthology were trained in creative writing workshops, these poets do not share the belief in "creativity." They do not believe that criticism is diametrically opposed to it, belonging to a separate right-hand "side" of the brain. They do not snicker that those who *can* . . . write poetry, while those who *can't* . . . write criticism. They do not shudder that criticism is parasitical, a leech upon the body of poetry. Instead, they agree with R. P. Blackmur, a leading pre-war influence upon them, who declared that the composition of a great poem is a labor of unrelenting criticism, and the full reading of it only less so; the critical act is what is called a "creative" act, and whether by poet, critic, or serious reader, since there is an alteration, a stretching, of the sensibility as the act is done.(1)

In a phrase, the poets in this anthology are united by the conviction that poetry is *a living whole*. To neglect any part of it is not to practice poetry, but to fiddle with a hobby. Poetry cannot be the creative writing of it *simpliciter*. If poetry is only the writing of poems, then it is written badly, because it is written ignorantly. What is worse, to reduce poetry to the mere writing of it is to contribute to what troubles all lovers of poetry—its decline into cultural insignificance. Poetry is not only written; it must also be *unrelentingly read*. If not it is genuinely insignificant, for then it is the self-indulgence of sensitive souls. In loafing and inviting the soul, most contemporary poets have disdained the mind. The poets in this anthology are dedicated to undoing this neglect. In brief, they are committed to literature itself, literature as a whole. The ultimate goal of their movement is to return criticism's unrelenting readings to the center of the poetry world.

Before these poets came upon the scene, criticism had been marginalized by the way it was pursued. In the years immediately following the Second World War, as one writer recalls,

Literary criticism was enjoying a vogue. As Randall Jarrell said, some people consulted their favorite critic about the conduct of their lives as they had once consulted their clergymen. The war had left a bitter taste, and literary criticism is the art of bitter tastes.(2)

A generation later, criticism had come to leave even more of a bitter taste in poets' mouths. In 1981, for example, in the first issue of their magazine the *Reaper*, Mark Jarman and Robert McDowell—two of the poets in this anthology, just venturing out on their literary careers—pondered the relationship between poetry and criticism, and offered four conclusions:

1. Poetry, more than ever, is harnessed by and subordinate to its criticism.
2. Criticism grows out of an arbitrary neurotic sensibility.
3. Critics are creating an exclusive audience for poetry, which consists only of themselves and the poets they promote.
4. When critics cease with explanations and turn to examples, more often than not, what they like is not good: they try to invent surprises where no surprise exists.

The true function of criticism had been lost to sight. "After all," said the *Reaper*, "the poet creates and the critic analyzes that creation."(3) In conceiving criticism in these terms, Jarman and McDowell were repudiating their education. Pretty much without exception these poets' teachers were second-generation New Critics, and like any second generation, the critics had begun to dissipate their inheritance. They taught their students that the criticism of poetry is identical with the analysis of it; criticism is nothing more than explication. Young and disgusted, many student-poets of the time concluded that criticism was arrogant and even aberrant. Only someone who hated poems and considered them beneath him would want to spend a life taking them to pieces. After all, the poets of the previous generation—Richard Hugo, John Haines, Alan Dugan, Donald Justice, Robert Creeley, James Merrill, W. S. Merwin, John Ashbery, Galway Kinnell, James Wright, Philip Levine, Gary Snyder, Charles Wright, Derek Walcott—had written little or no criticism. And so they were models as much in their rejection of criticism as in their practice of poetry. Moreover, the poets in this anthology, almost without exception, were trained in the creative writing workshops, which were founded upon a strict separation of the literary sexes—"the poet creates and the critic analyzes that creation." (In 1976 the American Philosophical Society ratified the separation by reclassifying "creative arts" as distinct from the criticism of them.) Embittered by the New Criticism, many poets who came of age in the 1960s and 1970s could not imagine that criticism might be something more than explication: that criticism might be another way of enlarging a capacity for poetry.

The postwar vogue represented a betrayal of the New Criticism. Before the war, poetry, criticism, and teaching were nearly synonymous. What is now called creative writing, in fact, was originally a plan for bringing the three skills into one job description.(4) The first generation of poets to earn a living as teachers—Allen Tate, Yvor Winters, Louis Zukofsky, Robert Penn Warren, Stanley Kunitz, Theodore Roethke, Charles Olson, Josephine Miles, J. V. Cunningham, Karl Shapiro, Delmore Schwartz, Randall Jarrell—was also a generation of critics. In a book that serves as a sort of "prequel" to the volume you now hold in your hands, R. S. Gwynn has gathered the forebears of the men and women in this anthology: an entire generation of poets who were equally devoted to criticism.(5) It is an open question, in fact, whether some of them might not have been better critics than poets (more memorable, more profitable to read). Some who were primarily critics, like R. P. Blackmur and Kenneth Burke, also wrote poetry. Even publishers, like Alan Swallow and James Laughlin, doubled as poets. Indeed, when a major new critic like Cleanth Brooks appeared on the scene, it was a bit unsettling if he were *not* a poet. To an earlier generation, criticism and the writing of poetry were two aspects of the same activity, just as eating and conversation are two aspects of having dinner with someone. To the older poet-critics, in a word, the practice of criticism was *humane*.

The influx of poets back into criticism began around 1978, when the University of Michigan Press launched its series Poets on Poetry, edited by Donald Hall. Whether the Poets on Poetry were an improvement upon the bitter art of postwar criticism, however, is much to be doubted. While some poets turned to literary scholarship instead of criticism (6), most of the Poets on Poetry engaged in critical practices that very nearly entailed the abandonment of criticism. They did not write a *De Vulgari Eloquentia* or an *Apologie for Poetrie*; they gave an interview. As Bruce Bawer observes in his essay later in this volume,

> In one volume after another in this [Poets on Poetry] series, the interviews outnumber the essays; even extremely distinguished poets who have been publishing poetry for decades

. . . prove on inspection to have produced a
shockingly small body of critical prose.(7)

Even when these poets wrote an essay instead of giving an
interview, they were as likely to discuss their own poems—the cir-
cumstances under which something was written, where the inspi-
ration came from, how many drafts it went through, the back-
ground and references—as to draw attention to other poets. And
when they did get around to naming other poets, almost invariably
it was to praise them, and in the vaguest possible language ("the
poems are alive," they might say, "with rhythm and shape").
Contemporary poetry is a deluge of new books and magazine-
pieces. A fulltime specialist struggles to keep up. Not to sift
through the wreckage for what can be salvaged and not to submit
new poetry to the test of an unrelenting reading amount to
logrolling, a form of professional irresponsibility. But among the
Poets on Poetry, criticism was only rarely a sustained act of mind.
More often this criticism was a relaxing break from the day-to-day
business of writing poems, a specimen of the higher gossip. And
few seemed to suspect that this pointed to a fundamental defect in
their work. The weakening of criticism among poets denotes a dis-
dain of intelligence that will be obvious to anyone who has ever
read much contemporary poetry.

The problem is that most poets now belong to what might be
called the Creative Writing School of Literary Criticism. For "cre-
ative writers," criticism (when it is thought of at all) is thought of
as something that before anything else must be useful to them.
The poet Robert Morgan complains, for example, that since the
1970s, literary theory has had "no point of contact with the con-
cerns of most working poets."(8) The truth of this complaint is less
telling than the assumption behind it. Apparently, criticism is sup-
posed to have an instrumentalist or even vocationalist function,
assisting the professional practice of poetry. Anyone who reads
many Poets on Poetry cannot help but be struck by the absorption
with *technique*, narrowly conceived. In its extreme forms such
instrumentalist criticism overbalances into an almost compulsive
attention to details. The poet John Matthias tells of a workshop
that he took from John Berryman during a summer conference at
the University of Utah in 1959. Berryman turned to Stephen

Crane's "The Open Boat" for an example of a technique that could withstand close scrutiny. For an entire morning, he concentrated upon the first sentence of Crane's story, pointing out that it was written in iambic pentameter and repeating it over and over with varying stress:

> *None* of them knew the color of the sky.
> None of *them* knew the color of the sky.
> None of them *knew* the color of the sky.
> None of them knew the *color* of the sky.
> None of them knew the color of the *sky*.

What finally was the point of the lesson? Matthias isn't sure, but "it was a marvelous display of pedagogical virtuosity and critical ingeniousness. . . ."(9) Someone else might be struck by the deliberation, the sheer effortfulness, with which Berryman carried out the exercise. It is almost as if he believed that, by fixing his attention microscopically upon one element, he could *will* the technique to yield up its secret. Of course, this is a variation on the New Criticism's practice of "close reading." At the same time, though, it has drifted a good distance from New Critical practice, which was originally designed as a method for limiting the context of meaning to the text itself. There could be, it was argued, no knowledge of a text's subject-matter that was prior to a close reading of it; the text was the *whole* context of understanding. In Berryman's hands the context has shrunk to the scope of a sentence; there is no larger whole. And meaning is not at issue at all. The entire attention is absorbed by a technical detail. There is no answering of an argument with an argument, only with a formal analysis. A poet's vision of the human experience is seldom understood as true or false. This criticism stares past the vision to the technical features of visualizing.

Now it may be objected that this is to overstate the case because, as a matter of fact, contemporary poets are deeply suspicious of technique. In an essay on him, Henry Taylor quotes William Stafford as saying that poetry is

> not a technique, it's a kind of stance to take
> toward experience, or an attitude to take

toward immediate feelings and thoughts while you're writing. That seems important to me, but technique is something I believe I would like to avoid.

Taylor observes sharply, however, that Stafford tends to define technique in extremist terms with which few poets would ever agree:

> In one case, we have the desire to control absolutely every impulse, to work everything toward a predetermined effect or end; in another, we have a belief in rules. . . . The first method is obsessive, the second oversimplified and ignorant. Of course these ways of trying to write poems are doomed; and of course it is better to be ready for surprises. More conservative voices than Stafford's have been heard to say, for example, that a poem glides on its own melting, like a piece of ice on a hot stove, or that poetry should come as naturally as leaves to a tree.(10)

And yet Taylor is closer to confirming Stafford's dislike of technique than he realizes. On Taylor's own showing, poetry is something that glides and comes naturally; it is characterized by spontaneity; it cannot be controlled. No matter how badly someone wants to write a poem, it may still refuse to budge. Or the words may arrive when one is least expecting them, prickling the skin. Poetry cannot be written by an act of will. It is an attitude toward immediate feelings. Although he does not share Stafford's dislike for "technique," then, Taylor agrees that nothing must be allowed to mediate between feelings and the poem. His quarrel with Stafford is over terminology, not theory.

Some such romantic distinction between immediate feeling and rational mediation has a principled quality for many contemporaries. John Matthias advances another version, saying that poetry is at its best when it "seems to be demanded by the pressure of experience rather than just desired. . . ."(11) In an informational brochure, the Iowa Writers' Workshop advances yet another:

"Though we agree in part with the popular insistence that writing cannot be taught, we exist and proceed on the assumption that talent can be developed. . . ." This is very nearly creative writing's oath of office: while the mind can *control* the experience of poetry it cannot *create* it. Will, technique, rational control—these may assist a poet in developing his talent, but they cannot remedy an absence of talent. They belong to a different faculty of mind. To put it in readily familiar terms: there is a creative faculty and there is a critical faculty. Criticism is the deliberate and effortful part of a poet's life, whether he criticizes another poet or his own work in successive drafts, after the furor has cooled. Hence the absorption with technique. Technique is rational insight applied to poetry after it has been created.

The poets in this anthology reject this romantic distinction. Unlike so many Poets on Poetry, they understand clearly that the problem facing the criticism of poetry is one of unrelenting evaluation, including how to develop a vocabulary for evaluation. Although it is sometimes said that all criticism is divided into two sects—that which treats a poem as something *made* and that which treats it as something *said*—the new poet-critics find this to be a distinction with no real difference. The only way to judge how well a poem is made, they are convinced, is to judge how coherently it says what it has to say. To their minds, poetry must always be evaluated in respect to its intelligence. Their commitment is all the more remarkable because evaluation is largely without friends in contemporary literature. In academic circles all evaluation is seen as a conspiracy to dominate via the articulation of criteria. The consequence is that the criticism of poetry has been shrunk to two genres, both of which avoid intelligent evaluation—that of professional courtesy among poets, and unsmiling exegesis among academics. The poet-critics in this anthology prefer actually to read poems, and they know that this involves the hard work of evaluation.

In the decades following the New Criticism, a time during which poets' technique became their most important subject, what has gone largely unregarded are ideas. The new poet-critics are committed to sorting through contemporary poetry by means of evaluating it, usually in terms of its thinking. To assist their readers, they try to reduce another poet's work into the simplicity of order. Now this doesn't mean that they fall into the heresy of paraphrase, merely restating the "content" of poems in different words. The new poet-critics agree with Howard Nemerov that the purpose of too much superficial criticism is to turn poetry into prose as quickly as possible. The new poet-critics seek to translate the poetry not into prose but into a *view*. They are committed to ideas, not "themes." The difference is this. A literary theme is like foam; it is without edge; it offers nothing for the mind to take hold of. Instead of jerking haphazardly from theme to theme, unstitching a body of work and spilling it into a miscellany, the new poet-critics provide a generalizing structure of thought behind the cataloguing of themes. They are interested in the way a poet's entire body of work settles over time into a point of view, a firm and unmistakable response to the totality of experience.

This is not to say that the new poet-critics are not vitally interested in the question of form. All fifteen of this anthology's poets are adept at handling form in their own poems, after all. Most of them have, in one way or another, participated in the turn to "expansive poetry," the New Narrative and New Formalism.(12) But when they discuss another poet's form, they discuss the poet's mind; its movement, its rhythm, its disposition. For them poetic form is a way of *thinking*. It is a sibling to logic, prayer, algebra, or chess—a means of discovering and putting in order the truth about a portion of the human experience. Although they are practicing poets, they do not confine form, as so many of their contemporaries do, to an instrumentalist function. They do not confuse it with technique. Formal analysis is a way of *reading*—reading unrelentingly, which entails thinking along with the poet as he writes. Formal analysis is also, if need be, a way of thinking *against* a poet, answering a bad argument with a better one. The good critic reenacts the writing of a poem in the reading of it, but in doing so experiences technique as the stamp of individuality upon its thinking, the unique manner in which another person modifies an idea in handling it. Reading necessarily includes evaluation, then, because the good critic discerns a poet's individuality and assesses this poet's technical decisions in light of what he or she is trying uniquely to say.

But for the poets in this anthology, formal evaluation, as indispensable as it is, is only part of a critic's work. As in the past, the critical intelligence is also directed to two other primary tasks—a critical understanding of who the important poets are and a reflection upon the life of poetry. To sum up their movement while standing on one foot, the new poet-critics aim to redefine criticism as evaluation where "evaluation" is understood to mean not only the sorting and ranking of poets, but also the unblinking appraisal of poetry's place on the map of human experience. To use the classical terms, the critics in this anthology evaluate poetry under three headings—*poesis* (the general art of poetry), *poeta* (the individual poet), and *poema* (the poet's work, including its relationship to the culture at large).

And these are the three divisions of *Unrelenting Readers*. The first part of the book is given over to "The Art of Poetry." Elton Glaser opens the volume by reconsidering, from the perspective of a working poet, the beginnings and endings of poems. His purpose is to demonstrate the importance of "Entrances and Exits" to the means by which poems think their ideas. Louise Glück sets forth the overriding purpose of poetry, a purpose that so many contemporaries are in danger of neglecting—the pursuit of truth. Such a pursuit involves the application of intelligence to emotion to separate the honest from the merely sincere. Emily Grosholz is also interested in poetry's truth, but wishes to make clear that it belongs to practical wisdom rather than scientific knowledge—not a specialized truth, but an everyday one. In similar fashion, Jane Hirshfield associates poetry with memory and the spoken word, suggesting that humanity's one account of the whole of its experience is to be found in poetry. Rosanna Warren links the larger theoretical issues in the first part of the anthology to the formal experiments of one poet by showing how W. H. Auden both plays upon and disenchants readers' expectations for the classical alcaic.

The next section of the anthology extends the focus on individual poets. Rita Dove opens with a critical review of the whole of Derek Walcott's poetic accomplishment (a review of his *Collected Poems: 1948-1984*). For her, Walcott is important because of his bold refusal to serve as statesman-poet in the tradition of Neruda and because of his formal authority and (conflicted) cultural authenticity. Robert Hass turns to another of his generation's central influences—Robert Lowell. Hass discusses how political and cultural criticism are offered in ways purely poetic and dramatic, which again points to the larger moral purpose of poetry. Mark

Jarman discusses a third pervasive influence, the eloquent and trenchant elegist Donald Justice, whose tonally complex poems, Jarman believes, are radically under-appreciated. Robert McDowell introduces the first note of disapproval, puncturing the balloon of John Ashbery's over-inflated reputation by pointing to the pallid inconsequence at the core of Ashbery's mannered discontinuity. David Mason closes the section by returning to Derek Walcott. For him, Walcott is a poet whose "new world" perspective is created by the twin desires to be part of a contemporary literature as wide as the world and a particular literature of origins situated in the small Caribbean island of St. Lucia.

Following Mason's lead, the final section of *Unrelenting Readers* opens onto the larger world. The critics in this section consider poetry's relationship to history and culture. Mary Kinzie believes "The Poet's Calling" is to speak the truth and to recuperate the imagination's capability to speak with stamina, variety, and valor. Rachel Hadas explores the limitations and strengths of a restorative poetry. Bruce Bawer examines the interview phenomenon and its substitution of entertainment for ideas. Dana Gioia asks "Can Poetry Matter?" He answers yes, but only if it is publicly celebrated, intelligently criticized, honestly praised, and joyously performed. Finally, Robert Pinsky observes that the activity of poetry, while it may not unite American culture, remains valuable as an expression of whole personalities: the minds that think poetry—both the poet's and readers' minds—and the bodies that give poetry its voice.

Pinsky describes the wholeness upon which this volume's unrelenting readers insist. Again and again, the new poet-critics dramatize what has been lacking in contemporary American poetry: the whole personality, critical and creative, the mind of both the "creative writer" *and* the critic absorbed in one integrated calling. These critics are devoted to the whole of poetry: the ideas and the technique, the whole of the poet's collected work. The new poet-critics celebrate and enlarge poetry's place in our living culture.

1. R. P. Blackmur, "A Feather-Bed for Critics: Notes on the Profession of Writing," in *The Expense of Greatness* (New York: Arrow Editions, 1940), p. 302.

2. Anatole Broyard, *Kafka Was the Rage: A Greenwich Village Memoir* (New York: Carol Southern, 1993), p. 31.

3. *Reaper* 1 (1981): 52-53.

4. For a historical account see D. G. Myers, *The Elephants Teach: Creative Writing since 1880* (Englewood Cliffs: Prentice Hall, 1996).

5. R. S. Gwynn, ed., *The Advocates of Poetry: A Reader of American Poet-Critics of the Modernist Era* (Fayetteville: University of Arkansas Press, 1996).

6. E.g., Paul Breslin, *The Psycho-Political Muse* (Chicago: University of Chicago Press, 1987); Thomas Gardner, *Discovering Ourselves in Whitman: The Contemporary American Long Poem* (Urbana: University of Illinois Press, 1989); Timothy Steele, *Missing Measures: Modern Poetry and the Revolt against Meter* (Fayetteville: University of Arkansas Press, 1990); Wyatt Prunty, *"Fallen from the Symboled World": Precedents for the New Formalism* (Oxford: Oxford University Press, 1990); Jonathan Holden, *The Fate of Poetry* (Athens: University of Georgia Press, 1991); Laurence Goldstein, *The American Poet at the Movies: A Critical History* (Ann Arbor: University of Michigan Press, 1994); William Doreski, *The Modern Voice in American Poetry* (Gainesville: University Press of Florida, 1995); Michael Davidson, *Ghostlier Demarcations: Modern Poetry and the Material World* (Berkeley: University of California Press, 1997); and Lisa Steinman, *Masters of Repetition: Poetry, Culture, and Work in Thomson, Wordsworth, Shelley, and Emerson* (New Haven: Yale University Press, 1998).

7. See Bruce Bawer, "Talk Show: The Rise of the Literary Interview" (below).

8. Robert Morgan, *Good Measures: Essays, Interviews, and Notes on Poetry* (Baton Rouge: Louisiana State University Press, 1993), p. 18.

9. John Matthias, *Reading Old Friends: Essays, Reviews, and Poems on Poetics, 1975-1990* (Albany: State University of New York Press, 1992), p. 176.

10. Henry Taylor, *Compulsory Figures: Essays on Recent American Poets* (Baton Rouge: Louisiana State University Press, 1992), p. 147.

11. Matthias, p. 312.

12. See R. S. Gwynn, ed., *New Expansive Poetry* (Ashland: Story Line Press, 1999).

Part One:
The Art of Poetry

Entrances and Exits:
Three Key Positions in the Poem

ELTON GLASER

The problem with poetry today, as with so many other things in the 21st century, is that there is just too much of it. Who can keep up with the dozens of books published every year, let alone the thousands upon thousands of poems appearing in literary magazines? Any reader, and particularly any experienced reader who has absorbed a tradition of excellent poems in and out of the English language, soon grows frustrated and impatient at the prospect of winnowing the worthwhile poems from the chaff and the chatter and the shucks. The temptation is to throw up our hands and exclaim: *Life is short; art is too damn long.* There is for poets no shortcut to Parnassus—but might there be for readers a way of arriving at the peak of published poems without getting footsore in the foothills or dizzy on the switchbacks?

William Stafford, discussing the arrangement of poems in a book, offered some sound practical advice for the poet: "A person might pick up your book and look at the beginning to see if he likes it. And then he might look at the end to see if he still likes it—so if you have a couple of good poems, one at the beginning and one at the end, that might be a good thing."(1) What Stafford says about a collection of poems also holds true for individual poems: as readers, we look first at the entrance and exit, the poet's means of getting into and getting out of a poem, before we decide whether we want to follow the lines all the way through. We have a right to expect that any writer who makes a claim on our attention, as a poet does with a poem, should know enough about the craft to take special care with the most emphatic positions in a work, its opening and closing. If these positions are weak, what hope do we readers have that the rest of the poem will offer any recompense for our efforts?

Over the years, I have developed a test similar to the one suggested by Stafford, a kind of Early Warning System by which I quickly separate the immediately promising poems from the ones that seem unlikely to hold my interest for their entire length, even if they are relatively brief. (Many a ten-line poem can seem interminable.) Whenever I come across a new poem in a magazine, I scan three positions in the poem—the title, the first line or two, and the closing lines—to determine if the poet seems to have done anything exceptional with his or her writing. The title, the opening, the conclusion: these three elements should form a trinity of intrigue and intensity. If the poet has paid scant attention to these three positions, he or she is not likely to attract the busy, knowledgeable reader of poetry who has little time or tolerance for anything but what Marianne Moore recognized as "the genuine" in poetry.

Such a strategy, of course, is not infallible. Some good poems might be too easily dismissed because they start slowly or end not with a bang but a whimper. But I have to trust that, by playing the odds, I will not miss too many winners. Besides, it is the poet's task to invite me into the poem; I feel no obligation as a reader to plod through every work that happens to present itself to my eyes.

But the poet who wants to learn how to handle these important positions will find little help in published sources. In my own research, I have discovered no books or articles that focus on poetic titles, and only one essay on the beginning of poems, Howard Moss's "The First Line." The ending of poems is somewhat better served by Maxine Kumin's "Closing the Door," originally a lecture at the Bread Loaf Writers' Conference, and by Barbara Herrnstein Smith's thorough and valuable book, *Poetic Closure*, though even this *Study of How Poems End* is generally more appropriate for the professional reader of poems—critics or university professors— than for the poet seeking practical advice in writing poems. Scattered widely in interviews with or essays by poets, such advice may be happened upon, but only in an offhand sentence or two, not in any sustained investigation of these three crucial positions.

What I want to offer here is an account of the way titles, first lines, and last lines work in poems. I am not claiming these observations as a complete taxonomy or as a systematic inventory of initial and terminal devices; that would require an enterprising document even longer than this one. But my commentary—drawing, as it does, both on published discussions and on my own experience as poet and reader—might qualify as a modest user's guide to the effects, functions, and possibilities of these three key positions in the poem.

Titles

The first thing to be said about titles is that some very good writers don't use them. Ford Madox Ford argued that titles "as a rule do not matter much,"(2) and Robert Creeley put the point even more strongly: "It really speaks better of a poem not to have a title."(3) When we think of unlabeled poems, poets like Emily Dickinson and e. e. cummings come immediately to mind; from the evidence of their work, they apparently felt that titles were dispensable elements, perhaps even impediments that distracted the reader from the unmediated presence of the poem.

But the second thing to be said about titles is that they do get attached to poems, whether or not the poet put them there. If we want to refer to a poem by cummings, for instance, we call it by its first line, the standard editorial practice for designating any poem a poet left untitled. At its simplest level, then, a title is a "handle" by which we carry around a poem. Such handles can become cumbersome, not to mention redundant. Thus, a poem like cummings' "the Cambridge ladies who live in furnished souls" is usually abbreviated in casual references to a more easily portable title, the shorthand "Cambridge ladies."

We might argue that poets who do not use titles miss the point. First, they do not seem to realize that their poems have to be called *something*, so they might as well be the ones to christen the poems. Second, they pass up an opportunity to add an extra dimension to their work, another measure that will make their work more attractive or accessible or profound. Finally, they have not allowed themselves what Charles Wright calls the "particular pleasure in thinking up titles," titles which may even be "twice as good as the poem."(4) Look at what Wright himself has done. Whatever his poem called "Blaise Pascal Lip-Syncs the Void" might turn out to be, who could resist reading it after coming on a title like that? In the wit of its incongruous language, Wright's title holds out a promise of serious fun, reminding us that T. S. Eliot once

29

described poetry as a superior form of entertainment.

For me, the most appealing titles approach the poem at an oblique angle, piquing the reader to imagine how the title and the following lines could possibly be linked. As Jane Miller recognizes, the mind begins immediately to test out the relationship between the title that "hints and presages" and the poem that is to come: "Even a straightforward title invites conjecture about its possible use beyond a conventional, obvious meaning."(5) We most appreciate those titles that at first seem distant from the poem we are reading and then slowly reveal their unforeseen connections to it. I would confess to the same sympathies as Marvin Bell when he says that he "always liked titles that are odd . . . which offer a little surprise in the space between the title and the first line."(6) Such titles, like Bell's own "Drawn by Stones, by Earth, by Things That Have Been in the Fire," become little mysteries, miniature poems in themselves. We savor them first for the tang of their pungent phrasing, for their gnomic imagery.

Chutzpah and panache are not required, but these qualities can bring to titles a sharp pleasure that is hard to deny, as in James Tate's "Tragedy's Greatest Hits" or Charles Simic's "Baby Pictures of Famous Dictators." The poet whose titles most delight me is Wallace Stevens; in his books, the table of contents is more exciting than the collected poems of many other poets. To borrow a distinction that Tess Gallagher makes about one of her own poems: the typical Stevens title "doesn't explain, but *illuminates* the poem in the way a kite tells us the currents of wind by its swoops and feints toward earth."(7) His titles tease and float, astonish and amuse. They exemplify I. A. Richards' insight that "Words in titles operate in a peculiar suspension."(8) Stevens's titles range from "The Emperor of Ice-Cream" to "No Possum, No Sop, No Taters," from "Saint John and the Back-Ache" to "The Desire to Make Love in a Pagoda." Early in his career, Stevens claimed that his favorite poem was "The Emperor of Ice-Cream" because it exhibited something of "the essential gaudiness of poetry."(9) It's that liveliness, that flash of bright color, that love of the offbeat and the unpredictable that make his titles so immediately attractive.

Though every title ought somehow to arrest the moving eye of the reader, titles do serve many other purposes in a poem. Robert Wallace, in his useful textbook *Writing Poems*, briefly lists a few of these functions: titles may indicate a poem's subject or theme; or set the scene; or address a person or object; or highlight a crucial image; or present necessary information withheld from the body of the poem.(10) Titles may also introduce the poem's tone, or even begin the first sentence of the poem. Some of these purposes, and others not included in Wallace's list, are important enough to merit further discussion.

In a *New York Quarterly* interview, John Ashbery imagined the title as "a very small aperture into a larger area, a keyhole perhaps, or some way of getting into the poem."(11) In this metaphor, the title becomes an entry point directing the reader to the poem's central situation and allowing the reader better to understand what will follow. This kind of title is almost a neighborly gesture by the poet, helping the reader to become oriented to a new territory, whether the location is as conventional as Margaret Atwood's "This Is a Photograph of Me" or as bizarre as Craig Raine's "Martian Writes a Postcard Home."

Some titles seem so accommodating that the reader may wonder what is left to be said in the poem. James Wright probably set the fashion for these long, self-explaining titles, as in his "Depressed by a Book of Bad Poetry, I Walk Toward an Unused Pasture and Invite the Insects to Join Me." Where can you go from there? Wright seems to have created for himself a difficult problem, as if he had given away the plot of a novel in the first paragraph. But providing the reader with such advance knowledge of what will happen allows the writer to work on more subtle aspects than action, letting him concentrate on the implication of details, the nuance of sound and rhythm. In this case, Wright moves from the situation announced in the title, with its irritation and plain statement, to a quieter closing tone in which suggestive imagery replaces explicit declaration: "Then lovely, far off, a dark cricket begins / In the maple trees." As in many excellent poems, we find part of our pleasure in the distance traveled between the initial premise and the unpredictable resolution.

Titles can also work by changing our reading of the poem itself. As Ashbery noted, "The title is something that tips the whole poem in one direction or another . . . a satirical title can give a different color to a poem that might be very different if it were titled something else."(12) Of course, the perspective-altering title need not be satiric; it need only indicate how we should properly respond to the details of the poem. In this abrupt little piece by Jack Gilbert, what are we to make of the speaker's condition?

> Woke up suddenly thinking I heard crying.
> Rushed through the dark house.
> Stopped, remembering. Stood looking
> out at the bright moonlight on concrete.

The mystery of this quatrain lies in its lack of information: if we only knew what the speaker was "remembering," we could fit the actions into a meaningful context. That is, we clearly understand what he is doing, but not why he is doing it. Once the title is supplied, the lines take on a human resonance that was missing before: "Divorce." Now we can adjust the details to the emotional tone struck by the title, and the poem, though still reticent in its bare, telegraphic style, speaks of a pain and loneliness and longing that we can recognize because it is now grounded in a familiar circumstance. As Barbara Herrnstein Smith notes, titles "do not describe or define the contents of the poem so much as set it up. One may regard titles as among the linguistic resources of the poet or as more or less 'external' clues to context."(13)

Many poems make perfect sense without a title, of course, though the sense they make will be altered according to whatever title precedes the lines. In this poem by Janet Beeler Shaw, for example, the basic situation seems easily grasped:

> on the way home
> we stop at her picking garden
> gone wild since July
>
> tomato vines exploding fruit like nebulae
> red suns, green moons
> furry leaves parting
> handfuls of little gold tomatoes
> double handfuls of beefsteak tomatoes
> her whole field for our feasting
> spouts of hot juice in our mouths
> juice on our chins

seeds and juice on our clothes

eating her tomatoes the way she liked to
warm in the field
without washing

without salt

If we were presented with this poem and asked to come up with a title for it, what might we choose? "Eating Tomatoes" would certainly direct the reader to the poem's central activity, but it brings nothing to the poem that is not already evident in the lines; the title, then, would be superfluous. We might opt for a title that broadens the implications, something like "Last Taste of Summer," letting the details develop the mutability theme, with the tomato-eating as a perhaps desperate attempt to enjoy life before it expires. Coming from a slightly different—and sexier—direction, the title "Seeds and Hot Juice" would emphasize tomato-eating as a sensual pleasure akin to making love. Or, with a less erotic spin on the same theme, we could append an arch, mock-serious title in the early manner of Wallace Stevens: "Refutations of the Puritan Principle of Self-Denial."

Any of these titles would be credible, accounting for most of the particulars of the poem. But Janet Beeler Shaw's actual title is both more simple and more radical than these alternative versions; it is a title that makes us totally re-evaluate the poem, because it introduces a new context that colors every event. She calls the poem "Burial Day." Shaw's title does what M. L. Rosenthal argued that Pound's "Coming of War: Actaeon" does: it "explicitly spell[s] out the psychological pressure underlying its associative complex."(14) Reading the poem over again, we are now forced to focus on details that had slipped by before, or to recognize another significance than we had been prepared to find in our earlier interpretation. Now we understand the opening line in a new way: the speakers are "on the way home" from a funeral. Now we know why the picking garden has "gone wild since July": the gardener has died. Now we note the past tense of the verb in "eating her tomatoes the way she liked to." And now we can interpret the behavior of the tomato-eaters as a kind of ritual tribute to the dead woman, a communion feast that does not mourn the death announced in the title, but instead celebrates life in its on-going abundance, a rather pagan indulgence messy with the generative seeds and the blood-run of tomato juice spouting hot in their mouths. Shaw's title provides information that the poem itself does not have to include, a wide-angle view in which the lines take on a significance that the collective details could not convey on their own. Or rather, since the poem made sense even with our hypothetical headlines, what Shaw's title does is steer our attention down her specific course, giving coherence to individual parts that might otherwise have remained inert or puzzling, if noticed at all.

This desire to lead the reader to some special aspect of a poem also explains those titles in which the poet announces the poem's form, either to make the reader aware of the tradition which the poem continues, or to subvert the reader's expectations about a traditional form or a conventional treatment of a subject. This difference in attitudes towards tradition can be seen in the progression from Allen Tate's "Ode to the Confederate Dead" to Donald Justice's "Ode to a Dressmaker's Dummy." In our century, where the lofty is suspect and the ridiculous esteemed, poets are more likely to take the unconventional approach to literary conventions, as David Kirby does when he calls a poem "The Cows Are Going to Paris: A Pastoral."

But Tom Clark achieves something even stranger and more unsettling when he gives one of his poems the blandly generic title, "Sonnet." We come to a sonnet with a fixed sense of its form and lyric possibilities. We expect fourteen lines of iambic pentameter in any of a small number of rhyme schemes and logical structures; and we also remember that the original subject of the sonnet was romantic love, typically a male speaker's praise of his lover's beauty or his lament that the woman he loves has not returned his affections. With these expectations in mind, Tom Clark's "Sonnet" sets out to surprise the unwary reader:

> The orgasm completely
> Takes the woman out of her
> Self in a wave of ecstasy
> That spreads through all of her body.
> Her nervous, vascular and muscular

Systems participate in the act.
The muscles of the pelvis contract
And discharge a plug of mucus from the cervix
While the muscular sucking motions of the cervix
Facilitate the incoming of the semen.

At the same time the constriction of the pelvic
Muscles prevents the loss of the semen. The discharge
Makes the acid vaginal lubricant
Alkaline, so as not to destroy the spermatozoa.

Fourteen lines, yes: but where is the meter, the rhyme, the established order of the sonnet? Instead of the anticipated melody of heartfelt love, Clark offers us the flatfooted, dispassionate diction of a textbook in gynecology. His clinical language undermines the elevated romantic clichés that characterize entire volumes of bad sonnets in which lovers swoon and bosoms heave and the lines chirp as mindlessly as canaries sedated with Thorazine. When poetic forms or subjects become so familiar that they are revered without thought and duplicated without effort, then these forms and subjects must be stripped and restored until they can be seen plain again, without all the soupy varnish accumulated over the ages. Clark's impulse in using the title "Sonnet" is the same as that of Marcel Duchamp when he exhibited a reproduction of the Mona Lisa on which he had painted a mustache. Both artists want to shake up an audience that has grown too complacent about what art is; and such an audience is most easily upset when its cultural icons are mocked or disfigured in some way that demands a reconsideration of the prevailing conceptions about art. In a droll and uncharitable aphorism, Roethke made a related point: "One of the virtues of good poetry is the fact that it irritates the mediocre."(15) Tom Clark, with that outrageously innocuous title, is not trying to trash the sonnet; he is attempting to cleanse and extend our perceptions about what poems are and what they can do.

Poets are often asked: What comes first, the title or the poem? And the answer is always that titles may arrive before, during, or after the writing of the poem. Sometimes they show up like orphans on a doorstep: titles in search of a poem. Most poets have lists of phrases they are saving to use as titles, though many of these poemless titles will undoubtedly remain forever tantalizing and unfulfilled. Charles Wright once joked that he has "a whole manuscript of those—poems I didn't write because the titles were so good."(16) But whenever they come, and however they are used, titles work best when the reader finds them intriguing, flamboyant, beautiful, oblique. In poetry, first impressions count as much as they do in love.

First Lines

Writers welcome anything that will help them get started on a new work. The narrator of Donald Barthelme's short story, "The Dolt," a man struggling to compose fiction, expresses the perennial complaint of every writer: "Endings are elusive, middles are nowhere to be found, but worst of all is to begin, to begin, to begin."(17) And Nancy Willard, in a metaphor that echoes Ashbery's image of the title as a keyhole, has emphasized the importance of a story's beginning: "The material of a story offers itself to the writer like a house in which all the doors and windows are locked. Whose story is it? Whose voice does it belong to? The opening sentence is the key, the way into the house. It may let you in at the front door like a homeowner or at the window like a thief, but it lets you in."(18) Never mind why a thief, if he had a key, would break in through the window—professional ethics, perhaps?—or even how a key could open a window. Logical or not, the figure attests to the crucial role that openings play in a literary work.

But what do we actually look for in a poem's beginning? What should it do for the reader and for the rest of the poem? The bottom line is that the top lines should always pull the reader into the poem. Robert Penn Warren, using a military metaphor that probably came naturally to a Kentuckian who was a student of the Civil War, said that "The great battle of the poem is won or lost in the first line, or the first five lines anyway. If you don't get into motion by then, it's probably going to be dead."(19) And experience confirms what Warren has noted: many a poem fails because it does not unlimber until it is too late.

In a world of limited time, we give what Frost called our "passionate attention" only to those poems that compel our participation from the start. As Marvin Bell puts it: "One of the tests of a first line in a poem is probably, simply, 'do you want to read on, or

36

do you want to go out for popcorn.' "(20) When an interviewer quoted an "old gossip" who lamented, "I never should have repeated that story," Bell responded to the gossip's rueful remark with enthusiasm:

> I want to use that line. That's terrific. What an opening line—"I never should have repeated that story." That to me is where poetry is. How could you not read the next line in a poem that began that way? That works like the opening of Wright's "The Old WPA Swimming Pool in Martins Ferry, Ohio"—"I am almost afraid to write down / This thing." You have to read on. There's so much urgency, so much private power, such a sense of secrecy.(21)

Urgency, power, secrecy: these are qualities that, in the first lines of a poem, will draw us on. As readers, we react to a suspenseful beginning by moving deeper into the poem, hoping to see how the initial puzzle will be justified and resolved. We are magnetized by poems whose first attraction is an image that surprises or shocks, that promises an encounter beyond our normal experience. When Robert Bly starts off a poem with the line, "Inside the veins there are navies setting forth," we expect to get more than a recruiting pitch for the Marines—and we do. When Denise Levertov begins a poem by saying, "After I had cut off my hands," we cringe from the speaker's confession of self-mutilation, but at the same time we're too curious about this painful state of affairs to stop reading.

First lines do not have to be surrealistic or grotesque to hold a reader's eyes to the page. William Stafford has recognized that, both in the past and the present, a poet might make an effective beginning with "big initial claims"(22), citing as examples Milton's "Avenge, O Lord, thy slaughtered saints," and Ginsberg's "I saw the best minds of my generation destroyed by madness." The advantage of these forceful lines lies in their ability to command attention, to clear the mind of competing interests. The danger of such extravagant beginnings is that the fervency cannot be maintained throughout the poem, and the reader will feel conned as the lines fall off from their early intensity. "If the voice," as Stafford says, "makes extreme claims but demonstrates no quality commensurate with its demands, the poem gasps at once"(23)—and the reader lets it go, a fish that gave a mighty tug on the line but, when it was reeled in, proved too small to keep.

As readers, we react favorably to a voice that sounds much like a heightened version of our own, a voice in which we hear familiar speech renewed through some unexpected intensity or sudden torque of phrasing. M. L. Rosenthal explains that a "good many of the most memorable poems . . . seem to pick up from colloquial turns that hit the ear convincingly. One of Donne's poems begins with a shout: 'For Godsake [sic] hold your tongue, and let me love.' " (24) We might bring in, as additional examples of the living voice—either hortatory or restrained—these first lines from more recent poems: "Let's go—much as that dog goes" (Denise Levertov); "I have done it again" (Sylvia Plath); "You might come here Sunday on a whim" (Richard Hugo); "I don't know somehow it seems sufficient" (A. R. Ammons). In these openings, the diction defines one of the linguistic standards that Eliot raised in "Little Gidding": "the common word exact without vulgarity." But even vulgarity is not out of place, if that blunt speech sounds authentic, as it does in the sour beginning of Philip Larkin's "This Be the Verse": "They fuck you up, your mum and dad." In each of these cases, the ear catches something energetic and, perhaps, enigmatic, a summons to attend the poem.

The modern poet who was a genius at combining the singular inflections of a speaking voice with the echoes of the traditional iambic line was Robert Frost: we know immediately we are in the presence of a poet who can shape the language any way he wants to. We hear that relaxed authority in such lines as "You come to fetch me from my work tonight," and even in a line whose inverted syntax might sound precious or inept in the hands of a lesser writer: "Something there is that doesn't love a wall." Perhaps his greatest first line occurs in the last major poem of his career, "Directive," whose sinewy awkwardness gives it a poignant power that we do not easily forget: "Back out of all this now too much for us." Behind that line, of course, stands the opening of Wordsworth's sonnet, "The world is too much with us," but the strength of Frost's line comes more from the twisted simplicity of its syllables than from its Romantic reverberation. In "The Figure a Poem Makes," Frost argued that a "line will have the more charm for not being mechanically straight. We enjoy the straight crookedness of a good walking stick."(25) The beginning of "Directive" has that same sturdy, homemade effect.

All of these openings illustrate the advice that Richard Hugo gave to new writers in his "Nuts and Bolts" essay: "Make your first line interesting and immediate. Start, as some smarty once said, in the middle of things. . . . If Yeats had begun 'Leda and the Swan' with Zeus spotting Leda and getting an erection, Yeats would have been writing a report."(26) Hugo himself, of course, was known for the dramatic crackle of his opening lines, as in "Once more you've degraded yourself on the road," though in his later years he claimed that the "tough guy" stance was only a pose, and that even the poems that began with hard talk soon modulated into something softer: "Humphrey Bogart going in and Leslie Howard coming out."(27)

Whether the opening lines are violent or gentle, colloquial or bejeweled, they have to gain a reader's confidence through their mastery of language. In William Stafford's terms, "[R]eaders do not like to extend credit to poets: a poem must have early rewards. It must be eventful in language; there must be early and frequent verbal events."(28) The opening may be as playfully over-the-top as the first couplet of Stevens' "Bantams in Pine-Woods": "Chieftain Iffucan of Azcan in caftan / Of tan with henna hackles, halt!" Or it could eschew that startling bravura, and instead sidle into the reader's consciousness, like the beginning of Auden's "Musée des Beaux Arts," which John Berryman called the most admired lines of his generation: "About suffering they were never wrong, / The Old Masters." In either case, the poet's verbal authority makes us trust him enough to continue reading. Examples of these two stylistic extremes, what we might call the baroque and the plain-spoken, abound in 20th-century poetry. What they have in common is a savvy handling of language that is difficult to resist, whether the poem opens on something as exotic as Richard Wilbur's "Death of Sir Nihil, book the nth," or as unassuming as Donald Justice's musically melancholy line, "Everyone, everyone went away today."

In between these two poles is the voice that rings out firmly and evenly, a mid-range that arrests the ear with its solid tone—no gamelans or parlor piano, but a cello with its definite timbre grounded on the earth. This unadorned but resolute voice suggests someone who knows what he or she is talking about. Oddly, perhaps, we find this matter-of-fact voice characteristic of the generation that first grew up on modernism; Randall Jarrell, Elizabeth Bishop, Delmore Schwartz, and even Robert Lowell after the liturgical excesses of his early work. They all sing in this middle range with first lines like these: "The postman comes when I am still in bed" (Jarrell); "At low tide like this how sheer the water is" (Bishop); "Calmly we walk through this April's day" (Schwartz); "Two or three times a night, and for a month" (Lowell). The mildness, the uninsistent music of these beginnings, may owe much to the influence of Auden; whatever their provenance, they set up an atmosphere in which the reader feels comfortable and safe, in the hands of a reasonable and adult human being (though our knowledge of the poets' personal lives may temper that impression).

However much this soberness succeeds in attracting readers, it does not preclude the allure of its opposite, the poem in a comic key. Another writer from the Bishop-Lowell generation, John Berryman, often began his "Dream Songs" in a mode of reproachful or apocalyptic humor: "He stared at ruin. Ruin stared straight back," or "I don't know one damned butterfly from another." Anyone who can make us smile or snicker or guffaw will involve us in the poem. We warm up to the affectionately satiric view of the family eccentric with which Stafford opens one of his poems: "All her Kamikaze friends admired my aunt, / their leader, charmed in vinegar." Or the panache of Frank O'Hara's polished camp: "Ah nuts! It's boring reading French newspapers." Or Kenneth Koch's playful absurdities: "You were wearing your Edgar Allan Poe printed cotton blouse." The sly, the goofy, the uproarious, the witty: we are suckers for any opening that seems to guarantee the only wrinkles in our faces will come from laugh lines.

All these quotations show that there is no one right way to launch a poem. But anyone looking for a compact consideration of how good poems begin will find the best quick fix in Howard Moss's essay, "The First Line." Moss makes several very sensible points that are worth summarizing. First, he recognizes that the most successful openings "intrigue the ear *and* the mind"; they "are musical and contain an embryonic concept . . . a seed of expectation."(29) Frost, for instance, meets these criteria at the start of "An Old Man's Winter Night": "All out-of-doors looked darkly in at him." From that one line, with its tightly strung syllables that match the tension of the imagery, springs everything that develops in the poem.

Second, Moss notes that the first line, "if it is merely descriptive, . . . has to have something arresting—something implicitly dramatic, perhaps—no matter how subtly toned down."(30) Even the "drama of syntax" will do, or the drama of "the delayed verb."(31) Not very subtle, perhaps, but certainly arresting is the description with which Robert Graves opens "Recalling War": "Entrance and exit wounds are silvered clean." And e. e. cummings, that *enfant terrible* of syntactic drama, scored many successes in beginnings like "anyone lived in a pretty how town."

Moss also understands that the first line "has to allow for the possibility of going further, of going on, has to be a springboard but also to sound inevitable."(32) Williams's "By the road to the contagious hospital" exemplifies these traits, as it sounds both unfinished and complete. Finally, we are reminded that, in some poems, the opening need not be very striking: "The more narrative the poem the less dependent on the first line."(33) The narratives that comprise the later poetry of Louis Simpson, for example, usually begin with unemphatic lines, whether in a traditional story-telling form like "Once upon a time in California" or in the contemporary flatness of "At the post office he sees Joe McInnes."

Poets are caught, Moss contends, "between the desire to attain the first line and the desire to evade it."(34) He outlines three categories of first lines: the line "which is, in itself, a complete statement"; the line which needs two or three more to complete its effect; and the line which serves as a "syntactical diving board . . . with nothing particularly memorable in either the phrasing or the thought."(35) Each type has its own pitfall: "In the first kind of first line there is the threat of the grandiloquent and of stopping— of there being nothing more to be said. In the second, the danger of getting lost in a muddle—too much has been given at once. And in the third, the problem of banality—of drifting into prose."(36) Whether poets begin with the grand manner or a low mutter, the purpose is the same: to invite the reader into the poem.

Interestingly, Moss concludes the essay with a metaphor that resembles Ashbery's image of the title as keyhole and Willard's concept of a story's first sentence as the key to a locked house. For Moss, "[F]irst lines are introductions to worlds that never existed before and also parts of the world they introduce. We enter through them, but they are part of the structure, like doorways to houses."(37)

To Moss's observations about the function and effect of first lines, a few other principles might be added. The opening lines of a poem, for instance, usually set the tone and pace for what will follow. They become, in Donald Justice's phrase, "the model lines."(38) As soon as we read, "My mother would be a falconress, / And I, her gay falcon treading her wrist," we enter the rather formal, quasi-medieval world of Robert Duncan's poem. These two lines do more than establish the atmosphere and stately movement of the poem; they also announce the central relationship, conflict, and metaphor, elements which we expect the rest of the lines to maintain and extend.

In this sense, the opening of a poem can operate like the exposition in fiction, providing details that disclose the poem's context and introduce the dramatic situation. James Wright's "Blessing" does this by immediately signaling the time and place of the poem's action: "Just off the highway to Rochester, Minnesota, / Twilight bounds softly forth on the grass." Louis Simpson, always a canny poet, begins one of his poems with a sardonically self-conscious bow to this kind of conventional scene-setting:

> On the lawn at the villa—
> That's the way to start, eh, reader?
> We know where we stand—somewhere expensive—

Speaking of openings, Marvin Bell has said that the "start of a poem announces more than it knows. The very first line will often reveal the likely ratio of intelligence to feeling in what is to come."(39) Given that formulation, it seems clear that Wright's beginning suggests a more emotional approach than does Simpson's. Though both first lines are neutral, merely supplying details about location, the second lines vary in their effect, from Wright's warm metaphor to Simpson's complicitous sneer at the reader and the familiar props of literature.

If poems can begin with the kind of exposition that we are accustomed to in a short story, they can also begin with a thesis statement reminiscent—in this respect only—of a freshman essay assignment. What could be more direct than the first sentence of Denise Levertov's "Pleasures":

> I like to find
> what's not found
> at once, but lies
>
> within something of another nature,
> in repose, distinct.

Her poem goes on to develop that explicit theme through illustration, citing several examples (gull feathers, squid bones, etc.) to support the opening generalization. Despite Pound's warning, poets do not always go in fear of abstractions. In fact, probably the most celebrated opening lines of the last decade come from Robert Hass's "Meditation at Lagunitas" in which the "likely ratio of intelligence to feeling" manifestly favors intelligence: "All the new thinking is about loss. / In this it resembles all the old thinking."

Finally, we have to recognize that the opening lines make a contract with the reader about the external form and stylistic strategy of the poem, a contract that should be honored in the poem's unfolding. When Philip Larkin sets up the first four lines of "The Trees" like this—

> The trees are coming into leaf
> Like something almost said;
> The recent buds relax and spread,
> Their greenness is a kind of grief

—we notice that he has completed an iambic tetrameter quatrain rhyming a-b-b-a, and we expect that the rest of the poem will carry out this inaugural pattern. And when John Ashbery begins one of his surrealistic collage poems with this line, "The arctic honey blabbed over the report causing darkness," we know better than to wait for some sweetly tuned sonnet about the swaying grace of daffodils. Indeed, what we get are lines—long or cramped or frag-

43

mented—that defy normal analysis as they juxtapose some very strange items, including one line that ends, if not with a daffodil, then at least with another spring flower: "comfort of your perfect tar grams nuclear world bank tulip."

Like the title, then, the first line or two of a poem can work in many different ways. But these beginnings all must, in some fashion, engage the reader strongly enough that he or she will stick with the poem and not give in to the dozen other daily distractions that compete for our attention.

Last Lines

Entrances to poems have been likened to keyholes and keys and doorways. We should not be surprised, then, to find that the literary exit also has its architectural counterpart. In his *Paris Review* interview, Stanley Kunitz chose an apt metaphor for poetic closure:

> Merely to stop a poem is not to end it. I don't want to suggest that I believe in neat little resolutions. To put a logical cap on a poem is to suffocate its original impulse. Just as the truly great piece of architecture moves beyond itself into its environment, into the landscape and the sky, so the kind of poetic closure that interests me bleeds out of its ending into the whole universe of feeling and thought. I like an ending that's both a door and a window.(40)

A door and a window: in others words, a poem whose ending is also an opening, a way out. This is the paradox of effective closure: it should tightly wrap up the poem, not just let the words dribble away, but it should also be a jumping-off point for the reader, not stopping or contracting the perceptions, but expanding them, sending them out into the world again, enlarged and enriched. These contradictory qualities, along with other aspects of a poem's conclusion, deserve a closer look.

In last lines, we look first for authority and resonance. A finish should have *finish*, as on the treated wood of furniture: a gloss and a preservative. The language should seem lacquered, hard and clear and shining. And an ending needs weight, a heft that lets it anchor the whole poem. In the ideal instances, the conclusion also becomes separable and talismanic, an utterance with the force of a proverb or a gnomic revelation. The last line of Frost's "Directive," whose opening I have already praised, fulfills all these conditions: "Drink and be whole again beyond confusion." The sentence rings out with harmony and conviction. As James Merrill noted, "[Y]ou've got to end up saying the right thing . . . you don't *end* pieces with a dissonance."(41)

Certain concluding lines have a *gravitas* and polish that make them unforgettable. Tess Gallagher says that she has "always been struck by endings that fix a moment irrevocably in the memory, endings like Louise Bogan's, a line like 'The thin hound's body arched against the snow.' "(42) She also identifies such endings in her own work, where they "are allowed to rise to some peak of emotion that contemporary writers think unfashionable, as if we haven't a right to our own passions and should taper off and be noncommittal in order to sneak up on the truth,"(43) that latter point one that I will take up later. Here, what interests me is Gallagher's sense of her own "natural inclination, rushing the language into the experience until it overspills from the sheer impetus and urgency of the voice."(44) Whatever the judgment on Gallagher's own poems, the exhilaration she describes can be readily found at the end of poems like Hopkins's "God's Grandeur"— "Because the Holy Ghost over the bent / World broods with warm breast and with ah! bright wings"—or Hart Crane's "Voyages II": "The seal's wide spindrift gaze towards paradise." In both instances, pressure has been put on the language until it blazes: carbon concentrated into a diamond light.

Perhaps such examples tell us no more than that I am an admirer of the grand manner in poetic closure, the final line that is strong enough to stand on its own, the ending that has, in William Meredith's phrase, "commanding energy—dramatic, rhetorical, metaphoric."(45) If so, I am not alone. In a joint interview with Maxine Kumin, Anne Sexton remarked that both she and Kumin "have very strong feelings about a poem ending definitively. We don't like poems that trail off," to which Kumin added, "Oscar Williams said, anyone can write a poem, but who can end it? It's like slamming the door. And I said, you mean like having sex without orgasm?"(46) "Orgasmic" conclusions, whether as image or as strategy of poetic closure, are not hard to come by in either poet's work, as this sampling indicates:

> blooming, blooming, blooming
> into the sweet blood of woman.
> (Sexton)

> At night, alone, I marry the bed.
> (Sexton)

> and we are rammed home on the corkscrew gig
> one at a time
> and lugged off belly to belly.
> (Kumin)

Maxine Kumin, as I mentioned earlier, has organized her thoughts about poetic endings into a lecture presented at the Bread Loaf Writers' Conference. After complaining about "the poem that ends by simply falling off the page in an accident of imbalance, so that the reader, poor fish, doesn't actually know the poem has ended,"(47) she discusses several ways in which a poem might achieve "some definitive and actual sense of closure,"(48) and then reviews these methods in her peroration:

> Many poems succeed in shutting the door by turning back on themselves to unite beginning and ending. Pattern, rhyme, form of some sort probably serve their strongest purpose in this behest. It is possible for a poet to come down on an understatement that jars us to some apprehension of the truth; it is possible but perhaps more difficult to achieve the same goal with the anchor of prophecy, prayer, or shadow of the apocalypse. It is perhaps even harder to attain by turning or shifting the focus or tone or intent of the poem with a socket wrench just at the end.(49)

All those points and more are covered in Barbara Herrnstein Smith's impressive study, *Poetic Closure*. Though it is worth reading in its entirety, I am concerned here only with what Smith calls "special terminal features," which are considered after her long sections on "Formal Structure and Closure" and "Thematic Structure and Closure," both outside of my present focus: how to tell from the last lines whether or not a poem is worth reading. In other words, I am trying to isolate those non-structural, non-thematic qualities that make for strong closure. In a radical compression of her argument, let me briefly catalogue those special terminal features that Smith takes up, along with clarifying examples of their use.

Many of her observations stem from this insight: "The devices of closure often achieve their characteristic effect by imparting to a poem's conclusion a certain quality that is experienced by the reader as striking *validity*, a quality that leaves him with the feeling that what has just been said has the 'conclusiveness,' the settled finality, of apparently self-evident truth."(50) This "sense of an ending"—in Frank Kermode's phrase—seems aligned with what Smith terms our "sense of truth." And that alignment between closure and conviction can occur in several ways.

First, Smith states that an "utterance tends to seem valid . . . not only when it conforms to our expectations, but also when it confirms our experience."(51) We might expect such an ending to take the form of a statement, rather than an image or a metaphor, though these are not mutually exclusive possibilities. Charles Wright has argued that a poem "should end in the strongest manner possible. . . . The most interesting, of course, is an imagistic statement."(52) Smith provides no poetic examples to support her point, but I assume that this kind of ending would resemble the conclusion of Richard Wilbur's "In the Smoking Car"—"Failure, the longed-for valley, takes him in"—or Edgar Bowers's "Mountain Cemetery": "And what seems won paid for in defeat." Lines like these come close to sententiae, even when they employ figurative language, as Wilbur's ending does.

The second terminal feature that Smith addresses is the "occasional repetition" of formal elements, usually sound and rhythm, a feature distinct from the "systematic repetition" built up over the length of a poem.(53) When used in conjunction with the first type of device—the ending that seems valid because it fits our sense of what life is—occasional repetition adds a solid resonance to final lines. We can hear this effect in Louis Simpson's "To the Western World," whose ending combines both methods: "And grave by grave we civilize the ground."

Related to these devices of validity is a third quality of concluding lines: "the tone of authority," especially "the authority of unqualified assertion."(54) The authoritative line is recognized by "the relative frequency of universals, superlatives, and absolutes . . . and the relative infrequency of self-qualifying expressions,"(55) or by its reliance on "obvious hyperbole and overstatement."(56) For example, the word "only" at the end of John Ashbery's "Picture of Little J. A. in a Prospect of Flowers" helps give the lines a strong sense of closure: "And only in the light of lost words / Can we imagine our rewards." e. e. cummings goes even further at the end of "My Father Moved through Dooms of Love," with its "unqualified assertion" that "love is the whole and more than all."

Smith associates this tone of authority with lines that have a "striking sense of conviction and aphoristic rightness."(57) Her own example is the closing couplet of Shakespeare's 18th sonnet: "So long as men can breathe or eyes can see, / So long lives this, and this gives life to thee." Nearer to our own age, we might cite Stevens's "The Glass of Water," which proposes a new adage in its closure: "Among the dogs and dung, / One would continue to contend with one's ideas." The epigrammatic symmetry and concision of these endings give these lines their air of completion, of nothing left to be said.

Last lines also tend to strong closure if they exhibit "[m]etrical regularity . . . especially when accompanied by monosyllabic diction."(58) Monosyllables in a steady cadence slow down the line, a characteristic "associated with an approaching halt."(59) This effect, of course, occurs most often in accentual-syllabic poems, like James Merrill's "Timepiece": "For soon by what it tells the clock is stilled." But we can feel it, too, in free verse poems such as Philip Levine's "They Feed They Lion," where the powerful litany of lines issues in a menacing conclusion, made vivid by the sudden and inexorable footfall of iambic tetrameter "They feed they lion and he come."

Advancing her analysis, Smith explains how puns, parallelism, and antithesis can add to the impact of closure; these devices, akin to wit and epigrams, maximize other closural features in a line. Of the three, puns appear least often, possibly because the word play, to be successful, must depend on earlier lines in the poem. Look at what happens in the sixth and final stanza of Richard Wilbur's "Courtyard Thaw":

> This spring was neither fierce nor gay;
> This summary autumn fell without a tear:
> No tinkling music-box can play
> The slow, deep-grounded masses of the year.

The last line brings the earth to music as we hear a subliminal "ground bass" behind "deep-grounded masses"; it also contrasts the basso profundo tone with the "tinkling" sounds of the music-box in the preceding line. Wilbur has prepared us for this harmonious pun when he combines two seasons in the second line, giving autumn a "summery" ("summary") complexion.

Parallelism is a more common device; often occurring in the presence of alliteration, it seems to stabilize a closing line. Yeats's "Sailing to Byzantium" ends with a temporal series that typifies this effect: "Of what is past, or passing, or to come." When the parallel form displays antithesis, the sense of closure is especially strong, as these three final lines attest:

> Such violence. And such repose.
> (Richard Wilbur)

> more brave than me: more blond than you
> (e. e. cummings)

> Not public like mountains' but private like
>   companions'.
> (Donald Justice)

Smith goes on to demonstrate that many last lines earn their sense of completion through "closural allusion: references not [only] to termination, finality, repose, or stability as such, but to events which, in our nonliterary experiences, are associated with these qualities—events such as sleep, death, dusk, night, autumn, winter, descents, falls, leave-takings and home-comings."(60) Apparently, we respond strongly to last things in a last line, perhaps because, as Smith suggests, these "references to terminal motion" help us to "re-enact a physical event which itself terminates in repose or stability."(61) It is not difficult to find poems whose endings embody such closural allusions. I think immediately of Stevens's "Sunday Morning," which concludes with an image of pigeons sinking "Downward to darkness, on extended wings"; and of Wilfred Owen's "Anthem for Doomed Youth," which settles into "And each slow dusk a drawing-down of blinds"; and of Frost's "Stopping by Woods on a Snowy Evening," with its double-locked exit: "And miles to go before I sleep, / And miles to go before I sleep."

As useful and persuasive as Smith's insights are, however, they cannot account for every variety of closure. And not every ending that includes one or more of the terminal features she presents will satisfy the expert reader. Some poems, for example, go astray by closing with a strong rhetoric that seems forced. William Matthews has objected to the conclusion of James Wright's brief poem, "The Jewel," which I quote in its entirety:

> There is this cave
> In the air behind my body
> That nobody is going to touch:
> A cloister, a silence
> Closing around a blossom of fire.
> When I stand upright in the wind,
> My bones turn to dark emeralds.

Matthews characterizes the last four lines as "fancy writing," finding in them "something heraldic," so that a reader "almost expects a unicorn."(62) For him, the ending is an evasion, a retreat into fancy, a turning away from the "starkness and its challenge" of the poem's theme. While the last line offers a striking transformation in its image, it also seems unearned, ornamental, too precious to be taken seriously. Sometimes even a "deep image" can run shallow and rip the bottom out of a poem.

Those poems that try to undercut the "fancy writing" with something more colloquial can also show strain. Robert Bly, in a criticism of *kayak*, noted that often the magazine's contributors would, in closing, use "an image with literary resonance," and instantly follow that "with an off-hand remark from the world of truck-drivers."(63) Among the examples he cites is this conclusion: "Another beer truck comes to town, / chased by a dog on three legs. / Batman lies drunk in the weeds." In this type of poem, there is a deliberate attempt to avoid the risk of pomposity. But a poem that is determined not to soar often doesn't get off the ground at all.

The language of a last line does not have to be unusual or extravagant; it just has to be the right language for that particular place in the poem. Sometimes even a simple shift in syntax can turn a dull phrase into a memorable one, as at the end of Galway Kinnell's poem, "How Many Nights":

> and above me
> a wild crow crying *yaw yaw yaw*
> from a branch nothing cried from ever in my life.

The poignancy here comes from the masterful placement of the adverb "ever." In a more normal word order, the line would read: "from a branch nothing ever cried from in my life." But that conventional syntax renders the line rhythmically limp, and calls too much attention to the double use of the preposition "from," making the phrase sound a little clumsy and lethargic. Kinnell's subtly unorthodox word order puts a muscular emphasis on "ever," the emotional fulcrum of the line. The positioning of that small adverb makes us recognize again how mysterious the ordinary is, which is exactly what poetry ought always to do.

Even if a poem lacks dramatic closure, it need not be a failure. Barbara Herrnstein Smith recognizes an effect, especially in modern poetry, that she variously calls "closure without resolution"(64) or "anti-closure and hidden closure."(65) Poems of this kind "reflect a general preference for, and deliberate cultivation of, the *expressive* qualities of weak closure: even when the poem is firmly closed, it is not usually slammed shut—the lock may be secure, but the 'click' has been muffled."(66) Which is to say that the last-line test for assessing a poem's poetic value is not foolproof: the ending may be in itself relatively undistinguished, while the poem as a whole may be very successful. In our time, the poems of William

Carlos Williams and his diverse followers best exemplify this situation. If we made our judgment only on the final line of Williams's "Complaint," would we feel compelled to read the poem at all? Would an ending like "with compassion" stir us in any way? And yet, "Complaint" is a glorious poem, direct and human and decently exuberant in the midst of pain, its first line thrilling in its heroic resignation:

> They call me and I go.
> It is a frozen road
> past midnight, a dust
> of snow caught
> in the rigid wheeltracks.
> The door opens.
> I smile, enter and
> shake off the cold.
> Here is a great woman
> on her side in the bed.
> She is sick,
> perhaps vomiting,
> perhaps laboring
> to give birth to
> a tenth child. Joy! Joy!
> Night is a room
> darkened for lovers,
> through the jalousies the sun
> has sent one gold needle!
> I pick the hair from her eyes
> and watch her misery
> with compassion.

Smith suggests that the predilection for anti-closure stems from a poet's "effort toward poetic realism, where structural or other features that mark the work as a verbal artifact—rather than a direct transcription of personal utterance—are avoided."(67) That principle, however, may be valid only if we willfully deny the obvious—namely, that a poem, by its very nature, is always a "verbal artifact." We may have to admit that a few worthwhile poems have been written according to the aesthetic of "poetic realism," intentionally weak endings and all, but we should not encourage a theory which is proved so seldom in practice.

We could also argue, of course, that the opposite effect is equally true: a brilliant ending can salvage a poem that is otherwise mediocre or unattractive. As Maxine Kumin puts it, "some lapses can be forgiven the poet if he finishes well, just as they can be forgiven the lover."(68) What can't we forgive a poem that ends "With goddesses, mortal women, pigs, and homecoming," a series that makes perfect sense in context (Penelope's gloss on the return of Ulysses, in Alicia Ostriker's "Homecoming"), but thrills us first with its happy air of random selection? Nothing in the poem's preceding 34 lines is quite as good (even taken as mock-epic rhetoric, "Cold was his anger, and incredibly / Loosed was her burden of control at last" sounds stiff and manipulative), but those earlier lines take on a reflective glow from the strong conclusion.

M. L. Rosenthal makes the same point in his discussion of Philip Larkin's "High Windows." Rosenthal is disturbed by what he calls "the deliberate grossness and almost malicious irony of the first stanza"(69) which begins, "When I see a couple of kids / And guess he's fucking her and she's / Taking pills or wearing a diaphragm." Against those lines he sets "the contrasting purity of expression and paradoxical melancholy of the closing stanza":(70)

> Rather than words comes the thought of high
>   windows:
> The sun-comprehending glass,
> And beyond it, the deep blue air, that shows
> Nothing, and is nowhere, and is endless.

Rosenthal argues that "the closing stanza redeems the partial paltriness of what precedes it."(71) I do not have the problem that Rosenthal does with the casual vulgarity of Larkin's opening lines, but I can agree that the elevated ending "provides a strange balance, for it can hardly satisfy the human dream of a truly rich freedom although its phrasing presents the dream in appropriate terms."(72) Indeed, the final line has that quality of absoluteness that Smith noted as one hallmark of strong closure, along with a lilting rhythm that suggests freedom, not constriction. It is noteworthy that the last word of the poem, its very end, is "endless," as if Larkin is both closing and opening the poem at the same time.

Stanley Kunitz's favored ending, one that is "both a door and a window,"(73) appeals to many poets. Louis Simpson once told an interviewer: "I try to leave my poems at the end with a kind of openness about them. I never try to finish them."(74) Put another way, the end of a poem should make the same impact that a haiku does. The haiku, with its seventeen Japanese syllables, is so brief that it seems to be simultaneously a beginning and an ending. Just as the first lines of a poem ought to contain the seeds of the poem's development and conclusion, so the last lines ought to initiate a new train of thought or feeling that carries us well past the final period. As Lewis Mackenzie, translator of the poems of Issa, explains, the concentrated form of the haiku leads the reader on "to draw conclusions or to supply what is unexpressed."(75) The haiku, with its precise but unexplained image, offers a model for the closure of other poems, perhaps especially those that seek to conclude with key elements held in a state of harmonious tension. This haiku by Buson—

> A butterfly settles
> on the neckplate of
> a warrior in ambush—

operates on a principle of unresolved conjunction/disjunction that can also be found in a poet like Wallace Stevens, whose poems often concern themselves with that wavering area between the exact and the indefinite, sometimes isolating that ambiguity in the last line: "That fluttering things have so distinct a shade"; "In ghostlier demarcations, keener sounds." We see this reluctance to bolt the door even more clearly in the work of Charles Wright, whose frequent use of the ellipsis leaves things ajar even at the end of poems: "The land of the chosen has one door, there is no knob . . ."; "Angel, omega, silence, silence . . ."; "Released as a glint, as a flash, as a spark. . . ."

Whatever the mode of the ending, it must agree with a reader's sense of conclusion. (And a poet's: Tess Gallagher argues that "the way in which you finish a poem is the most important place in the poem, the place where you're going to satisfy or disappoint the urges that got you to write the poem in the first place."[76]) As

54

Yeats famously said, the poem must close like the click of a box lid—though today we might change the desired sound to the solid thunk of a Mercedes-Benz's door slamming shut. But if we first feel drawn to a poem because the language of its ending promises pleasure in the prior lines, we will ultimately have to judge that ending in its context; in Barbara Herrnstein Smith's terms, we need to evaluate the structural and/or thematic closure of the poem.

Howard Nemerov, in his essay, "Bottom's Dream: The Likeness of Poems and Jokes," provides an interesting explanation of the way that poetic endings relate to the rest of the poem. He reasons that the enjoyment we find in poems and jokes "must come from the fulfillment of an expectation that the resolution in both instances will make use very purely, indeed exclusively, of the given materials, plus our surprise at the use made, which as straight men for the occasion we should not have thought of."(77) As his comic example, he calls up an old schoolyard riddle:

> Question: How do you catch lions in the desert?
> Answer: You strain off the sand, and the remainder
> will be lions.

In Nemerov's analysis, the punchline works because it is an economical revision of the joke's beginning—the same elements occur, but in a changed relationship. This surprising resolution of recycled material is also a feature of poetry. One of Stephen Crane's simple and disturbing poems can serve as the poetic counterpart to the lion joke; it even uses the same setting:

> In the desert
> I saw a creature, naked, bestial,
> Who, squatting upon the ground,
> Held his heart in his hands,
> And ate of it.
> I said: "Is it good, friend?"
> "It is bitter—bitter," he answered;
> "But I like it
> Because it is bitter,
> And because it is my heart."

There's nothing funny about that piece. But, as Nemerov notes, the essential linkage between poems and jokes is not laughter, it is "the quality of decisiveness and finish, of absolute completion to which nothing need be added nor could be added: not laughter, but the silence with which we greet the thing absolutely done."(78) In that passage, he might easily have been talking about the characteristics of strong closure. Nemerov further speculates that this shared virtue of decisiveness and finish "may seem to mean that their endings are somehow contained in their beginnings."(79)

And we, too, are back where we started, as closings return us to openings, and exits become entrances. Though I have been separating titles, first lines, and last lines from the poem as a whole, it is clear that these elements, important as they are, cannot define the entire work, any more than we could conjure up a collie with nothing more than a damp nose and a wagging tail. Still, if we encounter first only those elements that begin and end the poem, and then judge from their quality whether or not the whole poem is worth our attention, we will be doing ourselves a favor. Bad poetry does not, like bad money, drive out the good, but it certainly makes finding the good poems more difficult and time-consuming. Rejecting a poem because its opening is conventional and its ending is flat may not be an unerring way to judge the value of a complete poem, but, given the long odds against coming across an artful and rewarding poem in any miscellaneous gathering of poetry, that is surely the way to bet.

1. William Stafford, *Writing the Australian Crawl: Views on the Writer's Vocation* (Ann Arbor: University of Michigan Press, 1978), p. 115.

2. Nicholas Delbanco, "Judgment: An Essay," in *Writers on Writing: A Bread Loaf Anthology*, ed. Robert Pack and Jay Parini (Hanover, N.H.: Middlebury College, 1991), p. 30.

3. Robert Creeley, "Craft Interview with Robert Creeley," in *The Craft of Poetry: Interviews from the New York Quarterly*, ed. William Packard (Garden City, NY: Doubleday, 1974), p. 208.

4. Charles Wright, "Language, Landscape, and the Idea of God: A Conversation," *The Iron Mountain Review* 8 (Spring 1992): 27.

5. Jane Miller, *Working Time: Essays on Poetry, Culture, and Travel* (Ann Arbor: University of Michigan Press, 1992), p. 55.

6. Marvin Bell, *Old Snow Just Melting: Essays and Interviews* (Ann Arbor: University of Michigan Press, 1983), pp. 135–36.

7. Tess Gallagher, *A Concert of Tenses: Essays on Poetry* (Ann Arbor: University of Michigan Press, 1986), p. 84.

8. I. A. Richards, "Poetic Process and Literary Analysis," in *Poems in the Making*, ed. Walker Gibson (Boston: Houghton Mifflin, 1963), p. 232.

9. Wallace Stevens, *Letters of Wallace Stevens*, ed. Holly Stevens (New York: Knopf, 1966), p. 263.

10. Robert Wallace, *Writing Poems*, 3rd ed. (New York: Harper Collins, 1991), p. 335.

11. John Ashbery, "Craft Interview with John Ashbery," in *The Craft of Poetry: Interviews from the New York Quarterly*, ed. William Packard (Garden City, NY: Doubleday, 1974), p. 111.

12. Ashbery, 111.

13. Barbara Herrnstein Smith, *Poetic Closure: A Study of How Poems End* (Chicago: U of Chicago P, 1968), p. 18.

14. M. L. Rosenthal, *The Poet's Art* (New York: Norton, 1987), p. 65.

15. Theodore Roethke, *Straw for the Fire: From the Notebooks of Theodore Roethke, 1943–63*, ed. David Wagoner (Garden City, NY: Doubleday, 1972), p. 209.

16. Wright, 27.

17. Donald Barthelme, *Unspeakable Practices, Unnatural Acts* (New York: Pocket Books, 1976), p. 73.

18. Nancy Willard, "Close Encounters of the Story Kind," in *Writers on Writing: A Bread Loaf Anthology*, ed. Robert Pack and Jay Parini (Hanover, NH: Middlebury College P, 1991), p. 267.

19. Victor Strandberg, "Robert Penn Warren and the Search for Design," *The Gettysburg Review* 5 (Summer 1992): 497.

20. Marvin Bell, "Distilled from Thin Air," in *Acts of Mind: Conversations with Contemporary Poets*, ed. Richard Jackson (Tuscaloosa: University of Alabama Press, 1983), p. 154.

21. Bell, "Distilled from Thin Air," 68.

22. Stafford, 65.

23. Stafford, 66.

24. Rosenthal, 30.

25. Robert Frost, "The Figure a Poem Makes," in *Modern Poetics*, ed. James Scully (New York: McGraw-Hill, 1965), p. 57.

26. Richard Hugo, *The Triggering Town: Lectures and Essays on Poetry and Writing* (New York: Norton, 1979), p. 38.

27. Richard Hugo, "An Interview with Richard Hugo," in *Interviews with Contemporary Writers: Second Series 1972–1982*, ed. L S. Dembo (Madison: U of Wisconsin P, 1983), p. 312.

28. William Stafford, *You Must Revise Your Life* (Ann Arbor: University of Michigan Press, 1986), p. 17.

29. Howard Moss, *Whatever Is Moving* (Boston: Little, Brown, 1981), p. 86.

30. Moss, 86.

31. Moss, 86.

32. Moss, 86.

33. Moss, 93.

34. Moss, 96.

35. Moss, 94–96.

36. Moss, 96.

37. Moss, 97.

38. Donald Justice, *Platonic Scripts* (Ann Arbor: University of Michigan Press, 1984), p. 165.

39. Marvin Bell, "Homage to the Runner: 'The Grand Sense Necessary . . . ,'" *American Poetry Review* 20.5 (September/October 1991): 43.

40. Stanley Kunitz, *Next-to-Last Things: New Poems and Essays* (Boston: Atlantic Monthly, 1985), pp. 113–14.

41. James Merrill, *Recitative* (San Francisco: North Point, 1986), pp. 76–77.

42. Gallagher, 25.

43. Gallagher, 25.

44. Gallagher, 25.

45. William Meredith, *Poems Are Hard to Read* (Ann Arbor: University of Michigan Press, 1991), p. 138.

46. Anne Sexton, *No Evil Star: Selected Essays, Interviews, and Prose* (Ann Arbor: University of Michigan Press, 1985), p. 169.

47. Maxine Kumin, *To Make a Prairie: Essays on Poets, Poetry, and Country Living* (Ann Arbor: University of Michigan Press, 1979), p. 127.

48. Kumin, 127.

49. Kumin, 139.

50. Smith, 152.

51. Smith, 155.

52. Charles Wright, *Halflife: Improvisations and Interviews, 1977–87* (Ann Arbor: University of Michigan Press, 1988), pp. 167–68.

53. Smith, 157.

54. Smith, 157.

55. Smith, 158.

56. Smith, 185.

57. Smith, 159.

58. Smith, 160.

59. Smith, 160.

60. Smith, 175–76.

61. Smith, 178.

62. William Matthews, *Curiosities* (Ann Arbor: University of Michigan Press, 1989), p. 126.

63. Robert Bly, *Talking All Morning* (Ann Arbor: University of Michigan Press, 1980), p. 161.

64. Smith, 145.

65. Smith, 244.

66. Smith, 237.

67. Smith, 238.

68. Kumin, 128.

69. Rosenthal, 14.

70. Rosenthal, 14.

71. Rosenthal, 15.

72. Rosenthal, 15.

73. Kunitz, 114.

74. Louis Simpson, *The Character of the Poet* (Ann Arbor: University of Michigan Press, 1986), p. 45.

75. Lewis Mackenzie, "Introduction," in *The Autumn Wind: A Selection from the Poems of Issa,* (New York: Kodansha International 1984), p. 1.

76. Gallagher, 205.

77. Howard Nemerov, *Reflexions on Poetry and Poetics* (Chicago: University of Chicago Press, 1972), pp. 9–10.

78. Nemerov, 14.

79. Nemerov, 16.

Against Sincerity

Louise Glück

Since I'm going to use inexplicit terms, I want to begin by defining the three most prominent of these. By *actuality* I mean to refer to the world of event, by *truth* to the embodied vision, illumination, or enduring discovery which is the ideal of art, and by *honesty* or *sincerity* to "telling the truth," which is not necessarily the path to illumination.

V. S. Naipaul, in the pages of a national magazine, defines the aim of the novel; the ideal creation, he says, must be "indistinguishable from truth." A delicious and instructive remark. Instructive because it postulates a gap between truth and actuality. The artist's task, then, involves the transformation of the actual to the true. And the ability to achieve such transformations, especially in art that presumes to be subjective, depends on conscious willingness to distinguish truth from honesty or sincerity.

The impulse, however, is not to distinguish but to link. In part the tendency to connect the idea of truth with the idea of honesty is a form of anxiety. We are calmed by answerable questions, and the question "Have I been honest?" has an answer. Honesty and sincerity refer back to the already known, against which any utterance can be tested. They constitute acknowledgement. They also assume a convergence: these terms take for granted the identification of the poet with the speaker.

This is not to suggest that apparently honest poets don't object to having their creativity overlooked. For example, the work of Diane Wakoski fosters as intense an identification of poet with speaker as any body of work I can think of. But when a listener, some years ago, praised her courage, Wakoski was indignantly dismissive. She reminded her audience that, after all, she decided what she set down. So the "secret" content of the poems, the extreme intimacy, was regularly transformed by acts of decision, which is to say, by assertions of power. The "I" on the page, the all-revealing Diane, was her creation. The secrets we choose to betray lose power over us.

To recapitulate: the source of art is experience, the end product truth, and the artist, surveying the actual, constantly intervenes and manages, lies and deletes, all in the service of truth. Blackmur talks of this: "The life we all live," he says, "is not alone enough of a subject for the serious artist; it must be a life with a leaning, life with a tendency to shape itself only in certain forms, to afford its most lucid revelations only in certain lights."

There is, unfortunately, no test for truth. That is, in part, why artists suffer. The love of truth is felt as chronic aspiration and chronic unease. If there is no test for truth, there is no possible security. The artist, alternating between anxiety and fierce conviction, must depend on the latter to compensate for the sacrifice of the sure. It is relatively easy to say that truth is the aim and heart of poetry, but harder to say how it is recognized or made. We know it first, as readers, by its result, by the sudden rush of wonder and awe and terror.

The association of truth with terror is not new. The story of Psyche and Eros tells us that the need to know is like a hunger: it destroys peace. Psyche broke Eros's single commandment—that she not look at him—because the pressure to see was more powerful than either love or gratitude. And everything was sacrificed to it.

We have to remember that Psyche, the soul, was human. The legend's resolution marries the soul to Eros, by which union it—the soul—is made immortal. But to be human is to be subject to the lure of the forbidden.

Honest speech is a relief and not a discovery. When we speak of honesty, in relation to poems, we mean the degree to which and the power with which the generating impulse has been transcribed. Transcribed, not transformed. Any attempt to evaluate the honesty of a text must always lead away from that text, and toward intention. This may make an interesting trail, more interesting, very possibly, than the poem. The mistake, in any case, is our failure to separate poetry which sounds like honest speech from honest speech. The earlier mistake is in assuming that there is only one way for poetry to sound.

These assumptions didn't come from nowhere. We have not so much made as absorbed them, as we digest our fathers and turn to our contemporaries. That turning is altogether natural: in the same way, children turn to other children, the dying to the dying, and so forth. We turn to those who have been dealt, as we see it, roughly the same hand. We turn to see what they're up to, feeling natural excitement in the presence of what is still unfolding, or unknown. Substantial contributions to our collective inheritance were made by poets whose poems seemed blazingly personal, as though the poets had performed autopsies on their own living tissue. The presence of the speaker in these poems was overwhelming; the poems read as testaments, as records of the life. Art was redefined, all its ingenuities washed away.

The impulse toward this poetry is heard in poets as unlike as Whitman and Rilke. It is heard earlier, in the Romantics, despite Wordsworth's comment that if he "had said out passions as they were, the poems could never have been published." But the idea that a body of work corresponds to and describes a soul's journey is particularly vivid in Keats. What we hear in Keats is inward listening, attentiveness of a rare order. I will say more later about the crucial difference between such qualities and the decanting of personality.

Keats drew on his own life because it afforded greatest access to the materials of greatest interest. That it was *his* hardly concerned him. It was a life, and therefore likely, in its large shapes and major struggles, to stand as a paradigm. This is the attitude Emerson means, I think, when he says: "To believe your own thought, to believe that what is true for you in your private heart is true for all men—that is genius."

That is, at any rate, Keats's genius. Keats wanted a poetry that would document the soul's journey or shed light on hidden forms; he wanted more feeling and fewer alexandrines. But nothing in Keats's attitude toward the soul resembles the proprietor's investment. We can find limitation, but never smug limitation. A great innocence sounds in the lines, a kind of eager gratitude that passionate dedication should have been rewarded with fluency. As in this sonnet, dated 1818:

When I Have Fears

When I have fears that I may cease to be
Before my pen has gleaned my teeming brain,
Before high-pilèd books in charact'ry,
Hold like rich garners the full-ripened grain;
When I behold, upon the night's starred face,
Huge cloudy symbols of a high romance,
And think that I may never live to trace
Their shadows, with the magic hand of chance;
And when I feel, fair creature of an hour!
That I shall never look upon thee more,
never have relish in the fairy power
of unreflecting love!—then on the shore
of the wide world I stand alone, and think
Till Love and Fame to nothingness do sink.

The impression is of outcry, of haste, of turbulent, immediate emotion that seems to fall, almost accidentally, into the sonnet form. That form tends to produce a sensation of repose; no matter how paradoxical the resolution, the ear detects something of the terminal thud of the judge's gavel. Or the double thud, since the sensation is especially marked in sonnets following the Elizabethan style, ending, that is, in a rhymed couplet; two pithy lines of summary or antithesis. "Think" and "sink" make, certainly, a noticeable rhyme, but they manage, oddly enough, not to end the sonnet like two pennies falling on a plate. We require the marked rhyme, the single repeated sound, to put an end to all the poem's surging longing, to show us the "I," the speaker, at a standstill, just as the dash in the twelfth line makes the necessary abyss that separates the speaker from all the richness of the world. Consider, now, another sonnet, akin to this in subject and rational shape, though the "when" and "then" are here more subtle. The sonnet is Milton's, its occasion, the fact of blindness, its date of composition, 1652:

When I Consider How My Light Is Spent

When I consider how my light is spent
Ere half my days in this dark world and wide,

And that one talent which is death to hide
Lodged with me useless, though my soul more bent
To serve therewith my Maker, and present
My true account, lest he returning chide
"Doth God exact day-labor, light denied?"
I fondly ask. But Patience, to prevent
That murmur, soon replies, "God doth not need
Either man's work or his own gifts; who best
Bear his mild yoke, they serve him best. His state
Is kingly: thousands at his bidding speed,
And post o'er land and ocean without rest:
They also serve who only stand and wait."

When I say the resemblance here is sufficient to make obvious
the debt, what I mean is that I cannot read Keats's poem and not
hear Milton's. Someone else would hear Shakespeare: neither echo
is surprising. If Shakespeare was Keats's enduring love, Milton was
his measuring rod. Keats carried a portrait of Shakespeare every-
where, even on the walking tours, as a kind of totem. When there
was a desk, the portrait hung over it: work there was work at a
shrine. Milton was the dilemma; toward Milton's achievement,
Keats vacillated in his responses, and responses, to Keats, were
verdicts. Such vacillation, combined with inner pressure to decide,
can be called obsession.

The purpose of comparison was, finally, displacement; in
Keats's mind, Wordsworth stood as the contender, the alternative.
Keats felt Wordsworth's genius to lie in his ability to "[think] into
the human heart"; Milton, for all his brilliance, showed, Keats
thought, "less anxiety about humanity." Wordsworth was exploring
those hidden reaches of the mind where, as Keats saw it, the intel-
lectual problems of their time lay. And these problems seemed
more difficult, more complex, than the theological questions with
which Milton was absorbed. So Wordsworth was "deeper than
Milton," though more because of "the general and gregarious
advance of intellect, than individual greatness of mind." All this
was a way for Keats of clarifying purpose.

I said earlier that these sonnets were like in their occasions:
this statement needs some amplification. The tradition of sinceri-
ty grows out of the blurring of distinction between theme and

occasion; there is a greater emphasis, after the Romantics, on choice of occasion: the poet is less and less the artisan who makes, out of an occasion tossed him, something of interest. The poet less and less resembles the debating team: lithe, adept, of many minds.

In the poems at hand, both poets have taken up the question of loss. Of course, Keats was talking about death, which remains, as long as one is talking, imminent. But pressingly imminent, for Keats, even in 1818. He had already nursed a mother through her dying and had watched her symptoms reappear in his brother Tom. Consumption was the "family disease"; Keats's medical training equipped him to recognize its symptoms. The death imminent to Keats was a forfeit of the physical world, the world of the senses. That world—this world—was heaven; in the other he could not believe, nor could he see his life as a ritual preparation. So he immersed himself in the momentary splendor of the material world, which led always to the idea of loss. That is, if we recognize movement and change but no longer believe in anything beyond death, then all evolution is perceived as movement away, the stable element, the referent, being what was, not what will be, a world as stationary and alive as the scenes on the Grecian urn.

In 1652, Milton's blindness was probably complete. Loss makes his starting place; if blindness is, unlike death, a partial sacrifice, it is hardly a propitiation: Milton's calm is not the calm of bought time. I say "Milton's" calm, but in fact, we don't feel quite so readily the right to that familiarity. For one thing, the sonnet is a dialogue, the octet ending in the speaker's question, which Patience answers in its six sublime lines. In a whole so fluent, the technical finesse of this division is masterfully inconspicuous. It is interesting to remark, of a poem so masterful, so majestic in its composure, the extreme simplicity of vocabulary. One-syllable words predominate; the impression of mastery derives not from elaborate vocabulary but from the astonishing variety of syntax within flexible suspended sentences, an instance of matchless organizational ability. People do not, ordinarily, speak this way. And I think it is generally true that imitations of speech, with its false starts, its lively inelegance, its sense of being arranged as it goes along, will not produce an impression of perfect control.

And yet there is, in Milton's poem, no absence of anguish. As readers, we register the anguish and drama here almost entirely subliminally, following the cues of rhythm. This is the great advantage of formal verse: metrical variation provides a subtext. It does what we now rely on tone to do. I should add that I think we really do have to rely on tone, since the advantage disappears when these conventions cease to be the norm of poetic expression. Education in metrical forms is not, however, essential to the reader here: the sonnet's opening lines summon and establish the iambic tradition, with a certain flutter at "consider." No ear can miss the measured regularity of those first lines:

> When I consider how my light is spent
> Ere half my days in this dark world and wide. . . .

The end of the second line, though, is troubled. "Dark world" makes a kind of aural knot. We hear menace not simply because the world is described as "dark," alluding both to the permanently altered world of the blind and, also, to a world metaphorically dark, in which right paths cannot be detected: the menace felt here comes about, and comes about chiefly, because the line that has been so fluid is suddenly stalled. A block is thrown up, the language itself coagulates into the immobile, impassable dark world. Then we escape; the line turns graceful again. But the dread introduced is not dissolved. And in the fourth line we hear it again with terrible force, so that we experience physically, in sound, the unmanageable sorrow:

> And that one talent which is death to hide
> Lodged with me useless. . . .

"Lodged" is like a blow. And the next words make a kind of lame reeling, a dwindling. As I hear the line, only "less" receives less emphasis than "me." In these four words we hear personal torment, the wreckage of order and hope; we are carried to a place as isolated as Keats's shore ever was, but a place of fewer options. All this happens early; Milton's sonnet is not a description of agony. But loss must be vividly felt for Patience's answer to properly reverberate.

The most likely transformation of loss is into task or test. This conversion introduces the idea of gain, if not reward; it fortifies the animal commitment to staying alive by promising to respond to the human need for purpose. So Patience, in Milton's sonnet, stills the petulant questioner and provides a glimpse of insight, a directive. At the very least, corrects a presumption.

Great value is placed here on endurance. And endurance is not required in the absence of pain. The poem, therefore, must convince us of pain, though its concerns lie elsewhere. Specifically, it proposes a lesson, which must be unearthed from the circumstantial. In the presence of lessons, the possibility of mastery can displace the animal plea for alleviation.

In Milton's sonnet, two actions are ascribed to the speaker: he considers, and, when he considers, he asks. I have made a particular case for anguish because we are accustomed to thinking the "cerebral" contradictory to the "felt," and the actions of the speaker are clearly the elevated actions of mind. The disposition to reflect or consider presumes developed intelligence, as well as temperamental inclination; it further presumes adequate time.

The "I" that considers is very different from the "I" that has fears. To have fears, to have, specifically, the fears on which Keats dwells, is to be immersed in acute sensation. The fear that one will cease to be is unlike the state of chronic fearfulness we call timidity. This fear halts and overtakes, it carries intimations of change or closure or collapse, it threatens to cancel the future. It is primal, unwilled, democratic, urgent; in its presence, all other function is suspended.

What we see in Keats is not indifference to thought. What we see is another species of thought than Milton's: thought resistant to government by mind. Keats claims for the responsive animal nature its ancient right to speech. Where Milton will project an impression of mastery, Keats projects a succumbing. In terms of tone, the impression of mastery and the impression of abandon cannot co-exist. Our present addiction to sincerity grows out of a preference for abandon, for the subjective "I" whose impassioned partiality carries the implication of flaw, whose speech sounds individual and human and fallible. The elements of coldness to which Keats objected in Milton, the insufficient "anxiety about humanity" correspond to the overt projection of mastery.

Keats was given to describing his methods of composition in terms implying a giving-in: the poet was to be passive, responsive, available to all sensation. His desire was to reveal the soul, but soul, to Keats, had no spiritual draperies. Spirituality manifests the mind's intimidating claim to independent life. It was this invention Keats rejected. To Keats, the soul was corporeal and vital and frail; it had no life outside the body.

Keats refused to value what he did not believe, and he did not believe what he could not feel. Because he saw no choice, Keats was bound to prefer the mortal to the divine, as he was bound to gravitate toward Shakespeare, who wrote plays where Milton made masks, who wrote, that is, with an expressed debt to life.

It follows that Keats's poems feel immediate, personal, exposed; they sound, in other words, exactly like honesty, following Wordsworth's notion that poetry should seem the utterance of "a man talking to men." If Milton wrote in momentous chords, Keats preferred the rush of isolated notes, preferred the penetrating to the commanding.

The idea of "a man talking to men," the premise of honesty, depends on a delineated speaker. And it is precisely on this point that confusion arises, since the success of such a poetry creates in its readers a firm belief in the reality of that speaker, which is expressed as the identification of the speaker with the poet. This belief is what the poet means to engender: difficulty comes when he begins to participate in the audience's mistake. And on this point, we should listen to Keats, who intended so plainly that his poems seem personal and who drew, so regularly and so unmistakably, on autobiographical materials.

At the center of Keats's thinking is the problem of self. And it is on the subject of the poet's self that he speaks with greatest feeling and insight. Those men of talent, he felt, who impose their "proper selves" on what they create, should be called "men of power," in contrast to the true "men of genius," those men who, in Keats's view, were "great as certain ethereal chemicals operating on the mass of neutral intellect—but they have not any individuality, any determined character." Toward the composition of poems that would seem "a man speaking to men," he advocated the opposite of egotistical self-awareness and self-cultivation; he recommended, rather, the negative capability he felt in Shakespeare, a capacity for suspending judgment in order to report faithfully, a capability of submission, a willingness to "annul" the self.

The self, in other words, was like a lightning rod: it attracted experience. But the poet's obligation was to divest himself of personal characteristics. Existing beliefs, therefore, were not a touchstone, but a disadvantage.

I referred, some time ago, to our immediate inheritance. I had in mind poets like Lowell and Plath and Berryman, along with many less impressive others. With reference to the notion of sincerity, it is especially interesting to look at Berryman.

Berryman was, from the first, technically proficient, though the early poems are not memorable. When he found what we like to call "himself," he demonstrated what is, to my mind, the best ear since Pound. The self he found was mordant, voluble, opinionated, and profoundly withheld, as demonically manipulative as Frost. In 1970, after *The Dream Songs* had made him famous, Berryman published a curious book, which took its title from the Keats sonnet. The book, *Love and Fame*, was dedicated "to the memory of the suffering lover & young Breton master who called himself 'Tristan Corbière.' " To this dedication, Berryman added a parenthetical comment: "I wish I versed with his bite."

We have, therefore, by the time we reach the first poem, a great deal of information: we have a subject, youth's twin dreams, a reference, and an ideal. But this is as nothing compared to the information we get in the poems. We get in them the kind of instantly gratifying data usually associated with drunken camaraderie, and not with art. We get actual names, places, positions, and, while Berryman is at it, confessions of failure, pride, ambition, and lust, all in characteristic shorthand: arrogance without apology.

It can be said of Berryman that when he found his voice he found his voices. By voice I mean natural distinction, and by distinction I mean to refer to thought. Which is to say, you do not find your voice by inserting a single adjective into twenty poems. Distinctive voice is inseparable from distinctive substance; it cannot be grafted on. Berryman began to sound like Berryman when he invented Mr. Bones, and so was able to project two ideas simultaneously. Presumably, in *Love and Fame*, we have a single speaker—commentator might be a better word. But the feel of the poems is very like that of *The Dream Songs*; Mr. Bones survives in an arsenal of sinister devices, particularly in the stinging, undermining tag lines. The poems pretend to be straight gossip, straight from the source; like gossip, they divert and entertain. But the source deals in mixed messages; midway through, the reader is recalled from the invited error:

Message

Amplitude,—voltage,—the one friend calls for the one,
the other for the other, in my work;
in verse & prose. Well, hell.
I am not writing an autobiography-in-verse, my friends.

Impressions, structures, tales, from Columbia in the
      thirties
& the michaelmas term at Cambridge in 36,
followed by some later. It's not my life.
That's occluded and lost.

On the page, "autobiography-in-verse" is a single ladylike word, held together by malicious hyphens.

What's real in the passage is despair. which owes, in part, to the bitter notion that invention is wasted.

The advantage of poetry over life is that poetry, if it is sharp enough, may last. We are unnerved, I suppose, by the thought that authenticity, in the poem, is not produced by sincerity. We incline, in our anxiety for formulas, to be literal: we scan Frost's face compulsively for hidden kindness, having found the poems to be, by all reports, so much better than the man. This assumes our poems are our fingerprints, which they are not. And the processes by which experience is changed—heightened, distilled, made memorable— have nothing to do with sincerity. The truth, on the page, need not have been lived. It is, instead, all that can be envisioned.

I want to say, finally, something more about truth, or about that art which is "indistinguishable" from it. Keats's theory of negative capability is an articulation of a habit of mind more commonly ascribed to the scientist, in whose thought the absence of bias is actively cultivated. It is the absence of bias that convinces, that encourages confidence, the premise being that certain materials arranged in certain ways will always yield the same result. Which is to say, something inherent in the combination has been perceived.

I think the great poets work this way. That is, I think the materials are subjective, but the methods are not. I think this is so whether or not detachment is evident in the finished work.

At the heart of that work will be a question, a problem. And we will feel, as we read, a sense that the poet was not wed to any one outcome. The poems themselves are like experiments, which the reader is freely invited to recreate in his own mind. Those poets who claustrophobically oversee or bully or dictate response prematurely advertise the deficiencies of the chosen particulars, as though without strenuous guidance the reader might not reach an intended conclusion. Such work suffers from the excision of doubt: Milton may have written proofs, but his poems compel because they dramatize questions. The only illuminations are like Psyche's, who did not know what she'd find.

The true has about it an air of mystery or inexplicability. This mystery is an attribute of the elemental: art of the kind I mean to describe will seem the furthest concentration or reduction or clarification of its substance; it cannot be further refined without being changed in its nature. It is essence, ore, wholly unique, and therefore comparable to nothing. No "it" will have existed before; what will have existed are other instances of like authenticity.

The true, in poetry, is felt as insight. It is very rare, but beside it other poems seem merely intelligent comment.

Poetry and Practical Deliberation

Emily Grosholz

What good is poetry? Why is it worth our time to write it or to read it? Is it really still possible that poetry furnishes wisdom about the world and the human heart? These questions seem thorny because contemporary conceptions of knowledge make the kind of knowledge that poetry embodies difficult to recognize and honor. In addition, many poets have so deeply internalized these conceptions that their own poems surrender the wisdom to which they might otherwise lay claim.(1)

A proof of the possibility of poetry's wisdom is best anchored in the existence of wise poems. In this essay, I will examine some current debates about the epistemic status of poetry and about knowledge in general. I will then argue that poetry ought to be seen as analogous to historical knowledge, not to scientific knowledge, and therefore as embedded in a process of practical deliberation, not theory construction. (This argument will make clear why I prefer the term "wisdom" to that of "knowledge.") Finally, I will illustrate and ground my position by examining in detail poems by Maxine Kumin, Donald Davie, and Eleanor Wilner, poets who make especially important contributions to the deliberative talk we are all caught up in, and which will one day include our children.

Two current versions of the epistemic status of language, and by implication of poetry as a mode of language, form a kind of Kantian antinomy. Plausible in themselves, they cannot easily be dismissed by ordinary empirical evidence, yet they are incompatible with each other, and that discrepancy casts a shadow of doubt on them both. The thesis in this case is that language imitates an already given reality, and does so truly or falsely. The antithesis is that nothing external to language exists, in particular no external world to which language could be truly or falsely correlated.

People who champion the thesis and reject the antithesis are generally concerned to establish the possibility of objective human knowledge, warranted in reliable ways and stably persistent. They tend to emphasize the importance of perceptual evidence, and to regard knowledge as causally engendered. Those who reject the thesis in favor of the antithesis, by contrast, wish to emphasize the constructedness of human cultural reality, which always recreates itself in unprecedented forms. They regard knowledge as the interpretation of an intrinsically significant and value-laden world.

Kant resolves the Third Antinomy in the *Critique of Pure Reason* by arguing that reality must be thought of as divided into a world of the senses and an intelligible world. The realm of noumena is physical nature encountered through and thus conditioned by our senses and the categories of the understanding. The realm of noumena must be further postulated as things in themselves, unconditioned by our limited modes of encountering them. Kant's thesis that freedom is possible, then, may hold true for noumena while the antithesis that all events are causally determined holds for the phenomena. The apparent contradiction between thesis and antithesis dissolves with the insight that they apply to different aspects of reality.(2)

I don't think that these venerable metaphysical opposites can be quite so neatly dispatched, nor do I espouse Kant's way of dividing up reality. But I would like to take a similar tack in locating the two versions of how language relates to reality, to mitigate if not entirely resolve their opposition. The thesis that language imitates an already given reality is most plausible when the object of knowledge is supposed to be inanimate nature. The antithesis that nothing exists outside of language applies pretty well when the object (and matrix) of knowledge is human history.

In the former case, we can admit that some aspects of nature exist apart from us, in the sense that they would all continue unperturbed and unaltered if every human knower disappeared tomorrow. The fall of boulders and the chemical interaction of oxygen and hydrogen involve items and processes that have no social relations with each other or with us. They recur and recur, always in the same lawlike way, with the same causal antecedents and the same effects. Their causal efficacy persists into the future inde-pendent of whether any one of us is around to observe the conse-quences. If the task of science is to use language to describe such items and events, the regulative ideal of a precise and neutral description of an independently given external reality seems not at all misleading and indeed quite appropriate.

In the latter case, the use of language to describe human his-tory must be very different, for we are embedded in the "essential-ly contested" events of our history in a way that makes neutral and detached description impossible in principle.(3) Human actions and institutions are in large part composed of talk, and are then modified and evaluated in various conflicting ways by further talk, in which disagreement as well as harmony lead to the constitution of further social realities. We the historians then enter into this evaluative, quarrelsome, and creative conversation to talk about past talk, and not merely because we have a theoretical interest in the actions of our forebears. Rather, since we are engaged in the practical work of presently constructing the future, we must con-front the manifold ways in which the past is alive in us and bears upon us.(4)

History can never be given independently of the interests and values of those who read and write history. No precise and neutral description of historical events exists, for there is no Arbitrator who could give the final pronouncement on what ultimate evaluation of events should emerge from the private, legal, parliamentary, and international debates that surround the events. And when certain philosophers attempt to rewrite history in terms of a physicalist reduction to matter in motion that might admit a sufficiently pre-cise and neutral description, they simply make the stuff of history, human action, and utterance disappear altogether.(5) History real-ly doesn't exist outside of language and of its own efficacious trans-lation in the utterances and actions of future human beings. If we perish, history and indeed all human culture die with us.

Thus some aspects of the reality we inhabit depend radically upon us, our talk and our existence. Other aspects don't. The aspects that do are no less real or indeed precious for all their dependence on us, but they are fragile and equivocal. And they are ours to create: because we create them, because they are not given externally and prior to us, they are ambiguous in meaning and potential; because they are ambiguously incomplete, we must always recreate them by means of our very contentiousness. Arguments around the kitchen table, courtroom dialectic, and parliamentary debate reinforce and recreate the social and political institutions in which our life takes place.(6)

The writing of history is thus set in a context of practical deliberation, not theory construction. Scientific theory, thoroughly mathematical and perhaps arranged as an axiomatic system, with first principles that apply universally and necessarily, is a reasonable model for describing the repetitive patterns of inanimate nature. But it is not a reasonable model for describing the familiar, indeterminate, and self-creating activity of people in history. Rather, the notion of practical deliberation —with its emphasis on practical goals and problem solving, and on orderly but polemical discussion—captures much more accurately what professional historians and indeed all of us in our unofficial but essential role of chroniclers are about.(7)

Although I am arguing here that we must forego axiomatic logical systems and the deductive-nomological model of explanation as ways of arranging our knowledge of human nature, I want immediately to point out that what remains is still richly structured.(8) Human disputes about meaning, which are the focus and oven of meaning-creation, are not chaotic free-for-alls. To review the obvious, domestic and social life are organized by bonds of affection, conventions, norms of conduct, and institutions; law courts, parliaments and diplomatic convocations are bounded by elaborate rules of evidence and procedure; the writing of history itself has its canons, rituals, and precedents. To live in the world is to be empowered by and subject to these structures. What we can dispute, our real choices and possibilities for interpretation, are actually very limited.

These structures are human inventions, called into existence by language, radically dependent upon us, fragile and debatable. But they are as real as we are, and in their relatively stable persistence constitute a realm of fact and principle that we encounter as objective, although we participate in its construction and find it rife with irresolvable disputes. (We are probably also constrained by the natural and the divine, which lie in different ways outside of human intention; however, such constraints lie filtered and netted in medicine and religion, and so for the moment I pass over the important questions they pose.) This contested territory in which we live and breathe and have our being is also the place of poetry.

Poetry must of course be distinguished from history. The historian works from the written and material record of the past, and must be faithful to its detail and mindful of methodology in ways that simply don't concern the poet. When we tell stories about the remembered past to a child, therapist, or friend, we strive for the historian's fidelity, even as the effort of reconstruction (selecting elements, organizing the narrative between a beginning and ending, exhibiting significance) proves once again that the story is our own. But the poet is allowed greater free play in the choice and handling of subject matter. He or she can distort the historical record for aesthetic ends, or abandon it altogether, inventing characters that live in variants of our world, distant lands, paradise, the forgotten past. And poetic character and plot are often schematic and abstract, *figurae* resembling the figures of mathematicians rather more than the painstakingly fleshed-out panoramas of historians.(9) The poet often appeals to what transcends history, retiring imaginatively to the desert or the mountains, or to the contemplation of veiled divinity. Finally, because the poet must honor formal dimensions of language to which the historian remains indifferent, he or she can play with the phonic and syntactic surface of language in patterns that would only distract from historical narrative.

The imperatives of aesthetic form—the drive to make phrases and stanzas so beautiful and schematic *topoi* so compelling that they will be preserved, as it were, outside of history—set the poet at odds with history and, to an extent, with the historian. Yet, I would argue, the differences are not as important as the similarities if we are to give the wisdom of poetry its rightful status. A poem is an interpretation of human reality, which is a by and large constructed sequence of talkative action. That poem is itself an action, an utterance constitutive of further social reality that invites further actions, interpretations, understandings, and social adjustments. Moreover, poems are written for practical ends that arise more or less directly out of the experience of the poet: seduction, mourning, critique, forgiveness, celebration. The free adventuring of the poet's imagination is tied to history (the poet's past and that of his or her society), to allegory and parallelism, and to metaphor and symbol. And this adventuring is curbed and enriched by its responsiveness to other voices, personal, political, and poetic. Poetry, like history, takes its place in a process of practical deliberation about what this life means, locally and globally, and what we should do about it.(10)

Reading poetry requires arts of interpretation similar to those required by reading history and by reflecting on one's own past in a thoughtful and hopeful way. By interpreting a poem we keep it alive, and it in turn repays us with a dose of reflectiveness, a new angle on the perennial concerns of men and women, an antidote to dogmatism and subjectivism, another voice. It does not, any more than a history book, give us the solution to the terrible quandaries and disturbances of this life, nor the truth about nature, humankind, or even language. It cannot furnish the ultimate facts about this world or any other, or the true first principles. It cannot offer reliable warrants that everyone can agree upon. It cannot have the final say. Yet it can help us order, illuminate, chastise, comfort, and redeem our own lives and societies—that is, it can offer wisdom.

But who would ever have thought that a poet was like, or at least ought to be like, a physicist? The prestige of science and the diffusion of popular conceptions of scientific knowledge should not be underestimated. That we might have some privileged access to the truth of things, that our endless bickering and the wearisome ambiguity of human social life might be capped by the proper theory in the hands of an informed and rational expert are delusive hopes that pervade the twentieth century and, I believe, do a great deal of damage. If political and social discourse is seen as scientific theory *manqué* and the work of poet and historian mere subjective prattle in the absence of a sufficient database, then we misunderstand the creativity and promise of our talkative action and of our art. And we allow ourselves to be silenced by allegedly reliable theories and experts.

Currently, at least two sets of people force poetry onto the Procrustean bed of the hard sciences for different reasons and with distinguishable results. First, there are the fashionable contemporary epistemologists, whose model of human knowledge is materialist and causal. The paradigm they set out from is the perception

78

of medium-sized dry goods (like apples or coffee cups); the distinction between natural unities and artifacts doesn't bother them much. The chain of events leading from what is known to who knows it is a causal triggering of media and mechanisms; the object of knowledge is, naturally, mute, and any requirement of interpretation is missing or rudimentary. In such cases, as I observed at the beginning of this essay, the possibility of neutral and precise description and of unobjectionable warrants is plausible. These philosophers would have a very difficult time fitting poetry into their paradigm. And so, rather than supposing that their paradigm is defective, they ignore poetry altogether or dismiss it as a confused, illusory, and relatively useless mode of knowledge.

Second, I am sorry to say, are the poets themselves, some of whom have succumbed to the phantom of scientific truth, although in a roundabout way. Their version of this misunderstanding is to scorn social conventions and institutions as uniformly oppressive and obscurantist, standing in the way of the truth of nature, God, human nature, or language (depending on which aspect of things they're most concerned with.) Rather inconsistently, they claim that social discourse is full of irresolvable arguments and so can't be a conduit to truth and that this discourse is only tyrannical and coercive.

Thus, neo-surrealist poets hope to get at the truth of things through perception and utterance liberated from the ego and its intentions. And language poets hope to uncover the truth by deploying a language that unmasks its own pretensions to referentiality at every turn. But the poetry written by such poets is signally obscure and so not to be shared or challenged. Seemingly uninterested in the possibilities of conversation, these poets appeal to an ideal of liberation that sits uneasily with their dogmatic subjectivism.

The epistemologists and the surrealists, I would say, have cut themselves off from discovering the sources of human wisdom by mistaking abstract structure and the confused immediacy of phantasm as *Leitfaden*. On the contrary, such guiding threads lead only to increasing dissociation. To understand the kind of knowledge that poetry offers and to recognize and profit from wise poems, we need to set poetry back in the context of practical deliberation.

What kinds of wisdom can we expect from poetry? Without

claiming that my informal taxonomy is unique or exhaustive, I would like to suggest three categories of human insight—personal, political and metaphysical—that I often find in the poems that I value most. Some poems illuminate the shape of a human life. Those that mourn and suffer fragmentation can be powerful and moving, but I prefer those that reveal the possibilities of human wholeness which can arise between the threat of dissolution and the illusion of strict completeness, between expansive confrontation with the great world and private rediscovery of one's origins. In such poems, the schemas of departure and return, of movement outward and movement downward, recur again and again, but each time are animated and made accessible through the rich detail of an individual life.(11)

Other poems take up the first principles of our political life, and test their consistency and justice against the experience of the times. First principles, by their very abstractness, are incomplete in meaning and must constantly be brought into relation with the unexpected, multifarious situations cast up by history. We do this in general by practical deliberation, and poets carry out their own versions of it. Finally, some poems are metaphysical or perhaps cosmic in their sweep and import. They take on the ancient questions of how we should maintain the balance between culture and nature, and between aggression and compassion, in our constructing of the world. How shall we understand evil? What are the grounds for hope? Clearly, these debates take on new poignancy and immediacy in the unprecedented conditions spawned by the twentieth century.

Stories like the Biblical episode of the prodigal son, the warfare and wanderings of Odysseus, the quests of Arthurian knights, and even the comic adventures of Tom Sawyer and Huck Finn treat the perennial theme of a young man's departure from home into the fascinating and dangerous expansiveness of the great world and his subsequent return. To grow up, one must seek out the alien and cosmopolitan, and come to terms with it; and then the consolidation of that hard-won maturity requires some kind of homecoming. But of equal importance, especially in our present age of longevity, is the process that goes on within the parent renounced and then recovered by the adventuring child. Parents experience an emptying out, abstraction, and reorganization of the familiar when their children leave home. And afterwards, just as much as the children, they must actively set their house in order again, and retrieve a new relation to their own origins. It's a time both to feel the mortality of one's advancing age and the resurgence of an uncannily wise youthfulness.

Maxine Kumin's "Leaving My Daughter's House" presents the paradoxical scene of a mother in a foreign land, visiting a daughter who has gone to such lengths to leave home that she has made a new home on the far side of the Atlantic ocean.(12) In the Flemish village of Hoeilaart, Kumin records a set of landscape features (horses, vegetables, sheep) that seem to correspond exactly to the elements of barnyard and field that we know from other poems that compose her farm in New Hampshire. And yet this correspondence gives her no comfort, for all the details are wrong and make the scene she looks out upon disturbingly estranged, like her translated daughter:

> And no matter how hard I run I know
> I can't penetrate my daughter's life
> in this tiny Flemish town where vectors of glass
> roofs run to the horizon. Tomatoes climb
> among grapes in all the greenhouses of Hoeilaart.
> Although it is March, the immense purple faces
> of last summer's cabbages, as if choleric
> from the work of growing, still loll in the garden.

The grooms speak Arabic, greenhouses adjust the rainy climate and allow unseasonable combinations of plants, and the cabbages and sheep are simply too big: "What a Crusoe place this is, juicily rained on, / emerald-thick!" Even worse, her daughter has become a European and a grown-up, hard to recognize in her lush, archaic, adoptive village. This poem is about the real loss and dislocation a parent feels when the child first definitively shakes off the dust of her beginnings. Only in the very last lines does Kumin offer the suggestion of reconciliation, as her daughter joins her at the window:

> Tomorrow . . .
> I will have crossed the ocean, gone beyond time
> where we stand in a mannerly pose at the window

watching the ancient iron strike flint from stones,
balancing on the bit that links us and keeps us
from weeping O God! into each other's arms.

The estrangement of mother and daughter is maintained not by an
attenuation of feeling—their attachment is still intense and lies
just under the surface—but by a sense of what is seemly, manner-
ly, that links them as it holds them apart. Parents must in fact let
their children go, and children must inflict the growing pains of
differentiation on their parents.

Donald Davie writes about the same kind of loss in the poem
"Seeing Her Leave," addressed to his daughter as she leaves
California to return to England.(13) The personal and cultural
geographies that lie behind this poem complicate the schema of
departure and return in important ways. Davie is a British poet
who has invested much of his professional life in the United
States, teaching first at Stanford and then at Vanderbilt. His vol-
untary but at times rather bitter exile was the theme of much of his
poetry and criticism, lending them the depth and multivalence of
two superimposed civilizations. Thus for a time Davie raised his
children in California, but his daughter, coming of age, decided to
return to England to begin her career as a nurse, returning
ambiguously to her own origins by leaving home.

The movement in this poem, inverse to that of Kumin's, is
from reconcilement to a quick sense of privation, for the father
finds much to admire in his daughter's strong-minded decision and
much that conforms to his own ambivalence about uncultivated
and frantic California and his nostalgia for England:

> Once more my tall young woman
> Has nerved herself to abandon
> This Greece for the Graeco-roman
> Peristyles of London,
>
> Where the archaic, the heated,
> Dishevelled and frantic Greek
> Has been planed and bevelled, fitted
> To the civic, the moralistic.

The activities of planing and bevelling, civilizing and moralizing, to be taken up by his daughter as a Londoner and a nurse, are just those that Davie most approved. Not only his critical essays defending the chaste and balanced language of neoclassicist poets like Pope and Dryden, but also the finely proportioned diction of his own poetry reveal an aesthetics of restraint that is grounded in historical and ethical commitments.

All the same, the grieving father cannot entirely approve his daughter's repatriation. The poem's ending forces a rereading of its opening stanzas. The metaphorical Greeks stand perhaps not only for the overwrought and all-but-uncontrolled Californians, but also for the father's emotional state as he begins to understand that his daughter has really left him. Not even Lloyds of London can provide indemnity, "security against hurt, loss or damage," in the case of daughters:

> So much of the price is missed
> In the tally of toil, ink, years;
> Count, neo-classicist,
> The choking back of tears.

The neoclassicist poet does what he can to plane and bevel his feelings in closely rhymed quatrains and in the seemly self-containment of a parent who really does believe that his daughter should be free to lead her own life. But the last word of the poem is still "tears."

One way in which children come home again (without necessarily making the return geographically) is to beget children of their own. Not only does this process return them psychically to their experience as children, to the landscape and personae dramatis of their youth, but it lends itself to a hopeful new identification with their estranged or distant parents. In the poem "Grandchild," Kumin returns to the same European context where in the earlier poem she had encountered great sadness and anomie.(14) But this poem is full of new understandings, integrations, and exchanges sparked by the advent of a new life.

Once again, the poem begins and ends with the speaker watching from a window. Kumin has just put her exhausted daughter to bed and taken over the tending of her week-old grandson.

For a moment she imaginatively identifies with her daughter, remembering her own fear and uncertainty as a new mother. And in that memory, the separation from her daughter is eased:

> I stand at the window
> watching the ancient boundaries that flow
> between my daughter's life and mine dissolve
> like taffy pulled until it melts in half
> without announcing any point of strain
> and I am a young unsure mother again. . . .

The baby's reality, the fear and expectation he inspires, recall her to the moment and to a recent dream she had just before he passed over the frontier from gestation to separate creature. In the dream, the local customs agent and official guardian of boundaries, the *douanier* at the French border just down the street, entered with the baby "buttoned and suited" like a bureaucrat in one hand, and in the other, a ripened brie cheese.

But no rational authority can transform the baby away from its monstrous unappeasability as "the twelve-limbed raw / creature" or its immense vulnerability as a "little feared-for mouse," aspects that have left its mother so anxious and tense that she can't rock it to sleep, even though she has fed it to brimfulness. Rather, what is needed, offered, and successfully applied in this situation is a grandmother's "monkey-wit," an easy body to body closeness flush with the tranquillity of experience:

> Age has conferred on me a certain grace.
> You're a package I can rock and ease
> from wakefulness to sleep. This skill comes back
> like learning how to swim. Comes warm and quick
> as first milk to the breasts. I comfort you.
> Body to body my monkey-wit soaks through.

Precisely because she is not her daughter, Kumin can offer a grace that allows her child and grandchild to get the sleep they need so badly, even though she must wakefully keep watch over them. Comforted in turn by her daughter's cupboard full of "calming teas," she sees the new light slipping past the *douanier*, every other earthly authority, and the cows coming down the hillside, redolent of "the lefthand gift of ripened brie," of a new baby full of milk. So through the window she looks forward to her grandson's childhood.

Parents whose children have flown are not only busy with reassessing their relationships to their offspring, but also to each other, for they find themselves suddenly, again, with world enough and time, as in their days of courtship. Donald Davie's "A Spring Song" is a delightful reversal of his own canons in the service of the higher truth of unruly spring: "the whole / diction kit begins to fall apart. / High time it did, high time."(15) Full of sentence fragments and exclamations, the poem is an invitation to his wife to leave home (for awhile) and go roaming with him through the valleys of France, the alien and licentious France of ancient warfare and Ronsard:

> Spring pricks a little. I get out the maps.
> Time to demoralize my song, high time.
> Vernal a little. *Primavera*. First
> Green, first truth and last.
> High time, high time.

This lyric is deeper than adolescent songs, however, for the lover shows a tender solicitude born of his sense of the hovering black sail of death. His wife is ill; he won't go anywhere without her, despite his vernal impatience. And she must put her glasses on to read the maps with their tracery of accurate, diminished places, remembered and still unknown. But if the accession to truth and the French itinerary are covered a bit more slowly than they were before, the lovers' mutual delight in discovery is no less vivid. And that vivacity unfurls the future before them: "High time, my love. High time and a long time yet."

Likewise, in "Relearning the Language of April," Maxine Kumin exults in the season's quickening, and finds it an appropriate frame for and mirror of her marriage. (16) Since she and her husband are farmers, the pathetic fallacy that launches the poem is unforced and well-grounded:

Where this man walks his fences
the willows do *pliés* with green laces,
eyelashes fly from the white plums,
the gaunt elms begin to open their frames.

Her husband is mythologized as an authoritative and sensual fig-
ure, a mixture of Orpheus and Bacchus, charming and calling up
the stirring life around him. As a farmer, he in fact recognizes the
trees along his fence line, inspires allegiance in his hounds and
horses, and has animated the fields by working them: "For miles
around, the plowed fields / release a sweet rancidness / warm as
sperm."

The poem pivots on the old metaphor of sex as plowing, and
swings back home to the wife, still abed and musing on the sur-
mised, unexpected turnings of love and the season. She sees her-
self as one more element (a field, dove, horse) in the wreath of
creatures surrounding her Orpheus, and as a center of content-
ment,, *umbilicus mundi*, a child of spring:

I lie in the fat lap of noon
overhearing the doves' complaint.
Far off, a stutter of geese raise alarms.

Once more, Body, Old Paint,
how could you trick me like this
in spring's blowsy arms?

It's not the first time that her body—familiar, responsive, and
quirky as one of the horses she trains and lives among—has sur-
prised her; and the poet knows, with all the imaginative monkey-
wit that comforted her grandson, it won't be the last.

The ancient schema of departure and return has taken on a
new cast in the modern age, one that puts the emphasis on depar-
ture. The young man's warlike or sentimental journey has become
his way of extricating himself from his roots, putting the past
behind him in order to make a wholly free choice concerning what
he shall become. In this new self-understanding, the attendant
danger is fragmentation, the jauntily launched small ship breaking
up on the reefs of the infinite variety of alien cultures and on the

abstractness of the cosmopolitan. But a noble principle whose influence on western politics cannot be underestimated also stands behind this revision of the ancient schema. John Stuart Mill expressed it with his characteristic eloquence: "For, what is the peculiar character of the modern world—the difference which chiefly distinguishes modern institutions, modern social ideas, modern life itself, from those of times long past? It is, that human beings are no longer born to their place in life, and chained down by an inexorable bond to the place they are born to, but are free to employ their faculties, and such favorable chances as offer, to achieve the lot which may appear to them most desirable."(17) Life, liberty, and the pursuit of happiness. In his book *On the Subjection of Women*, written under the influence and in memory of his wife Harriet Taylor, Mill presents this as a first political principle that his intended audience of literate, voting British males could not only accept but had indeed taken to heart. Then he points out that its application is oddly and inconsistently lopsided and proceeds to sue for the suffrage, education, and full employment of women under its auspices.

The schema of departure and return, even in its modern reformulation, has been instantiated mostly by men. Thus, I think it is especially significant that the poems just discussed, treating the departure of children, have concerned two strong-willed daughters. One way to defend the extension of Mill's principle to women is to argue by example, as judges do in case law, and show how particular young women have profited from the opportunity to set forth in the great world, win their fortune or bitter experience, and then return home all the wiser. The negative cases will depict gifted and energetic women for whom the schema was closed off, and the harm it did them.

Eleanor Wilner employs the latter strategy in her poem "Emigration," in which she presents the celebrated novelist Charlotte Brontë and her friend Mary Taylor, remembered by history only because of her link with Charlotte.(18) Charlotte is never really allowed to leave home; a conscientious spinster, she stays by her father's side and nurses her siblings as they die one by one from tuberculosis. Despite her friend Mary's jibes and exhortations: "you are all / like potatoes growing in the dark," Charlotte remains tangled in her roots:

87

> Charlotte stayed, and paid and paid—
> the little governess with the ungovernable
> heart, that she put on the altar.
> She paid the long indemnity of all
> who work for what will never wish them well,
> who never set a limit to what's owed
> and cannot risk foreclosure.

Even Charlotte's genius and the imaginative adventures it leads her on are little compensation for her deprived and provincial existence. By the time she is able to enter London's literary society she cannot engage it; and in her late attempt at marriage and motherhood, her frail body proves unequal to its task.

In a sense, Mary Taylor fares no better. Defiant and fed up, she departs without the possibility of return and reintegration, for British society has no place for an adventuress of her sort. The trip to Australia, in Wilner's retelling of the tale, takes her outside of discourse altogether, "in that godforsaken outpost past / the reach of fantasy, or fiction." She is left in silent anonymity, unable even to alter the social conditions at home that led to her splitting half-lives with Charlotte. Nor is the reader exempt from this dichotomy; Wilner warns us at the beginning, "There are always, in each of us, / these two: the one who stays, / the one who goes away –," and starts the last stanza with the invocation:

> God bless us everyone until we sicken,
> until the soul is like a little child
> stricken in its corner by the wall; so there is
> one who always sits there under lamplight
> writing, staying on, and one
> who walks the strange hills of Australia. . . .

The divisions between male and female, the uncoupling of the double movement of departure and return, the severance of imagination from the world of social discourse, conspire to catch us all up in a malaise that is one of the sicknesses of our phylogenetic childhood.

Our childhood diseases also apparently include murderous aggression and selfishness, though for centuries now we have been puzzling over the inscribed principles, "Thou shalt not kill," and "Thou shalt love thy neighbor as thyself." But to confer meaning on these half-empty imperatives by understanding how and when to apply them is still a struggle, and must continue to be so. Deliberating about their intent and scope is all the more urgent in the present era, when the object of our rage and ghostly, detached fantasies seems often to be the whole living mantle of earth. In our most far-fetched popular versions of the modern schema of the quest, the body (brain included) is replaced by a fancy computer and the machined self is catapulted off the face of the earth into the clean, orderly heavens. The space cowboy then just keeps heading west forever, freed from returning to the ambiguities of our mortal estate, "female" domesticity, and the messy woes of nature unbalanced.

Most poets, however, don't deal in such cold caricatures of escape, but offer us ways to think and talk about the dilemmas facing us, which cannot in fact be avoided. Indeed, the language of science, designed for inanimate and unresponsive phenomena, must be superseded when we try to talk about our obligations towards and social relations with the natural world. And even the languages of law court and marketplace are inadequate to the task, for it requires an imaginative leap and even, dare I say it, a sense of the transcendent which yet must find a sociable expression in words.

Maxine Kumin's "Woodchucks" is one of a series of bitterly honest reflections on the farmer's often adversarial relations to nature, in particular, the bright-eyed, intelligent animals he or she raises for slaughter or must control as pests.(19) In this account of her skirmishes with a family of woodchucks out to take over her vegetable garden, Kumin explores and exposes the murderousness that all of us harbor and are frightened by. Frustrated in her attempt to gas the creatures in their den, she goes after them with a pistol:

> The food from our mouths, I said, righteously
> thrilling
> to the feel of the .22, the bullets' neat noses.
> I, a lapsed pacifist fallen from grace
> puffed with Darwinian pieties for killing,

now drew a bead on the littlest woodchuck's face.
He died down in the everbearing roses.

She discovers that there are principles to cover and justify her action: "thieves must be prosecuted," Darwin's "only those survive which are fittest," "neatness counts." One reason why principles are effective only in the context of practical deliberation is that they do not wear their meanings on their faces. For example, they may be inconsistent with each other, as these are with the principle of the lapsed pacifist: "Thou shalt not kill." Which principles are relevant, which ones take precedence over others, and how are they meaningfully to be applied? These questions are not easily answered, and Kumin, dissatisfied with her earlier decision, appeals to her readers and her retrospective self for another judgment.

In the poem, Kumin also discovers the terrible thrill of self-righteous destruction:

> O one-two-three
> the murderer inside me rose up hard,
> the hawkeye killer came on stage forthwith.

That fierce wish lives in all of us, male and female alike, fueled by our blood-fears and ghostliest theories. We might as well admit that it plays on our heartstrings and haunts our dreams, along with our warmer, friendlier sentiments, since its unspoken persistence will only poison us. We simply cannot put our demons to sleep forever, "gassed underground the quiet Nazi way." But we do have various strategies to keep from acting on them, and one is to name them.(20)

Donald Davie situates the poet in a similarly troubled pastoral in "Skelpick," as he stands before his rented summer cottage in Scotland.(21) The poem begins with an almost perfectly idyllic view of the river valley below, recorded in flowing lines:

> . . . while over us all the clouds
> Choir the incessant the variously lovely
> Descants of shadows up and across the valley.

But the diminutive fisherman beside the river is idly tormenting the fish, and the local color is a history of tribal warfare. The vision of nature suffering because it cannot escape the circle of its own mechanisms suddenly fills Davie with disgust and distress; he kicks away the sheep-shit in front of his cottage, "silently cursing / The mindless machines that they are, cropping and cropping." Even though he remembers once attempting to save a lost lamb, the memory is ironic: his imitation of the Good Shepherd only preserved the lamb, after all, for a future as lamb chops or mutton.

What can redeem this world, full of unfairness and dumb suffering, blood and excrement? In the end, Davie appeals to freedom, the radical novelty human nature introduces into the world, the possibility of deliberative choice and of re-imaginings. He invokes freedom ("calling / For air, for air, for a distance") under the aspect of poetry, and in particular the poetry of Ovid. Davie wants to exhibit a liberty that is ordered and yet earthbound, a playful making that does not deny ruin, exile, carnality, or change, and yet recreates them in redemptive language, beautiful and moving:

> *Tristia*, the threads of a destiny woven
> From a black fleece when a poet was born in
> Sulmona;
> *Tristia*, the pipe pitch-bonded played
> From under a war-bonnet over the shudder
> ing flock;
> *Tristia*, the beldam black Chaldeans'
> Disastrous flocking torrent through the birch-
> trees.

In one of his most powerful, highly wrought stanzas, heavy with dark consonants and spondaic rhythms, Davie recalls what Ovid was able to make of his savage place of exile at the wrong end of the Mediterranean Sea. And thus this poem deserves to stand beside Davie's other great lyrics for the Russian poets Mandelstam and Pasternak, upon whose redemptive language in the midst of bitter dislocations he has long meditated.

The perspective of the last stanza of "Skelpick" is lordly, taking in half the Mediterranean from an unspecified point in the stratosphere. And this is in keeping with its cosmic import, for Davie is making an encompassing statement about how art places humankind with respect to nature. Eleanor Wilner in her poem "See-Saw" steps even further out in space to contemplate the fate of our earth. Her poetic cosmology is more impersonal than Davie's and more explicitly mythical. The authorial "I" is all but invisible except for the characteristic way that a new myth is woven around the Talmudic and Midrashic symbol of the *Shekhinah*, a cloud of glory, the female, immanent aspect of divinity that presided in the original temple.

Through a series of extraordinary images, we see the earth mantled in mist and poised on one side of a kind of Archimedean scales, balanced by the self-important human ego, a wisp of smoke. Then it becomes an empty, weightless sphere, the pure potentiality it was at the Beginning, "a crystal ball / that held the future, like an emerald seed, inside." What have we made of it? Wilner's answer is, not much; indeed, we have diminished it and put the whole circle of life, ourselves included, in great danger. The self-regarding ego, the cyclopean, martial, Cartesian ego, has carried out a terrible reduction:

> Like a volcano in reverse, it drew
> the whole world, flowing, to its cone—
> a funnel that made everything go small
> in passing through. And nothing
> was enough—so great its appetite, so great
> its gift for shrinking what it fed on.

And yet, Wilner concludes, we are not lost because we are caught up in a universal equilibrium (describable "by laws as yet unstudied") that must restore us to our senses and teach the inwardly telescoped ego-eye to weep. In the poem's mythical identifications, those tears become the weeping cloud of the *Shekhinah*, whose breast-milk of spring rain plumps up the earth and marries earth and heaven:

> And water-fed,
> the crops came back, the earth began
> to put on weight, the trees rose up

like steeples to the sky and birds came down
to feed and sing the summer into grass.
And over all, the arch of sun through rain,
the sign of healing sorrow
Shekhinah
whose covenant asks nothing
of tomorrow.

What kind of paradoxical covenant sets no conditions on the future? I suppose it is a law that submits to freedom and is based on trust, like the bonds of friendship. The political interpretation of this poem remains to be worked out, but its very presence in the midst of our conversations is useful, a highly colored signpost that, like the rainbow, gives directions as long as it is apprehended.

The wisdom of these poems, as I hope I have shown, is ethical, political, and cosmological. These poems are persuasions and understandings, committed to deepening our sense of the shape and place of human life. They allow the past to speak again for us; they converse sociably with neighbors who are familial, friendly, and poetic; and they expect our future somehow to flourish and find its own voice. Our life together may amount to little more than an earful of quarrelsome talk, singing, and belly laughter, with perhaps an iridescent echo. These poems testify that so much is enough.

1. This essay was first delivered as the Joyce Foundation Lecture at St. John's University Minnesota, in 1989. It is dedicated to the professors at the University of Chicago in the Analysis of Ideas and Study of Methods program who introduced me to the tradition of philosophical rhetoric: Eugene Garver, Wendy Omsted, David Smigelskis, and Charles Wegener, whose recent death I note here with sadness.

2. Immanuel Kant, *Critique of Pure Reason*, trans. Werner Pluhar (Indianapolis: Hackett, 1996), pp. 346-59, 473-79.

3. These insights come from W. B. Gallie, *Philosophy and the Historical Understanding* (New York: Schocken, 1964).

4. I make this argument in "Women, History, and Practical Deliberation," in *Feminist Thought and the Structure of Knowledge*, ed. Mary Gergen (New: New York University Press, 1988).

5. See the Chapter "Narrative Sentences" in Arthur Danto, *The Analytical Philosophy of History* (Cambridge: Cambridge University Press, 1965).

6. See Edward Levi, *An Introduction to Legal Reasoning* (Chicago: University of Chicago Press, 1949).

7. Here I draw on ideas of Eugene Garver and Joseph Schwab, succinctly expressed in Eugene Garver, "The Arts of the Practical: Variations on a Theme of Prometheus," *Critical Inquiry* 14 (1988): 165-82, and developed at greater length in Eugene Garver, *Aristotle's Rhetoric: An Art of Character* (Chicago: University of Chicago Press, 1995) and Joseph Schwab, ed., *Science, Curriculum, and Liberal Education: Selected Essays* (Chicago: University of Chicago Press, 1982).

8. For a clear discussion of this model of scientific reasoning see Carl Hempel, *Philosophy of Natural Science* (New York: Prentice Hall, 1966).

9. This point is made by Scott Buchanan in *Poetry and Mathematics* (Chicago: University of Chicago Press, 1962).

10. The relation between poetry and history is developed at length in two interesting studies: Robert R. Edwards, *Chaucer and Boccaccio: Antiquity and Modernity* (London and New York: Palgrave Macmillan, 2002) and James M. Redfield, *Nature and Culture in the* Iliad: *The Tragedy of Hector* (Durham: Duke

University Press, 1994).

11. Carl Vaught, *The Quest for Wholeness* (Albany: State University of New York Press, 1982).

12. Maxine Kumin, *Selected Poems 1960-1990* (New York: Norton, 1997), pp. 179-80.

13. Donald Davie, *Collected Poems* (Chicago: University of Chicago Press, 1990), pp. 278-79.

14. Kumin, pp. 203-204.

15. Davie, p. 304.

16. Kumin, p. 175.

17. John Stuart Mill, *The Subjection of Women*, S. M. Oller, ed. (Indianapolis and Cambridge: Hackett, 1988), p. 17.

18. Eleanor Wilner, *Reversing the Spell: New and Selected Poems* (Port Townsend: Copper Canyon Press, 1998), pp. 215-16.

19. Kumin, pp. 80-81.

20. This argument is developed in Israel Charny, *How Can We Commit the Unthinkable? Genocide: The Human Cancer.* (Boulder: Westview Press, 1982).

21. Davie, pp. 332-33.

Poetry as a Vessel of Remembrance

JANE HIRSHFIELD

The story of poetry has many beginnings. One is in Mnemosyne—Remembrance—earliest-born of the Greek goddesses, mother of the Muses and so also of the poem. Hesiod calls her the goddess of the first hour, as it would have to be: at the moment that time appears in the world, change appears in the world, and change alone, lacking memory's steadying counterweight, would mean Chaos. Without the power of memory as Mnemosyne manifests it—creative, flowing ceaselessly from the source of what is—what would connect each moment to the next? Through Mnemosyne, the knowable world continues from moment to moment, and through the poetry she engendered, words first learned to transcend time.

Reading and writing come late. First there is Mnemosyne's world, the oral world whose immense shadow we can see in the works of Homer and which lives on in virtually every characteristic by which we recognize poetry as poetry—all the qualities that work to hold language in place in time. For words themselves are vessels of consciousness, but before the coming of letters placed into clay tablet, papyrus, or book, verbal thought could live only in the fragile containers of inner contemplation and spoken language. Verse, at its most fundamental, is language put into the forms of remembrance. The earliest vessel for holding consciousness that has lasted, poetry is the progenitor of all the technologies of memory to come.

In Mnemosyne's time, memory was not yet imagined as a book or a storage room into which one could look. It was a being who spoke, and the way she spoke was in shapeliness, in verse. When poetry came later to be housed in the material realm of symbol and ink, how and why it was used changed, many of its means changed—but the fundamental sound of Mnemosyne's speech continued to permeate its nature, as does some echo, however faint, of her absolutely central place in human life.

To see how the requirements of memorability created poetry, we need first to imagine the nature of language and knowledge in a purely oral world. As a number of scholars have pointed out, before literacy, sound, not sight, is the sense-realm in which words exist. Perhaps the most striking difference between these two senses is their differing relationships to time. The visual world holds still through time—an oak tree or rock seen yesterday will remain to be seen tomorrow. Or if what we look at moves, we can follow that movement, or at least trust that the thing we have seen could still be found; one of the early, hard-earned lessons of infancy is that what goes out of sight does not cease to exist. Similarly, the written word—language placed into the realm of sight—remains stable over time, staying faithfully, reliably, in its place. Set down in a book on a shelf, it can be readily returned to hand and mind when needed.

Sound and the spoken word are different: the most fleeting of forms, existing only within the tenuous, present-moment decanting of breath. By the time we hear the last syllable of "moment," the first syllable has already vanished. The knowledge-realm of sound is so immediate that we dare not close it out even for an instant— our ears have no lids, no lips to seal shut. And further, sound is a sense not only of immediate time, but also of physical presence, of connection in space. Human vision divides. Depending as it does on the clear perception of boundaries, it creates a feeling of the outer as opposed to the self, of distinct and separate being. We say, and feel, that we look "out": from the center of our being, vision travels away from us and into the world. But a sound is perceived as coming toward and entering into us, bringing the outer within: sound lives in the movement of our own inner bones joining the resonance of its prior source. It is sound, not light, that summons us almost irresistibly to the linked celebration that is dance. Enveloping and seamless, sound—like taste, like smell—is intimate by its very nature. Yet, like taste, like smell, sound unshaped by human artistry is hard to recall with precision. It lives and vanishes in the instant of its presence.

What is heard—the cry of a child, the fall of a cougar's foot in dry leaves—is always the sign of something changing: only something active makes a noise. In an oral world, the word is indistinguishable from action itself, and so the world of speech is one with the world of deed, as we can see in ancient Hebrew, where the term *davar* means both "word" and "event." Spoken language, possessing a magical and fluid power, acts as a tool by which the ground of being can be worked. God says, "Let there be light," and there is light; Adam's task is to name the animals, and this creates his dominion over them. Both the world of being and the world of relationship are made by words.

Even silence has meaning: the name of the Hebrew God is secret, not to be spoken, and in many oral cultures the true name of any individual is believed to be identical with that person, and so is concealed for his or her protection. The names of the dead may not be uttered, for fear of drawing their spirits back to this world. To speak a name aloud is to declare oneself willing to summon—the spell, one of the earliest forms of poetry worldwide, is a calling of powers to one's aid by the saying of names. What is spoken is by that speaking made to exist, and what exists is conceived of as that which was once spoken. The earth itself, in many traditions, is a sacred utterance, the singing of the gods.

In Mnemosyne's world, in which words hold such singular power and yet come and go in a momentary flash, a quandary arises: how can thought and knowledge be preserved over time? There are only two ways, as Walter Ong has suggested in his book *Orality and Literacy*. One is to transmit an idea by speaking it aloud to someone else, who can then help remember it; this is what we do each time we say to a friend, "Don't let me forget to call Margaret about that." The other strategy is to "think memorable thoughts"—to put thought into a form that will be in itself an aid to memory. The most universal of such forms are the call and response of repetition within variation, and separately or together, meter and rhyme—the two repeating bases for verse—are found at the heart of every literary and oral tradition worldwide. We need only watch an infant learning to speak to see the innate satisfaction that repetition brings. Like dance, lyric and song come into being as original joys that confirm the body's own rhythmic life.

Repetition lies also at the heart of other linguistic devices we associate with poetry's beauty and sensual pleasure. The parallel structures and balanced sentence patterns seen especially in classical Chinese poetry; the alliteration found in the earliest English-language poems; assonance; the thought-patterns of the sonnet or the word-patterns of such rhetorical figures as chiasmus; lists, especially those using anaphora, in which each part begins with the same word—all serve to lead the mind with accuracy from one word to the next. They do this by helping to shape where a thought is going by the recall of where it has been. Consider the literal meaning of this synonym for the act of memory: "recall," to voice again. Repetition embracing variation is the thread of the cloth Mnemosyne wears.

The linguist Roman Jakobson did extensive work on Russian folk proverbs, exploring the ways condensation and the devices of patterned syntax and sound help them survive. In one essay, "Subliminal Verbal Patterning," he shows that highly sophisticated poetic figures and language patterns appear fully formed in the sayings and tales of illiterate peasants. He points out that even thoroughly literate users of memorable patterns do not always do so out of conscious intention—William Blake, for example, stated that complex verbal designs appeared in his work "without Premeditation and even against my Will." The essence of aphorisms and proverbs is to be both linguistically shapely and the briefest possible containers of their own meaning. "A penny saved is a penny earned" and "A stitch in time saves nine" are models not only of compression of content, but also of memorability in their patterns of syntax or sound—the first by repeating its grammatical form and rhythm, the second through half-rhyme and its interwoven *s*'s, *t*'s, and *i*'s. If one remembers such sayings at all, one will remember them not in approximation, but exactly. Unlike ordinary sentences subjected to the forces every child has seen at work in the game of "telephone," these will resist distortion and entropy as they pass from ear to ear.

For those who have been shaped by literacy, proverbs and especially mnemonics offer some sense of the way purely oral memory works. Trying to remember something, we search our minds not for the information itself but for the formulaic saying that holds it in place: "Thirty days hath September," we start to recite, or we hum the tune in which the alphabet is held. Yet these sayings work only for remembrance of the smallest units of meaning. Larger constellations of meaning need something more to survive over time, which has been clarified only in the past half-century by the attempt to understand how the Homeric poems were produced and maintained. What that research has made visible is this: if the threads of memory are spun of the sounds and structures of individual lines, physical embodiment and narrative are the loom on which the epic's astonishing garment is woven.

The seminal theory was worked out in the early 1920s by Milman Parry for a master's thesis at the University of California, Berkeley. Examining the *Iliad* and *Odyssey*, Parry realized that the choice of words and phrases at any given point are driven by what he called "the requirements of the shape of the hexameter line." From this insight, he concluded that the Greek poems, though they have come down to us through later transcription, were not originally written at all. Instead, he found in them the marks of a process of oral composition by rhapsodes—tellers of tales, or, literally, "stitchers."

Parry and a protege, Albert B. Lord, tested out this theory in the 1930s by traveling to Serbian villages; Lord's *Singer of Tales* holds a full account of their work. They found that lengthy narrative poems were still being sung by illiterate singers, to the accompaniment not of a lyre, but of another stringed instrument, the *gusle*. Though no historical situation can precisely duplicate another, what they saw and heard corroborated their hypothesis that the Homeric poems, for all their vastness, were orally composed and handed down. Not only were the twentieth-century bards, called *guslari*, unlettered, but our own age's conceptions both of original authorship and of verbatim memory were, if anything, antithetical to the way they accomplished their task. Rather than memorizing by rote, the guslari drew their songs from a storehouse of formulaic metrical phrases they had learned by listening to other singers since earliest childhood; these formulae were then woven into a web of similarly traditional narrative themes. The idea of individual words is itself a construct of written language—compare the English two-word *Good day* with the French *Bonjour*. One might say, then, that the formulae are the words of oral poetry: words that, taken together, form a specialized kind of language created to fulfill the needs of memorability.

A master guslar would perform his own version of a new tale, however lengthy, after only a single hearing, but he first required a pause of at least a night and a day, and preferably a week, in which the piece could "ferment"—precisely the opposite of the way that word-by-word memorization works. And though the guslari boasted they could recite a poem "exactly the same" as they had twenty years earlier, in fact Lord's tape recordings proved that each telling was unique. A rhapsode's real skill, according to Lord, consisted of his ability to weave the story at hand into a new whole appropriate for each audience and occasion of its telling.

If the songs had been found to be repeated verbatim, differences between rhapsodes would be more akin to the differences between actors than between "authors"—and in fact the truest description may lie somewhere between, for the rhapsode does not so much create his tale as offer himself up to become it. One might think also of literal stitchers, quilt-makers, in this context. Though they work with traditional patterns and materials available to all, it is the specific aesthetic choices and abilities of a relative few that mark them as artists. And, like quilt-makers, the rhapsodes are artists almost incidentally: their task is to make something useful for their community, the story that helps to hold it together over time.

Poetry was theater, library, university, on-line service in Mnemosyne's world—its role was nothing less than the preservation and transmission of human knowledge and culture. In his *Preface to Plato*, Eric A. Havelock describes how the Homeric poems served as the encyclopedias of the Greek world. Geography, genealogies, laws; descriptions of how a ship is launched or brought into harbor; accounts of how to behave at a banquet, how not to behave toward the daughter of a priest—all were preserved across both time and distance in the epic's hexameter lines. They were passed on and renewed through public gatherings in which the intermingled, powerful rhythms of voice, lyre, and body were absorbed physically as well as mentally by the listeners. Whether listener or reciter, each participant entered fully into a common dream of what it meant to be Greek and human—a dream larger than any individual mind, that had been put into the care of the

Muse. Verse spun a thread of continuity and identity a person could follow through the chaos of a largely unknown and unknowable world.

Sound-based mnemonics, supported by the rhythms of the lyre, hold details accurately in place at the level of the line. Remembrance of larger structures in the epic takes place not in mouth and breath, but within the imaginative mind. This is accomplished perhaps most powerfully by engaging the unfolding powers of plot. As we see in young children, the mind's first way of understanding the world is by story: rehearsing familiar tales, a child constructs a familiar self, as well as a sense of existence as rhythmic, progressive, and meaningfully structured. Narrative both lends itself to repeated tellings and is in itself memorable—listening to an interesting story, we project ourselves vividly into its characters, their experience becoming a part of our own. Narrative, then, uses the structure of time to defeat the ephemerality of time, and as Havelock has pointed out, a story's episodes can also serve the oral mind as table of contents and index.

The mind of oral memory dwells always in a physical body. Neither emotion nor ideas have yet been abstracted; they live instead in the form of gods and goddesses whose angers, desires, moralities, and jealousies affect human behavior in the form of furious storms, biting gadflies, and irresistibly beautiful singing. Such physical descriptions let us enter a story vividly, as if from within. We do not only receive a powerfully described world in our minds, we occupy it—sleeping in the cradle of its rocky harbors, eating of its honey cakes sprinkled with dark seeds of poppy.

In a culture that likes to think it is founded on the powers of logical, rational mind, the term "imaginary" has taken on overtones of the trivial or the frivolous. Yet the imagination was oral mind's earliest tool for conceiving of the abstract at all, by binding ideas into physical, visual form. Grief at the very existence of death becomes the image of Achilles' two immortal horses lowering their dusty heads to weep over the body of Patroclus. The concept of life's ceaseless abundance, difficult as well as joyous, is carved by Homer and the craftsman-god Hephaestus onto Achilles' shield of war: A bridal procession unfolds near a marketplace argument over the blood-price of a murdered man; ploughmen drink flagons of wine as they pause in their labors; lions tear into the slaughtered body of an ox, oblivious of the nearby baying of dogs; acrobats and courting couples flank the blood-drenched figure of Death, busy harvesting her pick of young men from amid a battle. And all is ultimately enclosed by the great river that bounds the edge of the shield—water circling the realm of what can be seen and heard and touched, beyond which oral consciousness could not go.

These life-holding devices of Mnemosyne, story and physical embodiment, can still be found in the familiar precept given new writers: "Show, don't tell." Now, as twenty-eight hundred years ago, a poet's task is to cast a convincing spell, to create in the mind of another a lasting and particular vision of human experience, whether as sweeping as Homer's or as tightly focused as a single fragment by Sappho. A poem's task is to seduce—its readers or listeners must find in it something irresistible, something to which they want to surrender. The power of beautiful sound and structured language is one such lure; the power of vivid imagining is another; and a third is the human curiosity called forth by story, which lingers not only in poems that are obvious narratives but also in the way good poems root themselves in specificity of situation and event. In any good lyric poem—even one as brief as a haiku—a tiny narrative exists: there is a moment of transformation. Something happens, to writer, to reader, over its course.

This, then, is the world of Mnemosyne, in which all knowledge has been hard won, braced against the erasures of time by generations of singers and their words. In creation stories and early songs and poems worldwide, the strategies of oral mind are the same. It is a mind in which knowledge is embedded in the recital of outward description and actions, and in which new information immediately becomes the basis for a new story. It is a mind in which the complex grammar of subordinate clauses and their finely honed logic has not yet appeared, but, to use Elizabeth Bishop's phrase, "everything [is] only connected by 'and' and 'and.'" Lastly, it is a mind carried through time by the artful weaving of sound. Then, writing arrives—and the possibilities of mind, thought, memory, and poetry are suddenly and irrevocably altered. Much will be retained of Mnemosyne's ways, particularly in the making of poems, but much will also be added to them. And at this moment, we come to another point of poetry's beginning and another Greek god: Hermes, complex and fitting symbol of what is to come.

Guardian of the crossroads and of communication, and inventor of poetry's tools—first the lyre and then the alphabet—Hermes is the patron god of writing. Born long after Mnemosyne, into a world already filled with beings, gods, and stories, he is the last of the gods to join the Greek pantheon and does so out of his own deliberate ambition. Mnemosyne's story is simple: she enters the world, brings her gift of remembrance, and gives birth to her daughters; that is all. The story of Hermes, like his character, is filled with complication and multiplicity. In the paradox that so often holds Greek truth, the messenger god is a trickster. He lies, he jokes, he speaks by indirection as often as he speaks clearly. Tricksters spill with the energy of creation, and true to the form, Hermes loves sex: when the other gods retreat in horror at the sight of Aphrodite trapped aloft in a net with her lover Ares, Hermes only desires her more. Like language, like unsocialized sexuality, he can travel between realms freely—what he wants, he goes after. And it is in his playfulness, irreverence, and disdain for the rules that his capacities for seeing things new, for invention, also reside. He is in many ways the opposite of Mnemosyne, whose power, though it rises in a vernal freshening, is primarily in the service of conservation and continuance. The power of Hermes is that of change.

As a precocious day-old infant, Hermes captures a tortoise outside the cave where he was born. He kills it, and with the immediate and instinctive curiosity of child-mind, guts it. He then proceeds to steal his brother Apollo's herd of fifty sacred oxen, killing two cows as a sacrifice to the gods; seeing some possibility in the material at hand, he uses the intestines of one to make strings for the tortoise's shell—and so fashions the first lyre. When the furious Apollo tracks him down, Hermes calms him by singing a song of praise to his brother; literally enchanted, Apollo agrees to trade the remaining cows for the lyre itself, and in this way becomes the patron god of poetry. Next, Hermes invents the first shepherd's pipe, which he again gives away, this time in exchange for the gift of augury, of "reading" the future. Called before his father Zeus, Hermes is cautioned to behave more maturely in the future. Zeus then assigns him his duties as a member of the pantheon: the job of messenger and also the care of treaties, commerce, and travelers. This initial meeting of Zeus and Hermes is an interesting moment; in it we can see how the powers of the existing order attempt not only to acknowledge and include but also to contain the new god, who is a force of liberating and chaotic change.

Having created the instruments of music and gained the art of divination—of reading the signs of the world—and with his new responsibilities in mind, Hermes next joins with the Fates in devising a number of new technologies: the alphabet, astronomy (another tool for augury and predicting the future), musical scales, boxing, a system of weights and measures, the cultivation of olives. As master of oaths, Hermes is the god of rhetoric and magical formulae. There is also a rather phallic tale about his invention of fire-making, a technology Prometheus will later steal for humans along with *grammata* (written letters). Throughout Hermes' stories runs the thread of energetic invention—his works are not only artistic but also artful: crafty, clever, and ingenious. What better patron for writing can we imagine than this god whose hallmarks are not only creativity and playfulness, but also the capacity for anarchistic duplicity and lies?

Many themes in the story of Hermes appear as well in that of the Chinese god Fu Hsi, who is also credited with the invention of writing. Creator of musical instruments, Fu Hsi also taught human beings how to domesticate animals and catch fish in nets, devised a system of writing by tying knots in strings, and invented the trigrams used in Chinese divination. Both gods are resourceful producers, holding sway in the realms of art and commerce, and both are strongly connected to the idea of augury as well. Further, the earliest writing known in China appears on the oracle bones of the Shang dynasty (1766–1122 BCE)—generally either the shoulder bones of oxen or the shells of tortoise. Surely the convergence between these two cultures' versions of the origins of writing cannot be entirely an accident. An overlap in the inventions and domains of expertise of the two gods makes a kind of intuitive sense, but why these particular animals reappear (once in myth, once historically) is more of a mystery. For the tortoise, an explanation may come from the markings on the shell, already so much like written signs. The oxen remain more puzzling— except that, as early givers of meat and milk and labor, they are powerful symbols of that moment in which the wild earth's gifts to humankind were domesticated and put to use. In any case, it is in the shape of their powerful heads that the Western alphabet begins—turn the letter A on its side and you can still see the vestige of its early Greek form, modeled on the head of an ox with its two protruding horns.

With Hermes and the advent of writing a sea-change comes to our relationship with words, time, and ultimately, thought. The flowing, present-moment stream of Mnemosyne's unselfconscious recital gives way to the ingenuity of the Trickster, and the mark of Hermes permeates this new way of being in the world. Though writing and reading come late to the world, the mind of reading arrives first, even in Hermes' own story. Part of reading's flavor has always been an association with both prediction and the solving of puzzles. Before consciousness learned to transcribe experience into written signs, it read the weather, the herds of wild animals, the first turning leaf, the words and the hearts of others. To read with accuracy the outer world is the most basic work of understanding, the initial action we must bring to the enigmatic data of raw existence. And the results of reading matter: hunters read scat, sailors read the sky, and lovers read one another's every gesture, word, and glance with an intensity of attention they may bring to little else in their lives.

The word *read* comes from Old English and Germanic words having to do with advice-giving, interpretation, and guessing. Further back there is the Latin *ratus*, past participle of the verb *reri*, meaning to count, calculate, or reckon. One cognate is the Middle English *redel*: riddle. This etymology, as well as the myth of Hermes, links the reader of written letters to the early astrologer scanning the star-sprayed darkness, or the priest peering into a slaughtered bird's entrails, interpreting signs. The reader, along with the interpreter of oracles, searches in what is read for an answer useful for going forward wisely in life. But symbols—and particularly words, as many Greek myths show—are perverse. In the face of our human desire for understanding, words pose riddles before which our ability to read the face of things must either deepen or fail—and how it fails is instructive.

In one myth, which surely dates from the literate age, King Midas inquires of the oracle at Delphi what will happen if he takes his army into battle. The answer returns: "A great kingdom will be overthrown." Confidently, Midas advances against Persia, and the kingdom soon overthrown is his own. If Midas had widened his perception of the statement, had "read" the reply to his question not with the self-serving mind of his desires but for what it might mean on its own terms, he might have seen the danger and been spared. Hubris is the tale of the near miss. If you read carelessly, shallowly, or selfishly, this story says, it is at your peril. To be anything less than absolutely attentive is to fail to come up to what the deepest nature of reading requires—not the least of these is the inclusion of the Trickster's complex ways.

With the arrival of Hermes and written language, as we have seen, speech moves from the tongue and ear into the sense-realm of the eyes. This shift frees the mind of its first, great work of simple remembrance, and at the same time makes of language something that can be held still, and so subjected to a new care: to new and deeper levels of reading. Though the devices of Mnemosyne continue to permeate written language, the medium (as Marshall McLuhan memorably, alliteratively put it) is also the message. Writing alters consciousness. Objectified and able to be held at a distance from the self, the written word makes possible a considered survey of the human mind and its contents: once a thought can be looked at once, it can be looked at twice.

Further, once words have been placed into the form of externally perceptible objects, those objects, like individual building blocks, can he moved about independently from one another and put into new relationships, vertical as well as horizontal. The chain of narrative structure can be broken, and thinking is freed of its bonds to time and event. Knowledge formerly held only within personified action expands to a dense field of ideas and propositions, nouns used abstractly, newly complex logical relationships. Thought itself, along with the means of its recording, becomes reified, an object seemingly equivalent to other "things." In the process, consciousness is both liberated and fragmented.

This new mode of thinking affects everyone born into a literate culture, not only those who can read—the ways of literate mind, like the contents of Pandora's box, affect the whole community once they are released. At the core is this: when not only the world of phenomena but also the world of the mind itself can be read, reflection and analysis emerge. With them comes a new sense of what it means to be human, to be a self who can think in a way outside of events and a culture's consensual understandings. Such an individual will be more private, more separate from others—will be able, in a wholly new way, to be not only a carrier of cultural knowledge but an author.

One caution: it may be that scholars have made more of this idea of the private self's roots in literacy than is quite warranted. Our knowledge of what the historical oral mind chose to preserve in verse can come only from the first written texts. And while it is true that the Greek epic poems and works such as *Gilgamesh*, *Beowulf*, or South African praise poems offer more a portrait of "types" than individual lives, the earliest folk songs of Chinese and Japanese literature and the hieroglyph-transcribed love songs of Egypt's New Kingdom (dating from 1300 BCE) are filled with the sense of personal, common life. A girl asks her lover to join her in a bathing pond while she wears her new dress of sheer Memphis linen; a man wishes he might dry himself with the towels that have touched his beloved's face. These long-vanished lovers scarcely seem emblematic of larger forces—they are wholly themselves. Conversely, highly literate twentieth-century societies have made fierce attempts to immerse the private individual into group mind. For many decades, Communist China, Romania, and the Soviet Union suppressed "personal" writing as socially dangerous; in this country, recurrent attacks on artists as "un-American" show that wariness of individualized expression is hardly confined to Marxist regimes.

What is considered worth remembering becomes what is considered important; even the limited democracy of ancient Athens could not have been conceived in a culture concerned only with accounts of leaders and gods. The personal *is* political. We may wonder whether the concept of self-governance could have arisen without the respect granted Sappho and Archilochus, who each used Mnemosyne's memorable meters to carry the passions of daily life.

A two-thousand-year record of diaries, journals, pillow books, and "confessions" shows the way putting thoughts on paper allows a person to develop a deepened sense of individual life as well as independence of opinion. Private reflection creates the freedom to venture past what is generally held to be true—within the refuge of a journal's bound pages, one can hold an opinion at odds with others and not pay an immediate social price. The Trickster's cultural role is to counter rigidity and the forms of authority, and the tricksterish effects of literacy arc ultimately personalizing and democratic, however slowly the process unfolds—which may be one reason that many cultures made writing a carefully restricted skill, kept especially from women. By allowing its practitioners to think, see, and act for themselves, as well as by its ability to safeguard the already known, writing allows originality and idiosyncrasy of perception and statement to emerge.

The same holds true for the effects of literacy on the more formal aspects of poetry. The memorability inherent especially in the printed word, which enables the exact reproduction of visual forms for the first time, allows the development of the concrete poem (poems written in the shape of what they describe, first used in English by the seventeenth-century poet George Herbert in his poem "The Altar," arranged in the shape of a cross), the free verse line, and eventually even more highly individualized arrangements of poems on the page. The typographical play in the poems of e. e. cummings or the over-printings and strike-outs of Susan Howe are only the most recent of the new branches that Hermes grafts onto poetry's oral roots. Relatively fresh, they still surprise; yet each of Hermes' inventions seemed revolutionary, odd, even threatening, at the time of its first appearance. Plato, who lived at the pivot point of the oral-literate transition in Greece, shows Socrates condemning not only the poets, symbols of the old oral culture, but also the newly common practice of writing, which he asserted would weaken both memory and the ability to search out truth—written words, unlike debaters, cannot argue back.

The old ways were designed to persist, and the goddess of continuity is powerful. Even this essay uses one of Mnemosyne's strategies for thought, in describing poetry's evolution through the personified figures of two Greek gods. Still, once preserved, thought was freed of the need to be memorable. The work of history, philosophy, theology, moral allegory, and science could be approached in ways outside the rhapsode's devices of meter and sound, and eventually these forms of thinking moved virtually entirely into prose. Quite late, the novel emerges—related to the epic in some ways and yet wholly different.

Over two and a half millennia of literacy, the topics poetry approaches have slowly shifted. Though a poet such as Robert Frost or Maya Angelou may at times be invited to contribute to a public occasion, the work of forging community has gone over to song—to cultural anthems such as "We Shall Overcome" or "Imagine," or to whatever song is chosen to accompany the current political campaign. Even poems contemplating larger cultural issues (Auden's "September 1, 1939," Eliot's *Wasteland*, Pound's *Cantos*) do so within a highly individualized frame. A few recent poems attempting to voice directly the experience of a community come to mind—Gwendolyn Brooks's "We Real Cool: The Pool Players" is one example, even its title subtly echoing the old Greek chorus. Still, this outwardly simple poem asks of the reader a far more sophisticated understanding than does preliterate oral work, and the same is true of the writing of recent experimental poets who seek to escape subjectivity in their work.

In the realm of the personal lyric, love poems, religious hymns, and elegies arrived early, but accounts of bearing and raising children have entered the main Western tradition only in the last few decades, along with descriptions of car repair, factory work, and air travel. These additions stem not only from the changed demographics of poets; they are also a sign of our altered conception of the lyric itself. Late twentieth-century writings wrestle with the perennial questions of poetry, but they do so from the point of view of the individual, not the tribe: Hermes' task is not to speak for the whole but to create new depth through disruption, question, introspection, challenge. Poetry has responded in kind. And yet—

One line of *The Homeric Hymn to Hermes* suggests that Hermes was, in fact, destined to be Mnemosyne's chosen consort. If a wedding of Mnemosyne and Hermes is the source of poetry as we now know it, how should we summarize what each partner brings to the nuptial bed? Mnemosyne shows us how to make thought memorable through the story, image, compression, linguistic structure, and sound; Hermes keeps language flexible, energetic, playful, experimental, and free. Mnemosyne provides the place of beginning, the world of human event, of what is and has been; Hermes's realm is revision, seeing what emerges when the mind is able to look back on itself—how a tortoise, seen freshly, might become a lyre. Mnemosyne gives the forms and strategies of verse a central authority and role that continue to resonate at poetry's core; Hermes forges of these forms a tool to sing of new knowledge, of new ways to know.

While Mnemosyne and Hermes bring different dowries to the poetry we now know, each also supports the other's gifts. Mnemosyne's eternal present does in fact accommodate change—like the old goddesses of Europe whose temples were later rededicated to Mary, the Muse is not only capable of changing her story, she will do so whenever the present situation alters its needs. Similarly, Hermes' ingenuity works also in the service of remembrance—both the lyre and written language are technologies that preserve words through time. Poetry's strategies remain a pendulum swinging between the gifts of both these figures, and each shift of aesthetic in poetry over time can be viewed as a negotiation between the desires of Mnemosyne and those of Hermes. By the friction and tensions these two approaches engender, poetry is continually renewed.

The turn to common speech by the English Romantic poets, for example, can be viewed as Hermes breaking loose from an overly codified and constricting poetic tradition. And in just the past few decades of American poetry, we have seen the aesthetic strategy of the deep image and its poetry of physical embodiment challenged by the more hermetic practitioners of language poetry; then, in the 1980s, neoformalists and proponents of the new narrative appeared to champion Mnemosyne's devices and to balance the rise of a highly conceptualized and page-based poetics. Charles Olson's projective verse, based on the rhythms of the natural breath, and Allen Ginsberg's "Kaddish" are recognizably in the lineage of oral poetry; John Ashbery and Jorie Graham work more in the tradition of subtle literate mind. Questions of fragmentation versus wholeness, of whether meaning and coherence are the products of a dominating cultural authority or the natural workings of mind, of infinitely open-ended possible readings or the degree to which an author's intentions matter—all are matters of passionately partisan debate, a literary Trojan War in which these two Olympians each have their chosen heroes. Yet every writer is nourished by the full spectrum, the full history of the tradition. New strategies take their revolutionary meaning from their relationship with the forms that have gone before, and however much memory may shift its devices, it does not ever completely abandon the old: each step of a journey enters and alters the body of the person who makes it.

For the Greek rhapsode, the idea of a poem as a poem may not even have existed—and certainly our conception of a poet did not. The "maker"—what the Greek word for poet literally means—was not the individual self, but the entire culture, re-presenting and remaking itself and the world in song, through the Muse. The golden age of poetry so often mourned was not the age of Eliot or Frost; of Wordsworth, Keats, Shakespeare, or Dante; or even of Sappho. The golden age was that of Mnemosyne, in which poetry was humankind's one account of the whole, and the poet was, in fact, the acknowledged legislator of the race. Yet how much has been gained by that wholeness's breaking into separate letters, into the many parts—not least the ability to hold the idiosyncratic music and knowledge of individual lives. And conversely, however strange each new development may seem, every poem remains an attempt to name with fidelity some complex aspect of the human experience and keep it available through time. We peer into the new poem with the old hope: that we might find there a few words to illumine more widely our passage through the dark woods and brightly lit cities of the fleeting, time-bound world. And the art of poetry remains a daughter of Remembrance—of our wish to feel joined to some fabric that both gives meaning to and is made meaningful by the part of it we are.

Alcaics In Exile: W. H. Auden's "In Memory Of Sigmund Freud"

ROSANNA WARREN

O n September 23, 1939, Sigmund Freud died in exile in London, a refugee from Nazi Austria. Within a month, Auden, who had been living in the United States since January of that year, wrote a friend in England that he was working on an elegy for Freud.(1) The poem appeared in the *Kenyon Review* early in 1940. A stately public ode, the poem mourns not only the death of a publicly significant individual, but the collapse of a world. Hitler had overrun Austria, Czechoslovakia, Poland; assaults on Jews had intensified; England and France had just declared war on Germany. There would be, indeed, many who would have to be mourned:

> When there are so many we shall have to mourn,
> when grief has been made so public, and exposed
>   to the critique of whole epoch
>   the frailty of our conscience and anguish,
>
> of whom shall we speak?. . .

Someone encountering this poem for the first time, on the page or in the ear, might be pardoned for puzzling over its form. It sounds prosy. It seems to have some recognizable English cadences, pentameters ("When there are so many we shall have to mourn"), tetrameters ("so many plausible young futures"), and even trimeters ("the frailty of our conscience and anguish"). But the pattern seems unruly, with some lines stretching out beyond five traditional beats, and ignoring any iambic order: "turned elsewhere with their disappointment as he." Groping for a more satisfactory principle of organization, a reader with some knowledge of versification may be moved to count syllables. Such a reader will discover that the poem is indeed organized syllabically in lines of 11, 11, 9, and 10 syllables. "Aha," says the reader, alert to Auden's intimacy with classical civilization: "A Horatian ode. Not inappropriate for a formal elegy." Reflecting further, and leafing through the pages of Horace, that reader will find, or remember, that two thirds of Horace's odes are in these quatrains, the alcaic stanza. Auden, it appears, has composed his elegy in some version of the meter of Alcaeus, the 7th century BCE Greek poet whose stanza became second nature to Horace. And we cannot enter the world of Auden's poem without asking, why alcaics? And how do they work here?

"In Memory of Sigmund Freud" is sometimes said to be Auden's first syllabic poem.(2) Others demur, proposing both earlier and later examples.(3) Whatever the spats about dating Auden's early syllabic practice, scholars conventionally agree that his turn toward syllabic composition reflects his evolving interest in a discursive poetry; in the poet as a private intelligence with a public voice; and in the work, respectively, of Horace and Marianne Moore. Having identified the poem as syllabic, many critics move on to heftier topics like psychoanalysis versus Marxism, Auden more than most poets having laid himself open to an overridingly thematic criticism of Big Ideas. But if, having acknowledged the influence of Horace and Moore in Auden's refusal of English iambic lyricism here, we stay with the question of meter, we are led back to the older progenitor, Alcaeus, a great poet of exile, whose stanza Auden adopts and adapts. I shall ask how it affects our reading to observe that the stanza itself has a genealogy, and brings its expressive burden to bear on Auden's poem.

"In Memory of Sigmund Freud" relies on a counterpoint of two metrical systems, the largely iambic accentual/syllabic system, traditional in English since Wyatt, and a flattened version of Greek quantitative meter, which was a musical notation of syllable length. For Auden, whose great prosodic facility was almost a handicap, the problem was, "not how to write in iambics but how not to write in them from automatic habit."(4) Throughout his poetic life, he reached for cadences to interrupt the "natural" iambics, sometimes recalling the Old English alliterative beat, and often turning to ballads and popular tunes for rhythmical variation. By the late thirties, he was not only disillusioned with the Spanish Civil War and his role as quasi-Socialist bard, but was seeking new compositional principles as well. Free verse was not an alternative: his ear required an evident prosodic order, a perceptible "law like love." On the other hand, Auden had been stirred by his encounter with Moore's syllabics in 1935. As he confessed later, he had at first been "unable to make head or tail of her poems. . . . A syllabic verse like Miss Moore's, in which accents and feet are ignored and only the syllables count, is very difficult for an English ear to grasp."(5) He persevered, however, sensing the integrity of her rule. The syllabic verse Auden eventually made his own hardly resembled Moore's, but she helped deliver him from habitual cadences and perhaps helped him imagine the shape of a modern Horatian ode in rhythms trained more on speech than on song.

It is no mystery why Auden should have been drawn to a Horatian stance. The Roman poet stood squarely in the center of his era and mastered it with the authority of his verse, as Auden appeared to have done in 1939. But Horace leads us back to Alcaeus, who haunts Horace's odes as a symbolic figure. In the declaration of his own poetic immortality (III, 30: "Exegi monumentum aere perennius"), Horace links his power to his having first brought Aeolian song into Latin verse, and specifically invokes contentious, exiled Alcaeus in many of his odes. More deeply than in mere reference, however, Horace honors Alcaeus in incorporating his stanza. He insists on the caesura after the fifth syllable in the first two lines, and lengthens that syllable in the first three lines, giving weight and stability where Alcaeus had often allowed a rapid forward trill of short syllables. By accentuating weight and pause, Horace points up the principal beauty of the alcaic, its shifts in rhythm in mid-course, its calculated imbalance as the iambic and choriambic first two lines yield to iambs in the third and resolve in racy dactyls in the fourth. As exemplum of poetry's task, to act out the dynamic equilibrium between order and disorder, the alcaic has no rival. Listening to it in Horace's Cleopatra ode will tune our ears for Alcaeus' Greek and Auden's English. Here, celebrating in disorder the imposition of order, is the pounding dance step of the Romans after Actium:

Nunc est bibendum,/ nunc pede li/bero

pulsanda tellus,/ nunc Saliar/ibus

ornare pulvi / nar deorum

tempus erat dapibus,/ sodales.

(Now is the time to drink, now with freed foot
to beat the earth, now, companions, we must
decorate the couches of the gods for the
feasts of Mars.)

And what of Alcaeus, to whom Horace owed his lyre? He was
born in Mytilene on Lesbos around 630 BCE; he was an aristocrat;
he lived during the collapse of the traditional political order in
Mytilene; with his brothers he fought the tyrant Pittakos, was
defeated, and spent years in exile. His poetry has the directness of
statement, clarity of image, and eerily swift transitions that should
be the envy of any modern. His social role as a poet allies him more
closely with Auden than with any other modern poet. For Alcaeus'
lyrics are so intrinsically social, the very distinction between pri-
vate and public loses its relevance in regard to them. His songs
were performed in and for the *hetaireia*, the aristocratic kinship
club of his clan. Song consecrated the fellowship, which was based
on the sacramental bonds of common drinking and fighting. But
hunted into exile, Alcaeus the social poet becomes a solitary man
among wolf-thickets, *lukaimiais*, as he says in poem 130.(6) In the
two poems of Alcaeus I offer here, the actual community has been
replaced by divine order, the ideal spiritual community visible on
earth in its temples where the exile prays for revenge and consola-
tion, and where, in the astonishing last stanza of poem 130, in an
aeolic meter related to the alcaic, the girls of Lesbos go to and fro
trailing their robes, being judged for beauty, and all around there
rings the wondrous sound of the loud, holy cry of women. In the
prose translation by Alcaeus' authoritative editor Denys Page, the
surviving fragments of the poem read as follows:

> (16 ff.) . . . I, poor wretch, live a rustic's life, yearning to
> hear
> Assembly summoned, O Agesilaidas,

And Council; what my father and my father's father have
grown old possessing, among these citizens who
wrong each other, therefore I am an outcast,
An exile on remotest verges; and like Onomacles, . . . soli-
tary I settled, a man among wolf-thickets. . . . war, for
it is ignoble (?) to renounce rebellion against . . .
. . . to the precinct of the blessed gods . . . setting foot on
the black earth . . . I dwell, stepping clear of troubles;
Where Lesbian girls go to and fro with trailing robes,
being judged for beauty, and all around there rings the
wondrous sound of the loud holy cry of women every
year;
. . . from many [toils] when will the Olympian gods [deliv-
er me]?. . .(7)

If we recall how Auden, all his life, sought some version of the *het-
aireia*, an ideal brotherhood; how he tried one form after another
of such a community—public school, Socialism, the fraternity of
art, the Anglican Church; how deeply embedded in his poetry and
prose was the dream of that brotherhood, of "the poet and the
city": we shall begin to sense the poignant relevance of Alcaeus,
the poet of exile, to Auden in 1939, mourning another masterful
exile. But we might then ask, as some of Auden's English readers
did, whether his continued residence in the United States after the
outbreak of war was not more a vacation than an exile proper in the
sense in which Alcaeus and Freud both suffered it; we might even
be tempted to see the formality of his ode as a refuge from, or a
displaced shape for, tormenting questions about his own status as
an exile.

Let us hear, now, Alcaeus' own music, the song from his bro-
ken world, in a meter which seems to lose its footing, mid-stride,
but recovers its balance, and heals in the order of the ear what on
earth and in politics remains in ruins. The alcaic is scanned:

$$\overset{\smile}{-} \: - \: \smile \: - \: \overset{\smile}{-} \: / \: - \: \smile\smile \: - \: / \: \overset{\smile}{-} \: - \qquad \text{1, 2}$$

$$\overset{\smile}{-} \: - \: \smile \: - \: \overset{\smile}{-} \: / \: - \: \smile \: - \: - \qquad \text{3}$$

$$- \: \smile\smile \: - \: \smile\smile \: - \: / \: \overset{\smile}{-} \: - \: - \qquad \text{4}$$

I give the first three stanzas of poem 129 in Greek transliterated from Page's text, and in Page's translation:

— ˘ ˘ — ˘ —
...ra....a tode Lesbioi

— — ˘ ˘ — ˘ —
..........eudei/lon temenos/ mega

— — ˘ — ˘ — ˘ — —
xunon ka[te]ssan,/ en de bomois

— ˘ ˘ — ˘ ˘ — ˘ — —
athanaton makaron / ethekan

— — ˘ — ˘ — ˘ ˘— ˘ —
kaponumassann/ antiaon /Dia

˘ — ˘ — — — ˘ ˘ — ˘ —
se d'Aioleian / [k]udalimen / theon

— — ˘ — ˘ — ˘ — —
panton genethlan, / ton de terton

— ˘ ˘ — ˘ ˘ — ˘ — —
tonde kemelion on/umassan

— — ˘ — — — ˘ — ˘ —
zonusson ome/stan. a[gi]t' eu/noon

˘ — ˘ — ˘ — ˘ ˘— ˘ —
thumon skethontes / ammetera[s]/ aras

˘ — ˘ — ˘ — ˘ — —
akousat', ek de ton[d]e/ moxthon

— ˘ ˘ — ˘ ˘ — — —
argaleas te phugas / r[uesthe...

(. . . The Lesbians founded this precinct, con-
  spicuous and great, for all to share, and
  therein set altars of the blest Immortals;
And Zeus they entitled God of Suppliants;
  and you, the Aeolian, Illustrious Goddess,
  Mother of all; and this third they named
  . . .
Dionysus, devourer of raw flesh. Come, with
  friendly spirit hearken to our prayer, and
  from these toils and grievous banishment
  deliver us . . .) (8)

Turning to Auden's poem, we hear nothing of the subtle kin-
ship between choriamb (— ˘ ˘ —) and dactyl (— ˘ ˘) so essential to

Alcaeus' music. Auden's poem is oratory, not song: "When there are so many we shall have to mourn . . . ." In fact, his elegy is an exercise in the sacrifice of song. We note that Auden has not followed the practice of most English poets adapting quantitative meter, aligning English stress with Greek long syllables as Tennyson does in his alcaics to Milton:

$$\text{/ \quad / \quad } \smallsmile \text{ \quad / \quad / \quad / \quad } \smallsmile \smallsmile \text{ \quad / \quad } \smallsmile \text{ \quad /}$$
"Oh mighty-mouth'd in/ventor of har/monies. . . ."

This was not for lack of know-how on Auden's part: he had spent years in school translating Greek and Latin into English and vice versa. But he thought "the attempts of Spenser, Harvey and others to be good little humanists and write English verse in classical meters" futile (9) (though he granted that "English poetry owes much to their forlorn attempt)(10); nor, clearly, did he want to make his Freud elegy a piece of pyrotechnic classicizing by reproducing stress analogues to Greek meter.

The alcaic stanza as Auden deploys it here allows him to sidestep an iambic tune, and to mark the progression of a prosaic rhetoric, moving logically through stanzas as through stages of argument: When—For—No wonder—Of course—Like weather—But—But. It also allows him an invigorating asymmetry, further to defy the consoling recurrences of English lyric. Yet the ghost of Alcaeus still haunts it, and one way to read this poem of disenchantment and reenchantment, of fracture and union, is to measure the ways in which it both invites in and resists the lyric ghost of its ancestor.

"In Memory of Sigmund Freud" is not, in fact, Auden's first poem in syllabics or even in adapted English alcaics. From the mid-thirties on Auden had been fooling around with the ode form, gesturing with stanza shape toward the sapphic and the alcaic, eschewing rhyme but retaining an iambic accentual/syllabic meter, in poems such as "Casino," "Journey to Iceland," "Oxford," and "Orpheus." These poems are not organized by syllable count. But in April 1939, Auden wrote a disciplined, numerical alcaic poem called "Crisis."

A sinister poem, "Crisis" seems as stilted in its habitation of the alcaic stanza as in its generalized drama of plural pronouns, "they" versus "we": "Where do they come from? Those whom we so much dread . . . ." The poem suffers, I think, in never breaking through its symbolic generalities. What energy it does muster derives from its semi-submerged imagery of rape and (perhaps) of homosexual dread as an allegory for the onset of fascism:

> For the barren must wish to bear though the
> Spring
> punish; and the crooked that dreads to be
> straight
> cannot alter its prayer but summons
> out of the dark a horrible rector.

By contrast, "In Memory of Sigmund Freud," composed five months later, has an urgently particular subject that is both individual and public—Auden's own intense experience of Freud's work giving him, no doubt, a sense of private loss at this death. The first-person plural pronoun here is far more charged and personal than in "Crisis": "we" are all those who mourn the passing of a great healer, we who mourn the dominion of Hate over family life and nations, we who have suffered privately our own demons. Similarly, the alcaic stanza is far more daringly managed, its prosaic potentiality liberated, syntactic units no longer packaged by line as they were for the most part in "Crisis," but allowed to flex over lines and stanzas where the argument needs to make a pointed move. Here, poetry is startled to life: a formal vernacular disposed in argument strains against the local constrictions of unrhymed quatrains with unequal line lengths. In that rejection of lyric narcosis, Auden has found a shape for a loss which should afford no easy consolation.

This very public poem builds off the interplay of singular and plural, the "he" and the "we." In theme, let us note briefly how the literal exile of line 24 ("an important Jew who died in exile") expands to embrace figuratively the objects of the unconscious in lines 82-85: "while as they lie in the grass of our neglect, / so many long-forgotten objects / revealed by his undiscouraged shining // are returned to us and made precious again." By the end of the poem, the image of exile extends to the fauna of the night, the psychic formations which, in being recognized, contribute to healing: ". . . With large sad eyes/ its delectable creatures look up and beg /

us dumbly to ask them to follow:/ they are exiles who long for the future // that lies in our power . . . ." It expands further, we might suggest, to include the not-quite-exiled poet-speaker who never writes himself into this poem in the first-person singular. Further, in our pursuit of theme, we should notice how Time structures the poem, not only in the classroom allegories of Past, Present and Future, but in the disposition of temporal adverbs and conjunctions and the play of tenses: "*Still* at eighty he wished . . ."; "For about him *till* the very end were *still* / those he had studied, the fauna of the night, / and shades that *still* waited to enter / the bright circle of his recognition / turned elsewhere . . . ." "They are *still* alive . . . ." In line 68, the adverb "now" takes hold of the poem, and the tenses shift from past to present as the absent one is called into his after-life: "To us he is no more a person / now, but a whole climate of opinion . . . ." The retrospective "still" gives way to the prospective "till" in line 75 as Freud is seen affecting not only the present, but the future:

> he quietly surrounds all our habits of growth
>   and extends, till the tired in even
>   the remotest miserable duchy
>
> have felt the change in their bones and are cheered,
>   till the child, unlucky in his little State,
>   some hearth where freedom is excluded,
>   a hive whose honey is fear and worry,
>
> feels calmer now and somehow assured of escape . . .

A fuller reading of the poem would explore how images swell into theme in the structural antitheses of private and public life; childhood and adulthood; small and large; night and day; imagination and reason; disorder and order. For our purposes, I will merely remark that, as Freud's triumph is seen here in his power to "unite / the unequal moieties fractured / by our own well-meaning sense of justice," restoring night to day, maternal feeling to son, and so forth, the poem's triumph is to unite its antitheses in a single encompassing movement. This it achieves through the alcaic stanza.

Auden's obsession as a poet was to tell the truth. Hence his draconian self-revisions. As he said in *The Dyer's Hand*, "Poetry is not magic. In so far as poetry, or any of the other arts, can be said to have an ulterior purpose, it is, by telling the truth, to disenchant and disintoxicate."(11) Freud was, for Auden, one of the great, liberating truth-tellers, and one way the alcaic honors him here is by disenchanting the lyric, by interrupting English iambic flow and forcing dissonant enjambments. A look at a few of those enjambments will show some of the pressure points of the poem, where the stanza shape is intrinsic to the motion of thought. At line 36, the break between stanzas reenacts the moment of clarification in therapy: ". . . he merely told / the unhappy Present to recite the Past / like a poetry lesson till sooner / or later it faltered at the line where // long ago the accusations had begun." The collapse of oppressive structures is reflected at line 47: "No wonder the ancient cultures of conceit / in his technique of unsettlement foresaw/ the fall of princes, the collapse of / their lucrative patterns of frustration." In line 54, "down," clamping the line fore and aft, carries us appropriately down to Dante's hell: "down among the lost people like Dante, down / to the stinking fosse . . . ." To adduce one last example, we can note how the exposed preposition "to" in line 95 suspends and intensifies the restoration of maternal energy to the son: ". . . would give back to / the son the mother's richness of feeling."

I should not want to suggest that Auden leaves no trace of accentual/syllabic meter in his poem. It is powerfully audible through the resistant syllable count and periodic syntax. In the last stanza, you hear, distinctly, two pentameters followed by two tetrameters, and John Hollander has beautifully observed how the suppressed dactyls, the trace of the original Greek lyric, rise again in the end-stopped concluding lines of quatrains, as in

$$/ \; \smile \; \smile \; / \; \smile \; \smile \; / \; \smile \; / \smile$$
"puzzled and jealous about our dying" (line 16).

But the life of the poem, I suggest, inheres in its play of prose against its lyric model. In "In Memory of Sigmund Freud," Auden made himself at home in the alcaic stanza, and happily so, since he used it in numerous later poems, most immediately in the "Prologue" and "Epilogue" to the long "New Year Letter" written early in 1940.

By September 1939, Auden had outgrown the fantasy of belonging to a literal community. He had accepted exile as the essential, not the accidental, human condition: "Aloneness is man's real condition," he wrote in "New Year Letter" (line 1542). To his friends Professor and Mrs. E. R. Dodds back at Oxford, Auden wrote a series of letters between September 1939 and March 1940 in which he strained to justify his stay in the United States during England's struggle in the war with Germany. "At least I know what I am trying to do, which most American writers dont [sic], which is to live deliberately without roots," he wrote in January. (12) In March, he sent the Doddses an invented questionnaire in which he argues with himself about his actions; he confesses to being "embarrassed at being so happy when many of my greatest friends are having an unpleasant time" (13), but he determines that as his responsibility is to the language, nothing a writer could do in England "justifies smashing his private life . . . I am neither a politician nor a novelist, rapportage is not my business."(14) From Edward Mendelson's account in *Early Auden*, it is clear that the decision to leave England preceded the outbreak of war by well over a year, and was motivated by inward, poetic urgencies, not by expediency. The same forces that brought Rilke as a guardian spirit into Auden's sonnet sequence "In Time of War" (1938) were leading him away from a poetry of partisan politics toward a stance at once more private and more cosmopolitan.(15) His trajectory, that is, runs counter to that of Alcaeus: the ancient poet longs to return home, while his modern cousin flees it. But they meet in the alcaic stanza.

However one judges Auden's position—and some English readers still hold him, and the Freud elegy, accountable for a shirking of duty—his adoption of the alcaic stanza coincides with his stepping clear not only of the nation of his birth, but of the very idea of community as a defining force. He found in Alcaeus' stanza what he would call in another context, a "civitas of sound."(16) If we think of the word "stanza" etymologically, as a room, we may think of Auden coming to celebrate an ageless cult at the *temenos*, or sacred precinct, marked out by Alcaeus. In that *temenos*, in the presence of divinities invoked by Alcaeus and Auden alike, we say farewell to Freud:

One rational voice is dumb. Over his grave
the household of Impulse mourns
one dearly loved:
sad is Eros, builder of cities,
and weeping, anarchic Aphrodite.

1. Katherine Bucknell and Nicholas Jenkins, *W. H. Auden: "The Map of All My Youth"* (Oxford: Clarendon, 1990), p. 106.

2. John Fuller, *A Reader's Guide to W. H. Auden* (London: Thames and Hudson, 1970), p. 176.

3. See Monroe Spears, *The Poetry of W. H. Auden* (New York: Oxford University Press, 1963), pp. 222, 248; Richard Johnson, *Man's Place: An Essay on Auden* (Ithaca: Cornell University Press, 1973), p. 29.

4. W. H. Auden, *The Dyer's Hand* (New York: Random House, 1962), p. 47.

5. Auden, 296.

6. Lucid and informed accounts of Alcaeus' poetry and his social role can be found in Anne Pippin Burnett's *Three Archaic Poets: Archilochus, Alcaeus, Sappho* (Cambridge: Harvard University Press, 1983), and in Bruno Gentili's *Poetry and Its Public in Ancient Greece*, trans. A. Thomas Cole (Baltimore: Johns Hopkins University Press, 1988). The two poems of Alcaeus I cite here for their particular beauty were probably not known to Auden, as they entered the scholarly literature in 1942; but the main body of Alcaeus' surviving lyrics, including many poems of exile and political diatribe, were available in texts dating from 1935 (Ernst Diehl), *Anthologia Lyrica Graeca*, I. vi., Leipzig: Teubner, 2nd ed. 1935) and from 1911 (Theodor Bergk, *Poetae Lyrici Graeci*, iii, *Poetae Melici*, Leipzig: Teubner, 4th ed. 1911). Alcaeus as a poet of exile was of course a figure well-known from Antiquity, not least in his appearances in Horace's odes.

7. Denys Page, *Sappho and Alcaeus* (Oxford: Clarendon Press, 1955), pp. 199-200. The translations of Alcaeus are quoted with permission from Oxford University Press.

8. Page, 162.

9. Auden, *Dyer*, 17.

10. W. H. Auden, *et al.*, eds., *An Elizabethan Songbook* (New York: Doubleday Anchor, 1956), p. xv.

11. Auden, *Dyer*, 27.

12. Bucknell and Jenkins, 111.

13. Bucknell and Jenkins, 113.

14. Bucknell and Jenkins, 115.

15. Edward Mendelson, *Early Auden* (New York: Viking, 1981), pp. 332-66.

16. "New Year Letter," line 50, in W. H. Auden, *Collected Poems*, ed. Edward Mendelson (New York: Vintage, 1991), p. 200.

Part Two:
Poets

Either I'm Nobody, or I'm a Nation
RITA DOVE

1. Why a Collected? Why this essay?

A celebrated poet reaches a point in his career where there needs to be a retrospective consideration of the work. Several choices can be made. A *Selected Poems* demands rigorous excerpting from previous books. A *New and Selected Poems* is a way of assuring the public that one is not yet an institution. A *Collected Poems* is like tossing in one's lot with the gods.

Derek Walcott's massive *Collected Poems 1948–1984* has an edge of defiance, as if to say, "Dismiss me if you can." But who would want to dismiss him? Walcott's poems stand out from the wash of contemporary American poetry (so much of it so *mild*, like half-whispered, devious apologies) because they are so boldly eloquent. The writing is some of the most exquisite in the English language, resembling the Caribbean in its many voices—sometimes crisp, sometimes tough, sometimes sweetly lyrical, or clear and treacherous as water in a stream. The syntax is often elaborate, frustrating yet seductive in the way it both reveals and obscures. When a Walcott poem fails, the writing is rarely at fault.

A true Renaissance man, Walcott has consistently resisted being cubbyholed. He has rejected neither his Caribbean heritage nor his British education. Although in recent years he divides his time between Trinidad and Boston, for a while he lived exclusively in the West Indies as director of the Trinidad Theatre Workshop. Although St. Lucia, his birthplace, forms his primary subject matter, he has also written about Manhattan and Mandelstam. In the eyes of the public, however, his unique position as the first

English-speaking Caribbean poet of international renown threatens to make him ". . . a man no more / but the fervour and intelligence / of a whole country" (*Another Life*). And so the girth of this *Collected Poems* is also a demand to consider the whole man—not just his skin or age or prosody or heart or mind.

2. Two Early Poems—Precocity's ars poetica

> ". . . the writers of my generation were natural assimilators. We knew the literature of Empires, Greek, Roman, British, through their essential classics; and both the patois of the street and the language of the classroom hid the elation of discovery. If there was nothing, there was everything to be made. With this prodigious ambition one began."
> —Derek Walcott, "What the Twilight Says: An Overture"

In the very first poem—titled, significantly, "Prelude"—the young poet looks down on his island from a distance and puts it into geographical and historical perspective:

> I, with legs crossed along the daylight, watch
> The variegated fists of clouds that gather over
> The uncouth features of this, my prone island.
>
> Meanwhile the steamers which divide horizons prove
> Us lost;
> Found only
> In tourist booklets, behind ardent binoculars;
> Found in the blue reflection of eyes
> That have known cities and think us here happy.

Although he enjoys a giant's viewpoint, the "variegated fists of clouds" constitute a larger, more threatening entity which has beaten the island into submission. The poet recognizes his place in a line of bullies.

He then vows not to make his life "public" "[u]ntil I have

learnt to suffer / In accurate iambics." This statement of aesthet-
ics is an act of survival as well: coming from a marginal culture,
Walcott realizes how quickly colonial attitudes would label the per-
sonal confessions of a West Indian impulsive, lecherous, and non-
intellectual. Any of the contradictions and ambivalent urgings
common to all human beings would be invisible to such a preju-
diced observer; the poet's only chance to be heard is to beat the
masters at their own game. With the practiced duplicity of a
guerrilla, he plans to

> Make a holiday of situations,
> Straighten my tie and fix important jaws,
> And note the living images
> Of flesh that saunter through the eye.
>
> Until from all I turn to think how,
> In the middle of the journey through my life,
> O how I came upon you, my
> reluctant leopard of the slow eyes.

Beneath the surface politeness, he is a cool customer whose
detached observations register human beings as subjects—not
merely objects but "living images of flesh," a double removal. Still,
these images "saunter," and the casual iambics of the next lines,
plus the tripping syllables of "In the middle of the journey through
my life," are lulling. The incantatory "O" brings us up short,
approximating the sudden intake of breath the poet makes when
he stumbles upon that which changes his life.

Dante's *Divine Comedy* also begins in the middle of a life. Is
Walcott suggesting that he is at the same point—at age twenty-
eight a precocious notion—or is he saying that once "boyhood has
gone over" the remaining years constitute a struggle to recapture
that beatific state? ("Never such faith again, never such innocence!"
he exclaims, twenty-five years later, in *Another Life*.) The image of
the leopard, moreover, is "reluctant," like "a shy lover or a Muse . .
." I think "Prelude," finally, welcomes passion—both sensual and
communal—while warning against the pampering of personality that
can lead to self-indulgent writing. Above all, it is the poet's vow to
admit paradox and conflict into his intellectual makeup.

"Origins," the fifth poem in the book, was originally published in *Selected Poems* (1964). It is like a quilt of West Indian history, introduced with an epigram from Aimé Césaire; the roll of surrealistic images imitates the roll of the surf and is reminiscent of Césaire's *Return to My Native Land*. To begin, the slate is wiped clean. Tradition, history, culture, and identity are erased:

> The flowering breaker detonates its surf.
> White bees hiss in the coral skull.
> Nameless I came among olives of algae,
> Foetus of plankton, I remember nothing.

Walcott's admiration for the Hart Crane of "Voyages" and "O Carib Isle" accounts for the acoustical flamboyance here. The "flowering breaker" bombards the shoreline through the use of explosive consonants and that masterful word "detonates," with its echoing vowels. The sonic boom of the first two lines gives way to the quieter chains of nouns. The neutral material (coral skull, algae) provides a fruitful bed for the bees, the "I" with neither identity nor history. On this ground, then, one can plant. Nothingness, for Walcott, does not imply negation but rather a *tabula rasa* from which one can start afresh.

Western civilization intervenes, and the poet struggles to unite conflicting traditions in himself. His first efforts at assimilation apply the Western myths to oral African traditions:

> Between the Greek and African pantheon,
> Lost animist, I rechristened trees:
> Caduceus of Hermes: the constrictor round
> the mangrove. . . .

Sections III and VI are italicized homages to island patois, the linguistical result of assimilation. Here the debt to Césaire is evident in the undulating string of images laid out for our delectation—the "clear, brown tongue of the sun-warmed, sun-wooded Troumassee / of laundresses and old leaves"—images which, however, become more jarring, near-surrealistic in the juxtaposition of sensations, such as the "cracked cobalt" of the "starched, linen seas," a rising agitation that subsides with the exclamation *"Ah, mon enfance!"*

Part VI most resembles the Césaire of *Cahier d'un Retour au Pays Natal* (*Notebook of the Return to My Native Land*) with its associative progression of images through history: "their alphabet of alkali and aloe . . . their bitter olive" have scoured the "sweet, faded savour of rivers" until we find a "twin soul, spirit of river, spirit of sea." This, however, is a positive process, a multiplication of strengths rather than a division.

Walcott's concerns, reflected in these two early poems, have not changed substantially over the years. Even when he evokes violent emotions—fury, love, grief—the writing is controlled, trenchant. In the midst of the most relentless self-scrutiny is the panning, photographic eye, returning to us flailed beachhead, yellowing coconut, the "padded cavalry of the mouse."

The primary vigor of patois informs poems like "The Liberator," "Parang," "The Schooner *Flight*," and "Pocomania," where the cadences of dialect syncopate the iambic line and patois words are liberally sprinkled without obliterating sense. In "Sainte Lucie," in the middle of a bilingual cataloguing of indigenous fruit, he cries, "Come back to me, / my language"; later in the same poem appear the lyrics of a native Creole song he once heard on the back of an open truck; he provides an English translation in the next section.

Walcott is a poet of circling and deepening; even the framing dates for this volume—1948 to 1984—hint that everything comes full circle. A prodigy and a black, he saw his dilemma early; a poet, he knew that the iambic line, with its thumbholds of word and image, was his thread out of the labyrinth.

3. Santa Lucia: The Raw Material

> "If your daily life seems poor, do not blame it;
> blame yourself, tell yourself that you are not
> good enough to call forth its riches. For any-
> one who creates there is no poverty and no
> poor, indifferent place."
> —Rilke, *Letters to a Young Poet*

I had to go away to college to discover that I was supposed to be ashamed of my hometown—for wasn't Akron, with its brick factories and sooty clapboard houses, deplorable? Didn't the smell of rubber make me sick? Wasn't it true that the only river had been forced underground? (The gorge remains, choked with dogwood, oak, hickory; in summer it wafts sickeningly with the floral bouquet of rotting garbage.)

Tourists love the Caribbean for its white beaches and opal seas, its glossy vegetation trailing across restaurant lattices. How delightful to snack on pomegranates, tucking a nameless exotic flower behind your ear! How could anyone regret all this!

Derek Walcott was born in Castries, St. Lucia, a small volcanic island between St. Vincent and Martinique. Then a part of Her Majesty's Empire, St. Lucia "enjoyed" a British imprint— Christianity, white manor houses. But behind the Great House sprawled the squalor of the poor blacks. All that a writer from St. Lucia could offer, in lieu of Thomas Hardy's cool and lonely heath, were bleached shores and, puffing toward them, steamers which "prove us lost: / Found only / In tourist booklets, behind ardent binoculars."

To get a hint of the complexity of the West Indian identity crisis, first look at the map. Register the distances between islands— "little turtles from Tortuga to Tobago"—and imagine the small towns trying to imitate suburban America, the capital cities wishing they were Washington or at least Havana; imagine the tiny communities separated by distances we find insignificant but they experience as absolute. Then look at a history book: the waves of conquests from Spain, the Netherlands, France, Great Britain; the African slave trade, the influx of cheap peasant labor from India and China. Imagine the Babel of languages, the frictions arising from different religions, eating habits, body gestures. Above all, imagine the northwestern hemisphere leaning its weight on the rest of the world, telling them that their ways are primitive, shameful, wrong, and must be changed.

Colonialism imposes on its subjects many indignities, but the most insidious one is a spiritual and cultural schizophrenia. (Walcott's dilemma is also biological, as one of his grandfathers was British. In the oft-quoted "A Far Cry from Africa" he asks: "I who am poisoned with the blood of both, / Where shall I turn, divided to the vein?"). Until Walcott realizes that assimilation

136

means embracing every culture around one, his early lyrics are often stilted and hollow. The sonnets reprinted from *In a Green Night* (1962) are technically skilled but lifeless. This description of a Caribbean harbor could have been written by a tourist rather than by someone who grew up with the fishermen and listened to their stories:

> The fishermen rowing homeward in the dusk
> Do not consider the stillness through which they move,
> So I, since feelings drown, should no more ask
> For the safe twilight which your calm hands gave.
> ("The Harbour")

Yet he is learning; in an elevated manner reminiscent of Crane's shorter lyrics, Walcott applies his talents to the landscape and people, faithfully recording; by the time *Selected Poems* is published (1964), the improvement is startling. "Parang" not only re-creates the language of the people but succeeds in catching the ironical humor—*laughin' just to keep from cryin'*—any member of a suppressed group well better practice for survival. "Tales of the Islands," a sequence of ten sonnets, compiles snatches of gossip, folkloric rituals—some devoutly believed, some performed for visiting anthropologists—saloon talk, and scenic views, resulting in a batch of mock-satirical "postcards."

In the struggle to prove Akron worthy of poetry, the lines of battle are at least clearly drawn. Walcott's task is complicated by that very postcard image of the West Indies. Every time he mentions the sea, we tend to sigh with envy. And so he gives us sea and shore and salt air in spades: blinding heat, stunned water, the smells of sweating humanity, the omnipresent galvanized roofs, the stars nailed into the sky, the rain like knives—he rams the scenery down our throats until we stop being thrilled and start to listen.

4. History Lesson

> "When there is no history
> there is no metaphor . . ."
> —Michael S. Harper

"[T]here is too much nothing here."
—Derek Walcott, "Air"

Derek Walcott claims time and again that the West Indies have no
history, that without history a new race is rising from these tourist-
ridden islands. He plays the devil's advocate by adopting the
Official Version of Events; his bitter jibes at his countrymen for not
making an impact on this record is his duplicitous way of attack-
ing the foundations of Western civilization. Arguing negatively, he
is permitted, through remorse and abuse, to lavish his attention on
people, communities, and landscapes that aren't historically
"important."

Michael Harper's history is a matrix of memory and responsi-
bility. He rejects the Official Version, for it has no vision or moral-
ity. It is not, humanely speaking, truthful. I can imagine Walcott
replying to Harper: "Without history, there is no memory." Or con-
versely: "Without memory, there is no history." The Middle Passage
obliterated family ties, tribal connections, and the religious and
communal rites that give sense to natural law. West Indian history
is a how-to manual for the brutal destruction of whole races' sys-
tems for sustaining memory.

The amnesia of the people is reflected in the island vegetation
whose rapid proliferation obliterates paths and manors alike.
Human accomplishment disappears with time, sun, and rain.
Uncontrolled growth is emblematic of the process of forgetting:

> when the axe spoke, weeds ran up to the knee
> like bastard children, hiding in their names,
>
> whole generations died, unchristened,
> growths hidden in green darkness, forests
> of history thickening with amnesia . . .
> (*Another Life*)

Walcott's primary metaphor is the sea. The sea is History or,
more precisely, a history book, her pages steadily turning, writing
and erasing themselves. Sometimes the sea is a book of poems, left
lying face down by an absent reader; more often, the sea is quin-
tessential Nothingness. The islands take their lessons from the sea.
As he points out in "The Sea Is History" (from *The Star-Apple*

Kingdom), any event not recognized for its true essence does not exist. To the question "Where are your monuments, your battles, martyrs?" the West Indian replies: "Sirs, / in that grey vault. The sea. The sea / has locked them up." A list of humiliations follows— slave trade, imported peasant labor, conquerors and exploiters—to which the narrator blithely assigns biblical metaphors: the slave trade is Exodus, poverty is Lamentations, the sun setting is the New Testament. Only with the break-up of the British Empire does the clock start to tick:

> then came the bullfrog bellowing for a vote,
>
> fireflies with bright ideas
> and bats like jetting ambassadors
> and the mantis, like khaki police . . .

"This," Walcott claims wryly, is the "rumour without any echo / of History, really beginning." In other words, History begins with self-determination, no matter how corrupt the struggle to prevail, which, after all, is the last thing any empire that "sneers at all thoughts in the future tense" wishes. More suitable to the colonial game plan is the scenario of "Return to D'Ennery; Rain":

> So azure and indifferent was this air,
> So murmurous of oblivion the sea,
> That any human action seemed a waste,
> The place seemed born for being buried there.

5. Portrait of the Artist as a Young Man

> The dream
> of reason had produced its monster:
> a prodigy of the wrong age and colour.
> —Derek Walcott, *Another Life*

I first met Derek Walcott in the basement of the Performing Arts Building at my undergraduate university. He was in town to give a poetry reading I would miss because of the dress rehearsal of my first play, a one-act incorporating pantomime, dream, and song into forty-five-minute recounting of the last thirty years of Afro-American history. It was spring 1973, the year Walcott's phenomenal narrative poem, *Another Life,* was published. We shook hands and I croaked a hello; I had read *Dream on Monkey Mountain* in the previous summer and couldn't believe that the author of that great play was standing outside the auditorium where my diluted imitation was struggling through missed cues and uncertain direction.

I did not read *Another Life* until much later. When I finally did, out of graduate school and on my way to Europe for the third or fourth time, I recognized its major themes as chords in my own life: loss of innocence, the search for a heritage; the schizophrenia of assimilation, the writer as exile to his homeland and to his own life.

Another Life's 4,000-plus lines are divided into four parts, which are then divided into twenty-three chapters. The narrative operates on many levels, often shifting times and perspectives in mid-line; it is a lyric *Bildungsroman,* Walcott's *Buddenbrooks* or *A la Recherche du Temps Perdu.* His usual rhetorical reticence disappears, and the telling is made more haunting by its elasticity; he cajoles, proclaims, rages, and whispers. There are straight descriptive passages, dramatic monologues, self-interviews, brief spurts of song. Walcott's experience as playwright and theater director finds a second life here, in poetry.

Part One, *The Divided Child,* recounts the first artistic stirrings. His ambition to become a great painter is undermined by the very literary metaphor that sets the opening scene:

> Verandahs, where the pages of the sea
> are a book left open by an absent master
> in the middle of another life—
> I begin here again...

The absent master refers equally to the dead father, the drawing teacher Harold Simmons, God (who is either indifferent or dead), and the absence of racial memory. The image of the sea as a book occurs again and again, charting Walcott's deepening relationship to literature:

> And from a new book,
> bound in sea-green linen, whose lines

matched the exhilaration which their reader,
rowing the air around him now, conveyed,
another life it seemed would start again...

By Chapter 3, the narration is firmly in the hands of dramatic literature; the "town's characters, its cast of thousands" are presented in alphabetical order, from Ajax the "lion-coloured stallion" to Zandoli, rodent exterminator. "These dead, these derelicts," claims Walcott, ". . . were the stars of my mythology." He involves this cast in a mini-drama, but by Chapter 7, the narrator withdraws with an ironic commentary on his own creation:

Provincialism loves the pseudo-epic,
so if these heroes have been given a stature
disproportionate to their cramped lives,
remember I beheld them at knee-height...

Is this sly disavowal prompted by embarrassment, or has Walcott anticipated our condescension? The ruse is Shakespearean, a clue that we will have to watch ourselves, a warning to avoid the easy judgment. Look at Caesar, Macbeth, King Lear—what are heroes but plunderers, murderers, and vengeful, foolish men?

Part Two, "Homage to Gregorias," recalls Walcott's boyhood friend Dunstan St. Omer and their years together as apprentices of the artist Harry Simmons. Dunstan's name is changed to Gregorias because "it echoes the blest thunders of the surf . . . / because it sounds explosive, / a black Greek's!"; it also suggests that St. Lucia, with its misted mountains and wilderness of ocean, has affinities to ancient Greece.

Soon realizing he does not have the gift for painting, the narrator envies "mad, divine Gregorias / imprisoned in his choice." But there is literature and the growing compulsion to articulate the dreams of his people who were "dazed, ignorant, / waiting to be named." Of Gregorias he says "He had his madness," then: "mine was our history." But where was this history to be found? Not in the school headmaster, "a lonely Englishman who loved parades, / sailing, and Conrad's prose," nor in the pupil's red-jacketed *History of the British Empire*. Not in the tapestry of Waterloo hanging in the house of one of his mother's sewing clients, not even in daydreams of Montparnasse in the twenties. (When I was ten I read an article in *Jet* about Dorothy Dandridge losing out to Elizabeth Taylor for the role of Cleopatra. Right then I knew that History didn't include me.) Taking a cue from Gregorias, the poet turns to his immediate environment for inspiration and sees "vowels curl from the tongue of the carpenter's plane." The two drink, talk through the night, criticize and praise each other's work, and make a vow:

> But drunkenly, or secretly, we swore,
> disciples of that astigmatic saint,
> that we would never leave the island
> until we had put down, in paint, in words,
> as palmists learn the network of a hand,
> all of its sunken, leaf-choked ravines,
> every neglected, self-pitying inlet
> muttering in brackish dialect,
> the ropes of mangrovesfrom which old soldier
> crabs slipped
> surrendering to slush,
> each ochre track seeking some hilltop and
> losing itself in an unfinished phrase...

The youthful fantasies accelerate, almost reveling in the squalor which they plan to extol—the endless sentence, so customary of Walcott, rolls through intricate couplings of landscape and language, finally slithering to a pause with the soldier crabs falling into slush . . . those crabs being a foreshadowing of the disillusioned older poet who, looking back on those days, would exclaim: "Yet, Gregorias, lit, / we were the light of the world!"

That pun, with its cocky tenderness, erupts in Part Three into the purging, catalytic nature of fire. A conflagration devastates the town of Castries. Now the world of their youth is gone: ". . . with the fierce rush of a furnace door / suddenly opened, history was here." Castries' resurrection as "a cement phoenix" is paralleled by the poet's discovery of sex and the possibility of education abroad:

> Tea with the British Council Representative,
> tannin, calfskin, gilt, and thank you vellum much...

I am hoisted on silvery chords upward,
eager for the dropped names like sugar cubes.
Eliot. Plop. Benjamin Britten. Clunk. Elgar. Slurp.
Mrs. Winters's cheeks gleaming. Polished cherries.
Lawns. Elegance. Remembering elms. England, then.
　　When?
Down on her speckled forearm. More tea.
Thank you, my mind burrowing her soft scented crotch.
First intimations of immortality.
Other men's wives.

First love also sparks with the appearance of Anna, "gold and white
. . . light / of another epoch." He makes her his lover and then, imi-
tating literature, idealizes her until she dissolves into all the liter-
ary Annas he has adored: Anna Christie, Anna Karenina, Anna
Akhmatova. Finally, inevitably, she loses out to Art: "The hand she
held already had betrayed / them by its longing for describing her."

He leaves for study abroad, praying that nothing will change—
a futile wish, for though he returns many times, he carries the guilt
of the prodigal son. In Part Four, "The Estranging Sea,"
Walcott—"One life, one marriage later"—encounters Gregorias
and finds him

unable to hold down a job, painting so badly
that those who swore his genius vindicated
everything once, now saw it as a promise never kept.
Viciously, near tears, I wish him dead.

This self-punishing rage rapidly turns outward: news of the suicide
of his mentor, Harry Simmons, prompts a scathing denunciation of
"the syntactical apologists of the Third World," those ill-wishers
who condemn their promising artists before they have even begun.
He envisions them prodding Simmons to his grave while exclaim-
ing "from such a man / what would you expect, / but a couple of
paintings / and a dog's life?"

Finally it is the sea which opens the way to hope. If the sea is
a book, then the most natural action is to pick up that book and
start to read; the next step is to write the book oneself:

for what else is there
but books, books and the sea,
verandahs and the pages of the sea,
to write of the wind and the memory of wind-
    whipped hair
in the sun, the colour of fire?

His fury spent, Walcott assesses his present position—"I was eight-
een then, now I am forty one"—and accepts what he has been and
become. The next visit home he is able to see that it "is not bitter,
it is harder / to be a prodigal than a stranger." He decides to visit
neither Harry's grave nor Anna; instead, he asks forgiveness of the
island for his desertion. Upon those who stayed so that he might
leave—Anna, Gregorias, Simmons—he wishes rest. His only desire
now is "to grow white-haired / as the wave, with a wrinkled / brown
rock's face . . . an old poet, / facing the wind."

6. *Childhood's Aftermath*

> "It is summer-gone that I see, it is summer-gone."
> —Gwendolyn Brooks, "A Sunset of the City"

Another Life took seven years to write, years in which America
exploded with student demonstrations and race riots. It is typical
of Walcott's contrariness that he chose "to row, but backward"; to
present an introspective exploration of his personal past at the very
moment so many Afro-American writers were writing "for the peo-
ple." Walcott insists that only through the particular fate can a uni-
versal one be posited; his response to the call for Black Pride is to
contribute his version of a life, another life, in all its ambiguities.

Sea Grapes (1976) is the calm after the storm, a resignation
borne of equal parts serenity and loss. These poems are *triste*—ele-
gant, spare constructions, almost classical:

> Desolate lemons, hold
> tight, in your bowl of earth,
> the light to your bitter flesh . . .
> ("Sunday Lemons")

If the green of the sea is the signature color of *Another Life,* the prevailing hue of *Sea Grapes* is gold—lemons, Valencia oranges, the goldsmith of Benares, "oaks yellowing October, / everything turning money." I am reminded of Yeats's "Sailing to Byzantium," in which a similar yearning becomes the wish to escape the body into a form of "hammered gold and gold enameling." Gold, the color of fervor and denouement, of the fire and its embers.

Which is not to imply that Walcott has given up—on the contrary, there is a sweetness to this dignity that, rather than softening the effect of his rigorous attention to craft, makes these poems all the more troubling, their severe forms filled with mutable living tissue. The youthful paradise is gone; one cannot return home. Hence the Adam poems—Adam heartbroken by Eve's betrayal ("Adam's Song"), Adam's comprehension of labor and profit in "New World." Concomitant with the construction of a New World in these poems is the proliferation of bitter fruit—lemons, olives, limes, sour apples, green grapes.

The labor begins here, outside the walls. Where a lesser poet would fall silent or imitate earlier successes, Walcott rolls up his sleeves. His unique experience as unlikely prodigy, apprentice painter, literature student, poet, dramatist, and theater director; his cognizance of the bogus glories of "fame" and "world citizenship" all this has prepared him for a new lesson: reconciliation with the irrevocable. As he says in "Dark August":

> . . . I am learning slowly

> to love the dark days, the steaming hills,
> the air with gossiping mosquitoes,
> and to sip the medicine of bitterness . . .

* * *

> I would have learnt to love black days like
>   bright ones,
> the black rain, the white hills, when once
> I loved only my happiness and you.

7. *The Star-Apple Kingdom*

"Shabine sang to you from the depths of the sea."

The Star-Apple Kingdom is a lyrical celebration, an explosion of breathtaking imagery. The duality Walcott described in an essay titled "What the Twilight Says: An Overture" as "two lives: the interior life of poetry, the outward life of action and dialect" reaches a reconciliation in two major works: the title poem and "The Schooner *Flight.*"

The volume opens with "The Schooner *Flight,*" a rare persona poem. Shabine, whose name is "the patois for / any red nigger," leaves the "dreamless face" of his lover Maria Concepcion and boards the schooner *Flight.* The names are not accidental: Shabine's ordeal is the allegory of Everyman, and his flight becomes a quest. Like Odysseus, he encounters terrors and defeats them; unlike Odysseus, he is running away rather than trying to return, although his ambitions are loftier:

> You ever look up from some lonely beach
> and see a far schooner? Well, when I write
> this poem, each phrase go be soaked in salt,
> I go draw and knot every line as tight
> as ropes in this rigging; in simple speech
> my common language go be the wind,
> my pages the sails of the schooner *Flight.*

The similarity between Shabine's aesthetic and Walcott's (a much earlier poem "Islands" states: "I seek . . . to write / Verse crisp as sand, clear as sunlight, / Cold as the curled wave, ordinary / As a tumbler of island water . . .") is intriguing; more important, however, are the differences between the two men: Shabine, never having left the islands, still belongs; the cab driver addresses him familiarly, and he suffers no agonizing sense of estrangement from the spirit of his community. Perhaps Shabine is the man Walcott might have become if he had stayed on St. Lucia; perhaps he is simply himself, one man in a nation of individuals. In any case, he embodies the universal in the particular. To those who would consider him exotic and look upon his culture with a vague nostalgia,

Shabine is quick to call their bluff: "either I'm nobody," he says, "or I'm a nation."

Shabine has escaped a web of corruption and betrayal—now, on the high seas, he "had no nation . . . but the imagination." A willing castaway, he is the privileged witness to miracles. God speaks through a harpooned grouper, and one dawn the ship enters the Middle Passage:

> where the horizon was one silver haze,
> the fog swirl and swell into sails, so close
> that I saw it was sails, my hair grip my skull,
> it was horrors, but it was beautiful.

The vision includes the ghosts of great admirals as well as slave ships, "our fathers below deck too deep . . . to hear us shouting." Here is contemplation rendered palpable; Shabine is not as painfully self-conscious as Walcott and so is able to travel backward, over the troubled waters, to become whole. Later, during a life-threatening storm, what sustains him is the memory of those slave ships, superimposed on a church episode from childhood "when the whale-bell / sang service" and

> proud with despair, we sang how our race
> survive the sea's maw, our history, our peril,
> and now I was ready for whatever death will.

His last vision is of Maria Concepcion in the wake of the storm, marrying the sea and drifting away. "I wanted nothing after that day," Shabine states:

> I stop talking now. I work, then I read,
> cotching under a lantern hooked to the mast.
> I try to forget what happiness was,
> and when that don't work, I study the stars.

All the selections from *The Star-Apple Kingdom* are vintage Walcott: the hypnotic limbo of "Sabbaths, W.I.," the grimly brilliant "The Sea Is History." "Koenig of the River," a weirdly poignant negative of Shabine's journey, depicts Koenig, the last surviving

147

crew member of a missionary group sent to inspect a camp in the swamp, as he succumbs to fever and delirium. But the real *tour de force* is the title poem, which Walcott rightly saves for last.

The protagonist of "The Star-Apple Kingdom" is more politically astute than Shabine, his introspection more bitter and cerebral. Hence his judgments are harsher, his visions more brutal, and revelation, when it comes, is more suspect. The poem begins with him perusing an old photo album; sepia snapshots from the Victorian era afford glimpses of "lily-like parasols" floating across a landscape dubbed "Herefords at Sunset in the Valley of the Wye." As dusk falls, he looks out over Kingston, imagining a silent scream from the oppressed—all those who were not included in the photographs—rising over the landscape. He falls asleep, finally, only to plunge into a nightmare procession of images from Caribbean history: the submerged cathedral of Port Royal, a "crab climbing the steeple"; Christianity contriving so that "the slave pardoned his whip." *La Revolucíon* comes in the form of a woman, "a black umbrella blown inside out," who is simultaneously "raped wife, empty mother, Aztec virgin / transfixed by arrows from a thousand guitars." Refusing the bleakness of her vision, he cries out for

> . . . a history without any memory,
> streets without statues,
> and a geography without myth. . . . no armies
> but those regiments of bananas, thick lances of canes . . .

Still within the dream, he awakens to a vision of the partitioning of the West Indian republic: seven prime ministers who buy up the sea—
> one thousand miles of aquamarine with lace trimmings,
> one million yards of lime-coloured silk,
> one mile of violet, leagues of cerulean satin—

and resell it at a profit to conglomerates. He then plunges into a deep sleep, one "that wipes out history." When he wakens—for real this time, his jaw still aching from the silent scream—he is able, finally, to cry out. The only person who hears him is an old woman scrubbing the steps of the cathedral; she hears his scream "as a dog hears, as all the underdogs / of the world hear." The acknowledged scream imposes on the world a silence lasting "for half an hour / in that single second"—and though we cannot be sure if the old woman's cracked and wrinkled face conceals a smile, the poem assures us that the smile, if it exists, is "the same smile with which he now / cracked the day open and began his egg."

This is virtuoso writing: the roll of fierce images, dense with consonance, imitates the roar of the sea; the relentless dactylics of the last nine lines attain the grandeur of an Old Testament prophecy. Still, there is no resolution of conflicting energies; the outlook is nearly as bleak as at the outset. For though the anguished consciousness has found a kindred spirit, she is mute and ultimately inaccessible; the old woman is not about to join him for breakfast. Where does the torn soul go from here?

8. The Prodigy Turns Prodigal

> I know the dark delight of being strange,
> The penalty of difference in the crowd,
> The loneliness of wisdom among fools . . .
> —Claude McKay, "My House"

The fate of any member of a minority who "makes it" is double-edged. As a model, he or she must be perfect; no slip-ups or "you've let us down." As a special case, he or she is envied, even reviled. Move away from the home court and you're accused of being "dicty"; return and you're a prodigal. Write about home and you blaspheme; choose other topics and you're a traitor.

In "The Spoiler's Return," a scathing portrayal of corruption, "the Spoiler" comes back to Laventille. He claims to have been to hell and back after leaving the West Indies with "no will / but my own conscience and rum-eaten wit." With Popian rancor he describes the Caribbean "scene": "Is crab climbing crab-back, in a crab-quarrel, / and going round and round in the same barrel . . ."

(In August 1963, my parents dragged us to Washington, D.C. We stayed with relatives, great-aunts and uncles with scores of children and sub-children. The day before the March, Aunt Louise organized a crab bake: more terrifying than the claws scratching against the galvanized tub was the sight of them whole, boiled as bright a red as white people the second sunny day of summer, brilliant corpses we were supposed to dismantle and devour. Aunt Helen held no truck with my squeamishness; she pulled me over to the tub and pointed. "Look at that," she said, chuckling. "Niggers just like that—like crabs in a bucket, not a one get out 'cause the other pull him back."

(I was impressed at the sight, and the curiously affectionate way she had used a word forbidden among the Negro bourgeoisie up North. The expression, I thought, she had made up herself. Now, forty years later, I find it again, at the source.)

Everyone wants a prodigy to fail; it makes our mediocrity more bearable. Even before leaving for study abroad, Walcott felt the first twinges of the Prodigal Syndrome: envy from the outside, insecurity and guilt from within. It doesn't matter if the prodigal returns in shame or glory—the time away from "home" will always be suspect and interpreted as rejection. Frustration with this double bind can erupt into hate. "Laventille" depicts a funeral in a poor section of town; the narrator is impatient and grieved at the backwardness he witnesses:

> The black, fawning verger,
> his bow tie akimbo, grinning, the clown-gloved
> fashionable wear of those I deeply loved
> once, made me look on with hopelessness and rage
> at their new, apish habits, their excess
> and fear . . .

Perhaps because he is confiding in a soulmate (the poem is dedicated to V. S. Naipaul, whose novels are grim studies of the squalor of the East Indian community in the Caribbean), Walcott allows hidden thoughts to burst through.

But that's not the end of the prodigy's tightrope act. There is the problem of being accepted on one's own terms in the larger world, where reactions can fluctuate from patronizing praise ("The best black writer since Ralph Ellison!") to outright disdain. Those "accurate iambics" are meant to legitimize Walcott's subject matter and to command respect both for his craft and his conclusions. The prosody can also help him contain his uneasiness with the dichotomy of mind and body—mind meaning English education and body referring to sensuality, connectedness. The traits of the body, however desirable, render one vulnerable. The attempt to dissociate mind from body is in Walcott's case complicated by the fact that Western civilization assigns the characteristics of the body—perceived as "feminine" and "inferior"—to the black race as well.

Walcott's struggle, internalized by his own mixed racial heritage, appears rather programmatically in the overquoted "I who have cursed / The drunken officer of British rule, how choose / Between this Africa and the English tongue I love?" When the body is denied, creative expression is diminished: "to be aware / of the divine union the soul detaches / itself from created things," he states in "The Gulf"; later, in *Another Life*, he laments: "my sign was Janus, / I saw with twin heads, / and everything I say is contradicted." The wish for a separation of mind and body finds apt metaphors: mind becomes a "ripe brain rotting like a yellow nut"; an Indian trundles his wheelbarrow of "hacked, beheaded coconuts"; "the lopped head of the coconut rolls to gasp in the sand." Bodies on the subway ("A Village Life") are seen "each in its private hell, /each plumped, prime bulk still swinging by its arm / upon a hook." Marc Antony, stretched out next to a sleeping Cleopatra ("quick fox with her / sweet stench"), feels "dismembered, // his head / is in Egypt, his feet / in Rome, his groin a desert / trench with its dead soldier." In the last poem from *Midsummer*, wood lice become seraphim, "all heads, with, at each ear, a gauzy wing."

Even the "civilized" desire to relieve stress by a "vacation in the sun" can become an existential nightmare:

> We came here for the cure
> Of quiet in the whelk's centre . . .
> To let a salt sun scour
> The brain as harsh as coral,
> To bathe like stones in wind,
> To be, like beast or natural object, pure.
> ("Crusoe's Island")

If you want to be "like beast or natural object, pure" you will also have to assume their negative qualities—to be a beast means to be less than human, less than reasonable; natural objects do not possess history, they do not have a sense of time—which, for man, is tantamount to oblivion.

The self-consciousness which comes from seeing yourself as unsuspecting others see you *and* knowing exactly what you're thinking at that moment becomes a technical innovation in Walcott's work, as he switches pronouns from "he" to "I" to "you" when discussing the self:

> for once, like them,
> you wanted no career
> but this sheer light, this clear,
> infinite, boring, paradisal sea,
> but hoped it would mean something to declare
> today, I am your poet, yours . . .
> ("Homecoming: Anse La Raye")

To change pronouns in mid-sentence not only shakes our complacency, our sense of knowing where we stand, but creates an intricate layering of remorse. Poem XI of *Midsummer* begins with the very traditional, almost clichéd, moment of self-confrontation in the mirror. What elevates a predictable moment to a dialectic is the matter-of-fact way Walcott calls this reflection his double, and then gives him a life independent of the real "other"—one of menial action, snipping hairs and shaving—while the other is condemned to remember "empty cupboards where her dresses / shone"—the small but "fatal" sadnesses born of introspection.

Walcott explores his reactions from all angles: from a distance, in "Prelude," as if watching a rare insect ("I go, of course, through all the isolated acts, / . . . Straighten my tie and fix important jaws"), or from deep in the belly of the whale, as in "Mass Man," when he rages, half to himself and half to the laughing, dancing carnival celebrants:

> Upon your penitential morning,
> some skull must rub its memory with ashes,
> some mind must squat down howling in your dust,
> some hand crawl and recollect your rubbish,
> someone must write your poems.

9. Names on the Sand

> Craftsman and castaway,
> All heaven in his head . . .
> —Derek Walcott, "Crusoe's Island"

A recurrent figure in Walcott's work is that of Robinson Crusoe, castaway: the man forced, as the sole survivor of a race, to become a God. The epigram to "Crusoe's Journal" invites us to see home as "a place I had lived in but was come out of." A repository of British education, this Crusoe returns to his island to find himself ship-wrecked among familiar surroundings; he discovers that intellect can establish the distance helpful for accurate description, but only at the expense of emotion:

> the intellect appraises
> objects surely, even the bare necessities
> of style are turned to use,
> like those plain iron tools he salvages
> from shipwreck, hewing a prose
> as odorous as raw wood to the adze . . .

The fate of being the West Indies' first internationally acclaimed poet bears with it the pressure of assuming the role of creator. As the first to "make it out," Walcott also has the dubious privilege of finding language that can "startle itself / with poetry's surprise / in a green world, one without metaphors. . . ." The Adamic mission of naming is both an invigorating and a lonely enterprise, typically masculine in its separation of the human animal from the environment. Although he never quite escapes the alienation such a role provokes, Walcott, from his marginal perspective, is capable of seeing the irony in this:

> Being men, they could not live
> Except they first presumed
> The right of every thing to be a noun.
> The African acquiesced,
> repeated, and changed them.
> ("Names")

Still, the star witness for the defense—the native West Indian who has stayed home, who has not experienced alienation—is mute. And so it is only one step farther to see Crusoe in any exile, from John writing *Revelations* on the isle of Patmos to a hungover poet suspended over Love Field in a Boeing 747.

In "Crusoe's Island," the privilege of naming swings rapidly around to the dark side:

> Craftsman and castaway,
> All heaven in his head,
> He watched his shadow pray
> Not for God's love but human love instead.

To become a god is to relinquish human ties, to lose the father and the Father. The freedom of being the sole spokesman is fraught with the burden of total failure with nothing to hang on to:

> I have lost sight of hell,
> Of heaven, of human will,
> My skill
> Is not enough,
> I am struck by this bell
> To the root.
> Crazed by the cracking sun,
> I stand at my life's noon,
> On parched, delirious sand
> My shadow lengthens.

No matter how many times the prodigal returns home physically, he cannot obtain the purity of the stone or the crab. He cannot dissolve into the landscape that has yielded to the pressure of his observation. He cannot, in fact, touch the very people who are his legacy. At the poem's end he notices "Black little girls in pink / Organdy, crinolines" walking on the shore; in a brilliant recognition he dubs them "Friday's progeny, / The brood of Crusoe's slave." Thus Walcott becomes both Crusoe and Friday, "Crusoe's slave." The West Indian who loves those girls is a slave to the artist who stands outside their lives:

And nothing I can learn
From art or loneliness
Can bless them as the bell's
Transfiguring tongue can bless.

10. In the Air

"I don't know the language
Of the cool country
And its pace is not mine."
—Else Lasker-Schüler, "Homesick"

As Walcott's list of publications and achievements lengthens, so does the amount of time spent away from the islands. "We're in the air," a Texan remarks upon takeoff in "The Gulf." The rootlessness of the islander is augmented by the homelessness of the traveler. The idea of being the artist in the air begins to take precedence over the concept of Crusoe, firmly rooted—however lonely—on his island.

The Fortunate Traveler (1981) is generously represented in the *Collected Poems*. Although it is natural to favor one's most recent work, in this case I'm sorry the poet gave in to temptation, for many of these poems suffer from superficiality and a touch of the maudlin. Walcott is spending more and more time in the United States, and his adopted country has seduced him. He admits, in "Upstate," to falling in love with America (Kate Smith, move over!), and decides he must become a student again:

I must put the cold small pebbles from the spring
upon my tongue to learn her language,
to talk like birch or aspen confidently.

But what a meek, eager-to-please student we have here! Wistfully he says, "Sometimes I feel sometimes / the Muse is leaving, the Muse is leaving America." And yet here comes the Muse by poem's end, arrayed in her traditional garb—virgin land smelling of just-baked bread.

Okay, one can't remain an angry young man forever—but I wish some of that indignant righteousness and impatience remained. The traveler seems weary, and several poems appear to have no *raison d'être* other than the fact that a writer should keep writing. Cruel? Perhaps, but it springs from disappointment; after *Another Life, Sea Grapes,* and *The Star-Apple Kingdom,* I will not be satisfied with imitation Lowell. And though there are gems ("Map of the New World," or the vivid personae in "The Liberator" and "The Spoiler's Return"), there are far more embarrassments, such as the bland "Easter" and "Early Pompeian," where the attempt to describe a stillbirth results in overwriting ("your sorrows were robing / you with the readiness of woman") and festooned clichés ("the lamp that was struggling with darkness was blown out / by the foul breeze off the amniotic sea"). Powerful oratory fizzles to rhetoric; I can only wince when, in "The Hotel Normandie Pool," a raindrop "punctuates the startled paper" and Walcott muses, as the pool surface wrinkles with rain, ". . . all reflection gets no easier."

The title *The Fortunate Traveller* is meant to be ironic—perhaps more than its author realized.

11. Questions of Travel

> CORPORAL: We cannot go back. History is in motion. The law is in motion. Forward, forward.
> SOURIS: Where? The world is a circle, Corporal. Remember that.
> —Derek Walcott, *Dream on Monkey Mountain*

With *Midsummer,* a sequence of poems published in 1981, Walcott returns to the West Indies for inspiration; or, more precisely, the West Indies return to him. No matter where he finds himself—be it Rome, Argentina, or Van Gogh's orchards—he carries his island inside. Emblematic of midsummer is scorching heat that dries up vegetation and a glare that flattens perspectives. "Midsummer's furnace casts everything in bronze"; similarly, each poem paints itself and stiffens into elegy. One would think Walcott were bronzing memories like baby shoes. The language is appropriately baroque, with weariness and repetition built into the composition, and there is a sense of *just keep moving and everything will be all right.*

But what is he running from that always pulls him back into

its gravitational field? Here and there, through the lush linguistic scenery, we're given glimpses: "[t]he hills have no echoes" in poem VII and by XXI, "the cloud waits in emptiness for the apostles." In the islands "noon jerks towards its rigid, inert centre." *Echoless, empty, inert*—modifiers for Death (dare we whisper its name?), the Great Negator. (In Western tradition, a "living death" is synonymous with a destroyed ego.) Wherever Walcott travels, whenever he lets his rhetorical guard down, the Void is waiting with its shining, blank face.

He fights back the only way he knows . . . by writing: "My palms have been sliced by the twine / of the craft I have pulled at for more than forty years." This compulsion can sometimes lead to bad writing, such as metaphors extended far beyond their initial freshness. "Here the wetback crab and the mollusc are citizens," he writes in poem XXVII, "and the leaves have green cards." Or, musing on the Holocaust, these lines, more suited for a John Belushi monologue:

> Brown pigeons goose-step, squirrels pile up
>   acorns like little shoes,
> and moss, voiceless as smoke, hushes the peeled
>   bodies
> like abandoned kindling. In the clear pools,
>   fat
> trout rising to lures bubble in umlauts.
> (XLI)

When the compass swings north and Walcott attempts to re-create tropical stasis in Northern cities, inertia comes off as jadedness. Efforts to fuse literature and landscape often misfire: Boston city blocks become "long as paragraphs" and ". . . boulevards open like novels / waiting to be written. Clouds like the beginnings of stories." There are, however, moments of originality and rightness that make up for these lapses.

After self-imposed exile in cities like Boston and a Chicago "white as Poland," after returning to England, land of his "bastard ancestor" (significantly, it is the grandfather who is the bastard, not Walcott himself), he finally writes himself out of the Hole. Here is the conclusion of the fiftieth poem:

These poems I heaved aren't linked to any
    tradition
like a mossed cairn; each goes down like a stone
to the seabed, settling, but let them, with luck, lie
where stones are deep, in the sea's memory.
Let them be, in water, as my father, who did
    watercolours,
entered his work. He became one of his shadows,
wavering and faint in the midsummer sunlight.
His name was Warwick Walcott. I sometimes
    believe
that his father, in love or bitter benediction,
named him for Warwickshire. Ironies
are moving. Now, when I rewrite a line,
or sketch on the fast-drying paper the coconut
    fronds
that he did so faintly, my daughters' hands move
    in mine.
Conches move over the sea-floor. I used to move
my father's grave from the blackened Anglican
    headstones
in Castries to where I could love both at once—
the sea and his absence. Youth is stranger than
    fiction.

What impression does Derek Walcott want to leave us with?
His insistence on the particular and personal precludes any sug-
gestion that he'd like to be seen as statesman-poet in the tradition
of Neruda. More likely, his intent is to frustrate all efforts at por-
traiture so that, closing the book, we can explain nothing except by
referring to individual poems. With its wise artistry this collection
also raises the presentation of a slick surface, shelf upon shelf of
well-wrought urns polished to blinding perfection. "All the lines
that I love have their knots left in," Walcott writes, and this edition
allows us a glimpse into the workshop. The early sonnet "A City's
Death by Fire," for example, is a stilted portrayal of the Castries
fire that is easily upstaged by "A Simple Flame" in *Another Life*.
Certain images are recycled—an easel rifled across shoulders, a
"galvanized roof with its nail holes of stars," the gull as a hinge in

the sky, the pages of the sea. The last section of "Tales of the Islands" is incorporated verbatim at the end of "A Simple Flame."

Repetition and embellishment—these are also the devices of the storyteller. Walcott's rhetorical insistence works because we can hear him talking *to* us; we hear the words being strung on a breath. The story line—and I use "line" in a concrete sense, a thread running through fabric or a labyrinth—is held together by the authenticity of the storyteller's voice. Though we know we are seeing the world filtered through the teller, though we know he is weaving a spell, we trust him to tell the truth in his own way. "You have / a grace upon your words, and there is sound sense within them," said Alkinoos in praise of Odysseus, another castaway.

After reading the bulk of Derek Walcott's poetry, I am a little saddened, for I find the recent work a slight diminishment of his power, the flame turned a little lower. Still, he has surprised us before, and *Midsummer* augurs a fresh outburst. A *Collected Poems* forces a writer to start again with Nothing. *Tabula rasa.* And as the seasoned traveler knows, one of the most dangerous, and intoxicating, moments of any trip is takeoff.

Lowell's Graveyard

ROBERT HASS

It's probably a hopeless matter, writing about favorite poems. I came across "The Lost Son," "The Quaker Graveyard in Nantucket" and "Howl" at about the same time. Some of the lines are still married in my head and they still have talismanic power: *snail, snail, glister me, forward; Mohammedan angels staggering on tenement roofs illuminated; this is the end of running on the waves.* I see now that they are all three lost son poems, but at the time I didn't see much of anything. I heard, and it was the incantatory power of the poems that moved me. Enchantment, literally. I wandered around San Francisco demolishing the twentieth century by mumbling to myself, *blue-lunged combers lumbered to the kill* and managed to mix up Roethke's *ordnung! ordnung! Papa's coming* with the Lord who survived the rainbow of his will.

You can analyze the music of poetry but it's difficult to conduct an argument about its value, especially when it's gotten into the blood. It becomes autobiography there. The other night in a pub in Cambridgeshire (named The Prince Regent and built just before the regency in the year when the first man who tried to organize a craft union among weavers was whipped, drawn, quartered, and disemboweled in a public ceremony in London) the subject of favorite poems came up and a mild-looking man who taught high school geology treated us to this:

> For it's Din! Din! Din!
> You limpin' lump o' brick dust, Gunga Din!
> Though I've belted you and flayed you,
> By the livin' Gawd that made you,
> You're a better man than I am, Gunga Din!

And he began to talk about his father's library in a summer cottage in Devon. I thought of how my older brother had loved that poem, how we had taken turns reading Vachel Lindsay and Kipling aloud on summer nights in California, in our upstairs room that looked out on a dusty fig orchard and grapevines spilling over the wooden fence.

Poems take place in your life, or some of them do, like the day your younger sister arrives and replaces you as the bon enfant in the bosom of the family; or the day the trucks came and the men began to tear up the wooden sidewalks and the cobblestone gutters outside your house and lay down new cement curbs and asphalt streets. We put the paper bags on our feet to walk back and forth across the road which glistened with hot oil. That was just after the war. The town was about to become a suburb in the postwar boom. The fig orchard went just after the old road. I must have been six. Robert Lowell had just published in the *Partisan Review* a first version of "The Quaker Graveyard in Nantucket."

Thinking about this a long time later made me realize that "Quaker Graveyard" is not a political poem. I had assumed that it was, that its rage against the war and puritan will and the Quakers of Nantucket who financed the butchery of whales was an attack on American capitalism. But a political criticism of any social order implies both that a saner one can be imagined and the hope or conviction that it can be achieved. I had by then begun to have a way of describing such an order, got out of a melange of Paul Goodman, Camus, and *To the Finland Station,* but what lay behind it was an imagination of early childhood, dusty fig leaves and sun and fields of wild fennel. Nostalgia locates desire in the past where it suffers no active conflict and can be yearned toward pleasantly. History is the antidote to this. When I saw that my paradise was Lowell's hell, I was forced to see that it was not a place in time I was thinking of, but a place in imagination. The fury of conflict is in "The Quaker Graveyard" but I went back to the poem looking for the vision of an alternative world. There is none. There's grief and moral rage but the poem imagines the whole of human life as sterile violence:

> All you recovered from Poseidon died
> With you, my cousin, and the harrowed brine

Is fruitless on the blue beard of the god . . .

and it identifies finally with the inhuman justice of God:

> You could cut the brackish winds with a knife
> Here in Nantucket, and cast up the time
> When the Lord God formed man from the sea's slime
> And breathed into his face the breath of life,
> And blue-lunged combers lumbered to the kill.
> The Lord survives the rainbow of his will.

There are no choices in this history of the experiment of evolution and so there can be no politics. "The Lost Son," all inward animal alertness and numbed panic, contains the possibility of a social order by imagining, return. And "Howl" wants to imagine a fifth international of angels.

It struck me then that the poem was closer in sensibility to someone like Robinson Jeffers than to most of the poets that I had come to associate with Lowell. Both poets are forced to step outside the human process and claim the vision of some imperturbable godhead to whom the long violence of human history looks small. But about the "Quaker Graveyard" it is important to say that imperturbability is the position where the poem *finally* arrives because it is a poem of process and anguish. Warren Winslow drowns, the Quakers drown, the wounded whale churns in an imagination of suffering and violence from which it is the imperative of the poem to find release, and each successive section of the poem is an attempt to discover this release. When I was beginning to read poetry to learn what it was and what it could be, these depictions and their rhetoric were the originality of the poem and its greatness.

And it's still hard for me to dissociate it from the excitement of that first reading. The poem leapt off the page. Its music, its fury and grief, haunted me:

> where the bones
> Cry out in the long night for the hurt beast
> Bobbing by Ahab's whaleboats in the East

By that time Lowell was writing in the later, more influential style, then controversial, now egregious orthodoxy:

> These are the tranquilized fifties
> and I am forty . . .

But I didn't know that, and I still find myself blinking incredulously when I read—in almost anything written about the poetry—that those early poems "clearly reflect the dictates of the new criticism," while the later ones are "less consciously wrought and extremely intimate." This is the view in which it is 'more intimate' and 'less conscious' to say "my mind's not right" than to imagine the moment when

> The death-lance churns into the sanctuary, tears
> The gun-blue swingle, heaving like a flail,
> And hacks the coiling life out . . .

which is to get things appallingly wrong.

Years later I heard a part of this judgment echoed in a curious way. I was listening to Yvor Winters, just before his death, lecturing on George Herbert. He was talking about Herbert's enjambments and, in one of his rare excursions into the present, he said in a bass grumble, "Young Lowell has got a bad enjambment which he got from Allen Tate who probably got it from Herbert." I thought of "The Quaker Graveyard":

> Light
> Flashed from his matted head and marble feet
> Seagulls blink their heavy lids
> Seaward

It lit up the poem all over again. Lowell had just published this in one of the fashionable journals:

> Only man thinning out his kind
> sounds through the Sabbath noon, the blind

swipe of the pruner and his knife
busy about the tree of life. . .

Non est species, but plenty of *decor.* I'm still not sure what I think
about these lines. There is enormous, ironic skill in the octosyllab-
ic couplets, and terrible self-laceration in their poise. It is probably
great writing in the sense that the state of mind couldn't be ren-
dered more exactly. But I wondered about the state of mind and
said a small prayer to the small gods—hilarity and carnality—that
I could escape it. The writer, among other things, is getting a cer-
tain magisterial pleasure from seeming to be outside the picture.
The writer of these lines is in it:

And rips the sperm-whale's midriff into rags,
Gobbets of blubber spill to wind and weather,
Sailor, and gulls go round the stoven timbers
Where the morning stars sing out together . . .

It is possible, I suppose, to object to the brilliance of the writ-
ing. Charles Olson is said to have complained that Lowell lac-
quered each of his poems and hung it in a museum. But this judg-
ment, like the 'confessional' revolution envisaged by the professo-
riat, seems to be based on the sociology of Kenyon College or the
fact of meter or Lowell's early models, on everything but a reading
of the poems. Finish in poetry is, as Olson insisted, a question of
form following function. "The Quaker Graveyard" is brilliantly
written, and in a decade of amazing poetry: the *Pisan Cantos,* the
first books of *Paterson, Four Quartets,* HD's *War Trilogy,* Stevens'
"Credences of Summer," Roethke's "The Lost Son." But its bril-
liance seems neither dictated nor wrought; it is headlong, furious,
and casual. There are moments that hover near grandiloquence—
"Ask for no Orphean lute . . ." but they didn't bother me then and
don't much now.

Everything about the sound of the poem seemed gorgeous on
first reading. "A brackish reach of shoal off. . ." sounded like an
impossible Russian word, sluggish and turbulent; the Indian-
Yankee "Madaket" bit it off with wonderful abruptness. I still like
to say it:

A brackish reach of shoal off Madaket, —

In the second line, the oddness of the sound, which is a substitution in the third foot, has a slightly startling effect:

The sea was still breaking violently. . .

The rhythm breaks "breaking," makes a violence out of slackness in a way that I had never seen before and it was clearly intended because *still* is an extra syllable:

The sea was still breaking violently and night

From here to the end of the stanza, the energy of the poem allows no rest—

Had steamed into our North Atlantic fleet,
When the drowned sailor clutched the drag-net. Light
Flashed from his matted head and marble feet,
He grappled at the net
With the coiled hurdling muscles of his thighs:

I loved the nervous restlessness of the rhyming, the way you accept "net" as the rhyme for "fleet" and "Madaket," then get the off-rhyme "light," so that when you arrive at "feet" it is hardly an arrival and you are pushed toward "net" again. It's like a man shooting at a target with such random desperation that the hits count for no more than the misses. This effect, together with "young Lowell's bad enjambment," transmute an acquired skill into articulate rage. And the colon after "net" is not a rest; it insists on the forward hurtle of the lines:

The corpse was bloodless. . .

Warren Winslow or not, it has always seemed to me that Lowell himself was the drowned sailor, just as Roethke is the lost son. Otherwise the sudden moments of direct address make no sense:

> Sailor, will your sword
> Whistle and fall and sink into the fat?
> In the great ash-pit of Jehoshaphat
> The bones cry for the blood of the white whale,
> The fat flukes arch and whack about its ears,
> The death lance churns into the sanctuary. . .

It is having it both ways to be the young man drowned in the "slush," in the "bilge and backwash," "the greased wash," "the sea's slime" where "the whale's viscera go and the roll of its corruption overruns the world" and to be at the same time the young poet who identifies with the vengeance of the earth-shaker, "green, unwearied, chaste" whose power outlasts the merely phallic brutality of the guns of the steeled fleet, but the impacted writing permits this and it is psychologically true. Distrust of birth is the beginning of one kind of religious emotion.

In the speed of the writing, the syntax comes apart; it dissolves into emotion, into music and the subterranean connections among images. Throughout the poem it is characteristic that the important associations occur in subordinate clauses or compounds so breathless that you have to sort your way back quite consciously to the starting point. This resembles the syntactical strategies of the French surrealists, particularly Desnos and Peret. The main clause is a pushing off place and the poem makes its meaning out of its momentum. It's a way of coming to terms with experience under pressure and not some extrinsic decision about style. Even the lines about the shark—

> Where the heelheaded dogfish barks its nose
> On Ahab's void and forehead

are not Clevelandizing; they are not even—in the period phrase—a metaphysical image because their force is not intellectual. The lines depend on our willingness to let barking dogs marry scavenging sharks in the deep places where men void and are voided. To complain about this is not to launch an attack on 'consciously wrought' but the reverse.

The current taste is for the explicit, however weird. Surrealism comes to mean the manufacture of peculiar imagery and not something in the sinews of a poem. The fish in "For the Union Dead" are a midpoint in this leveling process. They are transformed into sharks and then into cars as "a savage servility slides by on grease," but the delivery is slower, the context narrative and topographical. It is pretty much the same image as in "The Quaker Graveyard," but it has been clarified like broth, a fish stock served up as clam chowder to the peremptory gentleman in the cartoon who likes to see what he's eating.

And this won't do for Lowell because the power of his imagery has always been subliminal; it exists as the nervous underside of the thing said. Look at this, for example, from "Fourth of July in Maine." The poet is addressing Harriet Winslow:

> Dear Cousin, life is much the same,
> though only fossils know your name
> here since you left this solitude,
> gone, as the Christians say, for good.
> Your house, still outwardly in form
> lasts, though no emissary comes
> to watch the garden running down,
> or photograph the propped-up barn.
>
> If memory is genius, you
> had Homer's, enough gossip to
> repeople Trollope's Barchester,
> nurses, Negro, diplomat, down-easter,
> cousins kept up with, nipped, corrected,
> kindly, majorfully directed,
> though family furniture, decor,
> and rooms redone meant almost more.
>
> How often when the telephone
> brought you to us from Washington,
> we had to look around the room
> to find the objects you would name—
> lying there, ten years' paralyzed,
> half-blind, no voice unrecognized,

not trusting in the afterlife,
teasing us for a carving knife.

High New England summer, warm
and fortified against the storm
by nightly nips you once adored,
though never going overboard,
Harriet, when you used to play
your chosen Nadia Boulanger
Monteverdi, Purcell, and Bach's
precursors on the Magnavox.

This is affectionate, even cozy. And beneath that first sensation is deep pathos; and beneath that is something like terror, so that the force of the phrase "life is much the same" keeps changing—for the worse—as you read. The imagery of a life with fossil memory, a run-down garden, a propped-up barn, a devastated Troy and cursed Mycenae, a Barchester that needs repeopling, people who need to be nipped and corrected, or redone, a half-blind paralyzed woman (the syntax has a way of paralyzing her objects as well), the need to be fortified against summer (with nips: the carving knife lying suddenly across both the cozy drinking and the corrected behavior) all issue in, among time's other wreckage, a Magnavox, the great voice which reproduces a great religious passion in the form of a performer's art. Everything dwindles, is rendered. Boulanger's Monteverdi. Lowell's Harriet. It's easy to explicate poems and hard to get their tone. The tone here has one moment of extraordinary pathos that is deeper than the cat-like movement through entropy and corrosion:

half-blind, no voice unrecognized,
not trusting in the after-life,
teasing us for a carving knife.

High New England summer . . .

But in the end the tone has to do with rendering; the whole passage is majorfully directed. It is not the experience but a way of handling the experience. The imagery accumulates its desolating evidence, but in such a way that the terror in the poetry is perceived while the novelistic pathos is felt. The subterranean images, whether "consciously wrought" or not, are intellectual. In this way, it is exactly a metaphysical poem as nothing in *Lord Weary's Castle* is.

In the second section of "Quaker Graveyard" there's not much that could be called development. Four sentences, three of which use syntax only as a line of energy, do little more than elaborate an instance of what used to be called the pathetic fallacy, but they confront the experience of grief, of terror at the violence of things, directly:

> Whenever winds are moving and their breath
> Heaves at the roped-in bulwarks of this pier,
> The terns and seagulls tremble at your death
> In these home waters. Sailor, can you hear
> The Pequod's sea-wings, beating landward, fall
> Headlong and break on our Atlantic wall
> Off 'Sconset, where the yawing S-boats splash
> As the entangled screeching mainsheet clears
> The blocks: off Madaket, where lubbers lash
> The heavy surf and throw their long lead squids
> For blue-fish? Sea-gulls blink their heavy lids
> Seaward. The wind's wings beat upon the stones,
> Cousin, and scream for you and the claws rush
> At the sea's throat and wring it in the slush
> Of this old Quaker Graveyard where the bones
> Cry out in the long night for the hurt beast
> Bobbing by Ahab's whaleboats in the East.

The effect here is not simple, but for me it is the most beautiful moment in the poem. The whole of that first sentence relaxes. The lines break deliberately as if they were trying to hold the emotion in place. But the content is terrible and the perception is extraordinarily intense. The feathers of the gulls ruffling in the wind are made to hurt. And it's such an ordinary perception. "Whenever winds are moving": to my Pacific grounding, the winds move almost always, so that Lowell's image registers the steady pain of merely seeing. For some reason this connected in my mind with a thing Levi-Strauss says near the end of *Tristes Tropiques*: "What I see is an affliction to me, what I cannot see a reproach." The power of this image connects all the description in the poem with the eyes of the dead sailor and the gulls' eyes and the profoundly becalmed eyes of the Virgin of Walsingham. It connects the wind's breath with the breath of the poet which accelerates into violence again in the next sentence. And that sentence is a good example of the expressive power of syntax in the poem. In its fierce accumulation of images, you lose any sense that it began, rather gently, as a rhetorical question. This is a way of being lost, of drowning in the dissolution of syntax. Surrealism, I'm tempted to say, is syntax: not weird images but the way the mind connects them. Here they swell and gather toward violence, toward a continuous breaking like the breaking of waves on the shore and the effort of control is conveyed by the way "the entangled screeching mainsheet clears the blocks."

So the poem must slow down again: "Seagulls blink their heavy lids / Seaward." This fixity, the imperturbable consciousness of the gull whose feathers a moment before were trembling in "home waters," is an enormous relief. It is not the dead staring eyes of the drowned sailor and it is not yet the seeing of Our Lady of Walsingham. That heavy-lidded blinking of gulls seems to have a wonderful Buddha-like somnolent alertness when you look at it. It accepts things as they are. It's when gulls are perched on piers, heads tucked in a little, eyes blinking matter-of-factly, that I'm suddenly aware they have no arms, no hands. Even if they don't like what they see, they're not going to do anything about it. And this is the relief. But gulls are also scavengers. Their seeing doesn't hope for much, but it belongs to the world of appetite and their appetites are not very ambitious. That is why the sailors, grasping at straws in section IV, are only three-quarters fools. They want something, have heard news "of IS, the whited monster." So the lines accelerate again. The sea, godly in the first section, is consumed in the general violence in this one and the section ends in a long wail for Moby Dick, the object of desire, monster and victim.

Almost all of "The Quaker Graveyard" works in this way. It's hard to get at without a lot of tedious explication, but look at the third section of the poem. If you ask yourself how the language or the thought proceeds, it's not easy to say. First sentence: "All you recovered . . . died / With you. . . ." Second sentence: "Guns . . . / blast the eelgrass. . . ." Third sentence: "They died . . . / ; only bones abide. . . ." Characteristically, the Quaker sailors appear at the extremity of a dependent clause; then their fate is seized on, midway through the section, as a subject, and the stanza unravels again into violence as the sailors drown proclaiming their justification. And it does not seem arbitrary. It seems inevitable because this hopelessly repeated unraveling into violence is both the poem's theme and the source of its momentum. Hell is repetition and the structure of anger is repetition. In this poem history is also repetition, as it is the structure of religious incantation. They are all married here, desperately, and the grace of the poem has to exist in modulation of tone. This modulation, like the different textures of an abstract expressionist painting or like the very different modulations that create the texture of Whitman's poems—"Song of Myself" comes to mind—is the grandeur and originality of "The Quaker Graveyard"—not theme, not irony or intimacy or the consciously wrought, but absolute attention to feeling at that moment in the poem's process.

"They died / When time was open-eyed, / Wooden and childish." It takes a while—or took me a while—to see that this is the one moment in the poem that reaches back into childhood. The image has about it the helplessness of childhood. Time here must be the wooden, open-eyed figureheads on old whaling ships, probably seen in books or in a maritime museum. The look of the eyes on those old sculptures, their startled and hopeful innocence, dawns on you and it creates the state of mind of the child looking up at them. *Was* not *seemed*. The verb makes the child's seeing sovereign and irrecoverable. Lost innocence is not the subject of the poem. There is a kind of pleading between the poet and the innocence of his cousin, the ensign who went to the war and did his duty. "All you recovered . . . died with you." But the innocence of the child, of the ensign, of the figureheads is only one syntactical leap away from the stupidity and self-righteousness of the Quaker sailors— "If God himself had not been on our side"—who are swallowed up without understanding a thing. Their eyes are "cabin-windows on a stranded hulk / Heavy with sand."

Sections IV and V continue this riding out of violence but the con-
clusions of both take a turn that brings us to the religious issue in
the poem. It didn't puzzle me much in that first excited reading
because I ignored it. I was living down a Catholic childhood and
religious reference in poetry seemed to me not so much reac-
tionary as fossilized and uninteresting. But it is surely there in a lot
of what I was reading. Robert Duncan's work is thick with religious
imagery, and the "Footnote to Howl" exclaimed, "Holy! Holy!
Holy!" I didn't know Lowell was a convert to Catholicism or that
this was a momentous rejection of his heritage. For that matter, I
didn't know what a Lowell was. But I could see that the poem was
not Catholic in any sense that I understood. It is true that the
implicit answer to the question "Who will dance the mast-lashed
master of Leviathans / Up. . ." is Christ. Orpheus, the way of art,
is explicitly dismissed at the beginning of the poem. And the fifth
section, the most terrible, the one in which the whale receives the
sexual wound of all human violence, ends with a prayer: "Hide /
Our steel, Jonas Messias, in Thy side."

But the first of these passages is a question and the second is
a supplication, not a statement of faith. Insofar as the poem is
Christian, it seemed to me to be a very peculiar Christianity. I was
prepared to grant that the killing of the Whale was also an image
of the crucifixion of Christ, but in the poem this act is the source
and culmination of evil: "When the whale's viscera go. . . .its cor-
ruption over-runs this world." There is no sense here of the cruci-
fixion as a redemption. I can imagine that three or four pages of
theological explication could put it there, but it isn't in the poem.
Typologically, the legal torture and murder of the man-god is not
the fall; in the Christian myth it is not cruelty and violence but
pride and disobedience through which men fell. One can make a
series of arguments, threading back through the blasphemous
pride of Ahab to the dominion given man by God in the epigraph
to the poem, and emerge with a case for cruelty as a form of pride,
but cruelty is not pride. They're different things, and it is cruelty
and death, not pride and the fall, that preoccupy the poet, no mat-
ter how much of Melville or theology we haul in to square this
vision with orthodoxy.

Reading Robert Duncan has given me a way to think about this
issue in Lowell:

> There was no law of Jesus then.
> There was
> only a desire of savior. . . .

Somewhere in his prose at about the same time, Duncan had written that the mistake of Christianity was to think that the soul's salvation was the only human adventure. That was an enormously liberating perception. It put Christ on equal footing with the other gods. And the gods, Pound had said in a phrasing that seems now late Victorian, were "eternal moods," forms of consciousness which men through learning, art, and contemplation could inhabit. They were not efficacious. We were not Mycenean warlords, burning bulls and hoping the good scent of roast beef found its way to attentive nostrils; and the Mother of Perpetual Help did not, as my aunts seemed to believe, repair carburetors or turn up lost purses. But the gods were real, forms of imagination in which we could dwell and through which we could see. "The verb," Pound had said with the wreckage of his life around him, "is 'to see' not 'walk on'."

I got my Catholicism from my mother's side, Foleys from Cork by way of Vermont who drank and taught school and practiced law on the frontiers of respectability until they landed in San Francisco at the turn of the century. My father's side was Protestant and every once in a while, weary probably with the catechisms of his children, he would try to teach us one of his childhood prayers. But he could never get past the first line: "In my father's house there are many mansions. . ." He would frown, squint, shake his head, but that was as far as he ever got and we children who were willing to believe Protestants capable of any stupidity including the idea that you could fit a lot of mansions into a house, would return to memorizing the four marks of the true church. (It was one, holy, catholic, and apostolic.) But that phrase came back to me as a way through the door of polytheism and into myth. If Pound could resurrect the goddesses, there was place for a temple of Christ, god of sorrows, desire of savior, restingplace of violence. I could have the memory of incense and the flickering candles and the battered figure on the cross with the infinitely sad and gentle face and have Aphrodite as well, "the fauns chiding Proteus / in the smell of hay under olive trees" and the intoning of Latin with which we began the mass: "*Introibo ad altare Dei*." On these terms, Lowell's prayer moved me: "Hide / our steel, Jonas Messias, in Thy side." And I could accept cruelty as the first fall; cruelty was truer to my experience than pride or disobedience which the violence of the state has made to seem, on the whole, sane and virtuous. Lowell evoked not the old dogma, but a piece of the unborn myth which American poetry was making. And this is the sense of things in the poem. There is no redemption promised in the prayer at the end of section V. There is only the god of sorrows and the receiving of the wound.

Sexual wounding: it is certainly there in section V, both in the imagery and in the way the section functions, literally, as a climax to the poem. This is the fall, the moment when corruption overruns the world. And the rhetorical question, "Sailor, will your sword / Whistle and fall and sink into the fat?" wants to make us all complicit. The passage is Calvinist in feeling; every day is judgment day:

> In the great ashpit of Jehoshaphat
> The bones cry for the blood of the white whale

In sexual imagery, not only the penetration by the death lance but the singing of stars, the dismemberment of the masthead, we are all judged:

> The fat flukes arch and whack about its ears,
> The death-lance churns into the sanctuary, tears
> The gun-blue swingle, heaving like a flail,
> And hacks the coiling life out: it works and drags
> And rips the sperm-whale's midriff into rags,
> Gobbets of blubber spill to wind and weather,
> Sailor, and gulls go round the stoven timbers
> Where the morning stars sing out together
> And thunder shakes the white surf and dismembers
> The red flag hammered in the masthead. . .

This needs to be seen straight on, so that we look at the sickening cruelty it actually describes. It's a relief and much easier to talk about myth or symbolic sexuality. This is an image of killing written by a pacifist who was willing to go to prison. It makes death horrifying; it makes the war horrifying, and the commerce of the Nantucket Quakers whom Melville reminded his readers to think of when they lit their cozy whale-oil lamps. "Light is where the landed blood of Cain . . ."

But, just as there is disgust with the mothering sea in the bilge and backwash throughout the poem, there is a deep abhorrence of sexual violence, of sexuality as violence. I'm not sure how to talk about it. There is Freud's gruesome little phrase, as gruesome in German as in English but lacking the pun: the sadistic conception of coitus. But calling it that doesn't take us very far. The fact is that there is an element of cruelty in human sexuality, although that isn't the reason for the Puritan distrust of sex. The Puritans distrusted sexuality because the sexual act dissolved human will for a moment, because—for a moment—men fell into the roots of their mammal nature. You can't have an orgasm and be a soldier of Christ. Thus *Samson Agonistes.* And the Puritan solution, hidden but real in the history of imagination, whether in Rome or the Enlightenment, was to turn sex into an instrument of will, of the conscious cruelty which flowered in the writings of Sade. It is there in our history and Lowell is right to connect it with the annihilative rage of capitalism. Flesh is languor ("All of life's grandeur / is something with a girl in summer. . .") but it is also rage. It marries us to the world and the world is full of violence and cruelty. This is part of the bind of the poem that is also the Calvinist bind of determinism and free will. The way out is not-world, an identification at the end of the poem with the "unmarried" Atlantic and the Lord who survives the rainbow-covenant of evolution.

All of the above would be pretty grim if it were not for "Our Lady of Walsingham." It's a remarkable moment in the poem, the most surprising of its modulations, a little tranquil island in all the fury. I imagine that for a lot of younger writers it was the place where they learned how far you could go away from the poem and still be in it. Pound says somewhere, sounding like a surly Matthew Arnold, that a history of poetry that's worth anything ought to be able to point to specific poems and passages in poems and say here, here and here are inventions that made something new possible in poetry. This is one of those places.

Its occurrence makes emotional sense because it follows sec-

tion V. It is peace from the satisfaction of the body's rage, a land-
scape of streams and country lanes. The nineteenth century would
have described the writing as chaste or exquisite and I'm not sure
we have better words to praise it with. It's wonderfully plain and
exact:

> Our Lady, too small for her canopy,
> Sits near the altar. There's no comeliness
> At all or charm in that expressionless
> Face with its heavy eyelids. As before,
> This face, for centuries a memory,
> *Non est species, neque decor,*
> Expressionless, expresses God: it goes
> Past castled Sion. She knows what God knows,
> Not Calvary's cross nor the crib at Bethlehem
> Now, and the world shall come to Walsingham.

The scene is another temple, not of the god of sorrows but of the
goddess of an almost incomprehensible peace. It appears to be the
emphatically Catholic moment in the poem, which adds a peculiar
comedy to the idea that "Lycidas" was somehow its model. (I've
just visited the cathedral at Ely where Milton's friend Thomas
Cromwell personally beheaded all the statues in the Lady Chapel.
If the setpiece digressions of Alexandrian pastoral taken over by
Milton to scourge a Popish clergy have really become Lowell's
hymn to the Virgin Mary, it is the kind of irony—funny, too elabo-
rately bookish—that would please the author of *History*.) But I
don't think it is Catholic, or not especially Catholic, and in that is
its interest.

   The crucial phrase is "Past castled Sion." Lowell is not after
sacramental mediation but a contemplative peace beyond any
manifestation in the flesh, beyond thought or understanding,
and—most especially—beyond desire. This isn't incompatible with
Catholic theology, but it's not central to its spirit, which is embod-
iment: the Orphean lute and the crib at Bethlehem. Lowell's
apprehension of God—of a pure, calm, and utterly clear con-
sciousness—belongs equally to all mysticism, Christian or other-
wise. It has always seemed to me that the figure of Our Lady here
looks a lot like Guatama Buddha. She is the embodiment of what

can't be embodied. This is a contradiction, but it is one that belongs to any intellectual pointing toward mystical apprehension. It is the contradiction that made the world-denial of Buddhists and Cathars utterly compassionate toward and alert to the world and the flesh. (The expression of this contradiction also makes the Buddhist Gary Snyder our best poet of nature.) Lowell's poem is not a rejection of the world, as the last lines suggest. The poem offers something much more attractive as a possibility of imagination.

What the Lady of Walsingham represents is past contention. She's just there. The method of the poem simply includes her among its elements, past argument and as a possibility through which all the painful seeing in the poem can be transformed and granted peace. She floats; everything else in the poem rises and breaks, relentlessly, like waves.

I got to hear Robert Lowell read in Charlottesville, Virginia—in Jefferson Country where the roadsigns read like a rollcall of plump Hanoverian dowagers and America comes as close as it ever will to a munching English lane. The setting made me feel truculent anyway, and when he began by murmuring an apology for the earlier poems—'rather apocalyptic,' 'one felt so intense'—I found myself on the poems' side. And the voice startled me, probably because I'd been hearing the work in my own for so long. I thought it sounded bizarrely like an imitation of Lionel Barrymore. It was not a voice that could say, "Face of snow, / You are the flowers that country girls have caught, / A wild bee-pillaged honeysuckle brought / To the returning bridegroom—the design / Has not yet left it, and the petals shine," without sounding like a disenchanted English actor reading an Elizabethan sonnet on American television.

I had felt vaguely hostile toward Lowell's later work, although I admired it. I thought, for one thing, that the brilliant invention of "The Quaker Graveyard" had come about because he had nothing to go on but nerve and that, when the form cloyed in *The Mills of the Kavanaughs*, he had traded in those formal risks for the sculpted anecdote and the Puritan autobiography, a form about as original as John Bunyan's *Grace Abounding*. Out of that manner had come—not so much in Lowell himself as in the slough of poetry *Life Studies* engendered—a lot of narrative beginnings: "Father,

you . . ." or "The corn died in the field that summer, Mother / when
. . ." It struck stances toward experience, as if Williams had said,
"No attitudes but in things!" I wanted the clarity that "Our Lady of
Walsingham" looked toward and in "Waking Early Sunday
Morning" I thought he had come to something like that earlier
insight and abandoned it too easily:

> I watch a glass of water wet
> with a fine fuzz of icy sweat,
> silvery colours touched with sky,
> serene in their neutrality—
> yet if I shift, or change my mood,
> I see some object made of wood,
> background behind it of brown grain,
> to darken it, but not to stain.
>
> O that the spirit could remain
> tinged but untarnished by its strain!
> Better dressed and stacking birch. . .

As if you had to choose between them or tarnishing were the issue.
That glass of water interested me a lot more than the ironies about
electric bells ringing "Faith of our fathers."

Anyway, when he began to read, all this buzzing of the head
stopped. There was the sense, for one thing, of a body of work
faithful to itself through all its phases (early, middle, and ceaseless
revision). And there was the reading of "Near the Ocean." Hearing
it, I began to understand the risks attendant on backing away from
the drama and self-drama of *Lord Weary's Castle*. Pain has its own
grandeur. This disenchanted seeing was not serene neutrality—it
was not serene at all; it had the clarity of a diminished sense of
things not flinched at. I thought "Near the Ocean" was a brave
piece of writing and it revisits the territory of "The Quaker
Graveyard," so it seems like a place to end:

> Sand built the lost Atlantis . . . sand,
> Atlantic ocean, condoms, sand.
> Sleep, sleep. The ocean, grinding stones,
> can only speak the present tense;

nothing will age, nothing will last,
or take corruption from the past.
A hand, your hand then! I'm afraid
to touch the crisp hair on your head—

Ironic Elegies:
The Poetry of Donald Justice

MARK JARMAN

D onald Justice is the most mordant poet we have in this
country today. I can think of no living American counter-
part whose poetry has his ironic bite. If he has any con-
temporary with a similar style and vision, it is Britain's own unique-
ly caustic poet, Philip Larkin. My aim here isn't to develop all the
parallels between these two, but to develop the most distressing
one: one that certainly exists and is most distressing is that neither
poet is as greatly appreciated in his own country as many poets
who are less gifted and less unique.

The paltry number of reviews which have appeared for
Justice's Pulitzer Prize-winning *Selected Poems* and the narrowness
of their scope are an indication of this nearsightedness. Some of
the daft conclusions of the book's reviewers are additional evi-
dence. In *Parnassus*, Vernon Young, making a point that American
poets, as they begin to dry up, return to their families and child-
hoods for subjects, a silly enough notion, suggests that Justice is
guilty of this, too; and "in quiet desperation" is writing odes to him-
self "way back there in that swimming hole of innocence or terror."
Obviously, Young has not read Justice's recent poem "First Death"
with a subtlety equal to the poet's. But we lose faith in a critic who
does not recognize a variation on a pantoum, "In the Attic," when
he sees one.

All the same, the irony of history tastes bitterly of a certain
mindless optimism that the best will be known for its true worth in
its time. In fact, new fields of approval have been chalked and
happy teams are lining up to be counted as the children of
Whitman and Dickinson, our pair of odd and newly found parents.

Justice is not there. He would not go were he invited. Besides, he would only make the spectators and participants uncomfortable.

> This poem is not addressed to you
> You may come into it briefly,
> But no one will find you here, no one.
> You will have changed before the poem will.
>
> Even while you sit there, unmovable,
> You have begun to vanish. And it does not matter.
> The poem will go on without you.
> It has the spurious glamour of certain voids.
>
> It is not sad, really, only empty.
> Once perhaps it was sad, no one knows why.
> It prefers to remember nothing.
> Nostalgias were peeled from it long ago.
>
> Your type of beauty has no place here.

"Poem," from his third book *Departures*, has been pointed to as an example of Justice's minimalism. Yet to call this minimalist is to ignore the complexities of the poem's tone, its modulations between an apparent *froideur* and an underlying hostility. The speaker seduces the reader with indifference, even anticipating the reader's skepticism, while offering phrases that are nearly precious because they are so delectable, like the eighth and twelfth lines above, and then claiming to be doing no such thing:

> Listen, it comes without guitar,
> Neither in rags nor any purple fashion.
> And there is nothing in it to comfort you.

There is irony in this seduction, and its irony occasions reason for the poem's strength the poet is writing an elegy for his reader. Murmuring all the while, he puts the bite on in the penultimate stanza:

Close your eyes, yawn. It will be over soon.
You will forget the poem, but not before
It has forgotten you. And it does not matter.
It has been most beautiful in its erasures.

Then, in the final stanza, after a mocking exclamation on the lost reader's behalf, the most cutting shift of all is made, ending the poem with a repetition of the first line like an unheeded warning:

O bleached mirrors! Oceans of the drowned!
Nor is one silence equal to another.
And it does not matter what you think.
This poem is not addressed to you.

This is a singular accomplishment and a singular recognition of the inevitable effacement of a poet's readers and hence of his work and himself. It is singular especially for a poet commonly thought of as narcissistic. Such labeling apparently issues from the mirror-motif in Justice's work, but the mirror as a love object, to mix my own metaphors a moment, is a red herring; for as Justice has implied in "Fragment: To a Mirror," the mirror itself is merely a "half of nothingness."

Emphasis on a possibly narcissistic quality misleads the critic, who thus overlooks a more essential role Justice returns to in his most significant poems—that of the elegist. Throughout his thirty year career his mordancy and his ear for the musical lament have made a fortuitous union. While "Poem" has been their most original product, each elegy before and since has reflected its origins in them, from the opening lines of "On the Death of Friends in Childhood" ("We shall not ever meet them bearded in heaven,/ Nor sunning themselves among the bald of hell') to "Early Poems" ("The rhymes, the meters, how they paralyze") to "Variations on a rest by Vallejo" ("I will die in Miami in the sun"), an elegy for himself ironically recasting Vallejo's famous self-fulfilling prophecy. As the originality of approach has grown, so has the irony of mourning. What a critic like Young mistakes for impoverishment of subject matter in Justice's recent poetry is actually a taking on of a newly recognized challenge in certain childhood concerns.

One of these recent poems is "First Death." A complexly formal elegy of three parts, each of eight rhymed couplets sounds simple and balladic while moving deftly between acatelectic and catelectic iambic tetrameter. In the last part, the speaker sits beside his mother at his grandmother's funeral:

> The stiff fan stirred in mother's hand.
> Air moved, but only when she fanned
>
> I wondered how could all her grief
> Be squeezed into one small handkerchief.
>
> There was a buzzing on the sill.
> It stopped, and everything was still.
>
> We bowed our heads, we closed our eyes
> To the mercy of the flies.

The boy Rimbaud, taking aim at the foolery and righteousness around him, never displayed Justice's subtlety, and yet Rimbaud did better than anyone else. Justice's poetic tone is more like Mamillius' teasing of his mother's ladies-in-waiting ("I learned it out of women's faces"). What memory has retrieved here is the beginning of a way of seeing that will set the boy apart. Here mordancy fixes the coloring of this vision as it shows both the small irony of the mother's tears and the great one of the attendant flies.

The condensation of Justice's bitterness since his first book *Summer Anniversaries*, which critics seem to prefer and long for with unpeeled nostalgia, may be a reason he is so poorly understood. For in this condensation there has been a slight separation, too. Nothing in "First Death" is quite as acrid as "Unflushed Urinals":

> Seeing them, I recognize the contempt
> Some men have for themselves.
>
> This man, for instance, zipping quickly up, head turned,
> Like a bystander innocent of his own piss.

One wonders at the consideration of form by critics who, thinking

form is troublesome, believe they need not mention it but in foot-
notes. The first line break here leaves us with a (spine tingling)
ambiguity, as do the first two words of the third line. This is how
Justice pays attention to the form within the form or the seeming-
ly formless. Yet, the more elegiac recent poems appear in a less flu-
orescent light. "Thinking about the Past" has the fragmentary bril-
liance of a broken bundle of mirrors:

> Certain moments will never change, nor stop being—
> My mother's face all smiles, all wrinkles soon;
> The rock wall building, built, collapsed then, fallen:
> Our upright loosening downward slowly out of tune—
> All fixed into place now, all rhyming with each other.
> The red-haired girl with wide mouth—Eleanor—
> Forgotten thirty years—her freckled shoulders, hands.
> The breast of Mary Something, freed from a white
>   swimsuit,
> Damp, sandy, warm; or Margery's, a small, caught bird—
> O marvellous early cigarettes! O bitter smoke, Benton . . .
> And Kenny in wartime whites, crisp, cocky,
> Time a bow bent with his certain failure.
> Dusks, dawns; waves; the ends of songs . . .

Here, might we be reminded not of Rimbaud but of Laforgue? Had
he lived beyond the age of 27, the author of "Complainte de l'Oubli
des Morts," might have written, with this ironic forgiveness of
things, of the world where the dead hardly go out anymore, except
in poems. For unpleasant and unhappy as they seem, our elegies in
Justice's hands record our failures. "What of the dead?" we ask.
And out of the importunate, raging wind, Justice, like Laforgue
simply answers with the irony I have feebly tried to describe,
"They travel...."

The self-effacement of the elegist is traditional, at least since
Milton sang of his friend, the drowned poet Edward King, "For
Lycidas is dead, dead ere his prime,/ Young Lycidas, and hath not
left his peer." The irony with which Justice effaces himself is noted
by William Logan in his essay on the poet in *Crazyhorse* 20, for it
makes him "a modern turned inside out confession is silenced, rev-
elation masked, statement disavowed." This irony certainly does

make Justice modern, but the twist it puts on the tradition is what makes him individual.

Justice's complexity of tone requires a quality of attention on the part of a reader that is hard to give: in fact, it is hard to describe what we hear, except by quoting the poem itself or, as Randall Jarrell once said, just pointing. I think we hear the voice of a supremely skeptical romantic, not a cynic, but an ironic elegist who, in his paradoxical largess, can sing not only of your death, mine and his own; in "The Telephone Number of the Muse," he can even sing of the death of his own poetic gift.

> I call her up sometimes, long distance now.
> And she still knows my voice, but I can hear,
> Beyond the music of her phonograph,
> The laughter of the young men with their keys.
>
> I have the number written down somewhere.

How Good Is John Ashbery?

ROBERT MCDOWELL

"So I live with this paradox: on the one hand,
I am an important poet, read by younger writ-
ers, and on the other hand, nobody under-
stands me. I am often asked to account for
this state of affairs, but I can't."
—John Ashbery

John Ashbery is a winner. In the small, clubby world of con-
temporary poetry, he has published ten volumes of poetry
since 1955 and received a Yale Younger Poets Prize, two
Guggenheim Fellowships, a Pulitzer Prize, fellowships from the
Academy of American Poets and the Merrill Foundation, a
National Book Award, a position as Distinguished Professor at a
New York university, a National Book Critics Circle Award, mem-
bership in the National Academy and Institute of Arts and Letters
and the National Academy of Arts and Sciences, and a MacArthur
Prize Fellowship. Only the deceased (and not many among them)
may claim comparable expressions of public gratitude.

America loves a winner. The beleaguered American Academy,
taking its cue from the winner-producing machinery of sports and
popular culture, sees its salvation in its ability to create winners in
literature. As long as there are "great" writers, so the reasoning
goes, there will be "great" literature. "Great" literature is attended
by the need for dedicated study and explication, and this necessity
validates the Academy's mission. If John Ashbery did not exist, one
might almost say, the Academy would have to invent him. In the
sense that he has been more widely honored than any contempo-
rary poet, he is our "greatest" living example of someone who wins
with poetry.

The harrowing problems and pressures this status exerts on Ashbery must be enormous; it affects others among us who are poets too. For given Ashbery's ascendancy, what are we to make of our poetic climate? One pervasive message, delivered by the American Academy, and frequently by publishers as well, is that once the star-making machinery clicks on, it generates an enthusiasm that often approaches hysteria. An atmosphere of sober judgment evaporates. Poets who also write criticism must examine their roles in helping to create this carnival atmosphere. In each case, we must ask ourselves if we promote poetry or a personality, and we must be aware of the dangerous, exotic lure of giddy endorsement for its own sake.

Given this warning, it is appropriate to recall that every new volume published by John Ashbery has been widely praised, probed, pumped up, or put down by a host of critics and reviewers. This prodigious soap opera in prose ranges from the unequivocal enthusiasm of Richard Howard, Laurence Lieberman, and David Shapiro to the exasperation of James Fenton and Robert Boyers; the sparsely populated middle ground of calm evaluation is best exemplified by Marjorie Perloff, Ashbery's best sympathetic critic. Out of all of this attention, two dominant opinions of Ashbery's worth as a poet have emerged: 1) his is the poetry of obscurity and boredom, which ought not to be taken seriously; 2) his is the poetry of genius that creates "new" ways of imagining and "new" ways of expression for a "new" audience, and which must be taken very seriously indeed.

It is relatively easy to disprove the first opinion; it usually is when confronting pronouncements from the criticism of dismissal. Ashbery's poetry *is* sometimes boring, but so is much of the poetry written by everybody else. However, Ashbery's poetry is seldom obscure. His obsessions are clear enough, and his poems express them repeatedly in English that is not too hard to follow. Furthermore, in the volumes up to and including *Self-Portrait in a Convex Mirror*, Ashbery was the dominant figure in the revival of a historical channel in our poetry's tradition. To dismiss the poems, to refuse to take them seriously on some level, would be foolish if not stupid.

In the same sense that we ought not to dismiss Ashbery, we might turn a calm, critical eye on the second popular opinion. I am not sure that I know of a single poet or critic among us who would readily recognize the "poetry of genius." The "new" ways of imagining in Ashbery's poetry are found extensively in the literature of psychology and philosophy, and in poetry, Stevens and Auden in particular come to mind as intellectual precursors. The "new" methods of expression have a number of precursors in poetry—Stevens, Auden, Traherne, Browne, Reverdy, Rimbaud. Here we might correctly consider that the words genius and new are related to great—a trilogy of blitz-glitz words borrowed from show business. They represent the other side of the attitude that inspires the criticism of complete dismissal, and both ought properly to be discredited. The publication of Ashbery's *Selected Poems* marks the occasion of another season of strong debate about the poet, and it offers yet another opportunity for sober evaluation of a kind that can perhaps take Ashbery's true measure.

"Not *what* one dreams but *how*—this is Ashbery's subject." This assertion by Marjorie Perloff is accurate and useful in making sense of the body of John Ashbery's work. Examining poem after poem, we find that Ashbery is making the same case over and over. In it he demands that the audience perceive reality in alternate ways by denying the referential nature of language. Couplings of rhythms and images are deliberately sabotaged to create new meanings, which reflect the happenstance significance of the world of dreams.

This is an admirable goal in theory, and since the mid-seventies such young poets as Alfred Corn, John Yau, Jorie Graham, and others have followed Ashbery's lead, making the shadow-mind their special subject. At their best, all of these poets have succeeded in creating moments of linguistic epiphany in which a new connection becomes, for the reader, surprise reality. And no one has succeeded more ably in this endeavor than Ashbery himself.

But there is a catch. It resides at the root of the linguistic theory that makes such poetry possible. Specifically, no poet or critic promoting the poetry of discontinuity has successfully argued the diminished significance of referentiality in language. Instead they have unquestioningly embraced the disastrous assumption that the powers of language are inherently equal. Thus, they hold that discontinuous poetry is equal in power to referential poetry. But language is not a utopian system that makes its resources available to any creature that grunts. Marjorie Perloff, by association, attempts to dispel the popular notion that Ashbery's discontinuous poems are abstract by calling attention to the "net work of representational traces" in Picasso and Gertrude Stein, but she fails to prove that Ashbery's network of traces transmits as well. Furthermore, Perloff is right to expose the contention that Ashbery strives to eliminate meaning; she warns us against regarding meaning "as some sort of fixed quantity (like two pounds of sugar or a dozen eggs)." But again, she does not go far enough.

I am willing to grant the poet his alternative meaning and learn from it if I can; I am not convinced that *alternatives* equals *meaning* any more or less than fixed quantities do. Taken to its extreme, the argument for discontinuity in poetry allows for any form of writing to be called poetry. When referentiality is banished from poetry, so is restraint. The result is a loss in the power of language. In order to offset this loss, Ashbery and others of his school attempt to retain some referential threads that most often resemble stage directions—an announced progression of time, a brief description of setting or characte, an anecdote. Poetry that holds to this practice has been accurately put into the category of parody by Northrop Frye: "The prose element in the diction and syntax is so strong that the features of verse still remaining give it the effect of continuous parody. This is the area of intentional doggerel. . . . Here again, as with euphemism, we are moving in an atmosphere of paradox, and also discontinuity."

One needn't have read Frye to notice the overwhelming prose element in Ashbery's diction and syntax. One need only consider a chunk of his lines, such as these from his famous poem "Self-Portrait in a Convex Mirror," in which the narrator reflects on the gaze of Parmigianino:

> . . . the soul is not a soul,
> Has no secret, is small, and it fits
> Its hollow perfectly: its rooms, our moment of attention.
> That is the tune but there are no words.
> The words are only speculation
> (From the Latin *speculum*, mirror):
> They seek and cannot find the meaning of the music.

It is impossible to analyze the movement of these lines as poetry; their rhythm is that of chatty prose. The speaker is delivering a lecture, a familiar lesson, and in his zeal to link what he considers to be complicated ideas, he begins to rely on imagistic leaps familiar in poetry. Defenders of this poem will point to the progression of words becoming speculation, becoming mirror, then becoming something active (again)—something capable of seeking (eyes? a gaze?)—as inspired examples of metaphor. I find them to be examples of mixed metaphor. The parenthetical line, perhaps intended to create irony, awkwardly aids the leap from the *speculation* to *mirror*; it is also prim and self-congratulatory, trotting out the narrator's learning and cleverness.

The *meaning* of the music. . . . The meaning is elusive, perhaps, but not as elusive as the making of the music itself. Ashbery's lyric success, in the example above and elsewhere, is minimal. In this he is not alone. At least one generation of American poets, the generation that came to maturity in the fifties, has forgotten that the finest lyric poetry in English relied on simple direct speech. If one must be convinced, I suggest renewed contemplation of Yeats's lyric poems. Today, most poets, critics, and reviewers mistake awkward, mannered speech for lyricism and consign direct speech to the province of prose. This is sadly misguided, and it is much responsible for poetry's already small audience shrinking even further.

What John Ashbery does best is to parody the act of writing poems. His fondness for abstract nouns and shifting pronouns is well documented, but little has been said about the temperament of the man who is so fond of these discontinuous devices. To begin with, here is Ashbery himself: "I guess I don't have a very strong sense of my own identity and I find it very easy to move from one person in the sense of a pronoun to another and this again helps to produce a kind of polyphony in my poetry which I again feel is a means toward a greater naturalism." This absence of a "strong sense of identity" accounts for the lack of notable characters in Ashbery's poetry. This absence also explains in part the difficulty in gauging the character of the poet himself. Instead. we must be content with watching him struggle to turn a fatal weakness into a strength, which he almost never does. Thus it becomes absolutely clear why Ashbery squeamishly veers from the referential realm, where characters are essential and character must assert itself if language is to achieve a powerful effect on the reader. Secure in his discontinuous universe, Ashbery repeatedly expresses contempt for our moment in history by systematically denying consequence. Without history and consequence, events slosh in and out of one another, continuing without end, as in these lines from " Pyrography":

> If this is the way it is let's leave,
> They agree, and soon the slow boxcar journey
>   begins,
> Gradually accelerating until the gyrating fans
>   of suburbs
> Enfolding the darkness of cities are remem-
>   bered
> Only as a recurring tic. And midway
> We meet the disappointed, returning one,
>   without its
> Being able to stop us in the headlong night
> Toward the nothing of the coast. At Bolinas
> The houses doze and seem to wonder why
>   through the
> Pacific haze, and the dreams alternately glow
>   and grow dull.
> Why be hanging on here? Like kites, circling,
> Slipping on a ramp of air, but always circling?
>
> But the variable cloudiness is pouring it on,
> Flooding back to you like the meaning of a
>   joke.
> The land wasn't immediately appealing; we
>   built it
> Partly over with fake ruins, in the image of
>   ourselves: . . .

Every image summons up the negative. Critics are observed in "darkness" and remembered as "recurring tic"; an individual is "disappointed"; dreams "glow and grow dull"; the land is not "appealing," so we construct "fake ruins, in the image of our-selves." The bitterness cloaked in mannered utterance is still bitterness. Redemption, for the poet, comes only in the act of assembling his discontinuous catalogue.

Another example occurs in Ashbery's poem " Litany":

> You were a secretary at first until it
> Came time to believe you and then the black man
> Replaced your headlights with fuel
> You seemed to grow from no place.

If we met these lines in the work of any other writer, wouldn't we call it mixed metaphor? If we were charitable, wouldn't we call strained surrealism? In Ashbery, it is often referred to as "genius."

This passage (among innumerable others) persuades one that it is, not in assertion, but in tone that so much of Ashbery's work is derogatory when it attempts to examine individual American character types. Ultimately, it does not matter that one prefers the poetry of the city over that of the farm, the poetry of the village over that of the small town. At the best, these diverse poetries share one essential element—a governing sense of community. This is what convinces us of a poem's value. Even if the poet's focus is inwardly directed, his language and point of view acknowledge a larger reality in which all of us play a part. Without this sense of community a poem's audience evaporates, its dialogue falls silent. Without it the poet settles for the role of a lost and lonely individual who talks only to himself.

This is Ashbery's most severe handicap as poet, and it is nowhere more obvious than in "Daffy Duck in Hollywood," which is based on the famous Chuck Jones "capic" (cartoon epic). In the animated short, Daffy is repeatedly erased and redrawn. With each new appearance, in guises he sometimes approves of, sometimes not, he must work his way out of a serious crisis. Ashbery uses this cinematic springboard (frequently, he turns to film for *subjects*, not *effects*, as has been inaccurately posited) to dive into an examination of appearances—how we look, how others appear to us—and their ramifications. Jones's work is more successful, which is not to suggest that Ashbery was mistaken in trying to write the poem. However, the poem should stake out its own ground, making the reader forget its precursor. The poem ought to be as funny, visual, and disturbing as the capic. In the latter, theme is powerfully understated; in the former, it is plainly announced again and again with all the force of a buried headline:

All life is but a figment; conversely, the tiny
Tome that slips from your hand is not perhaps the
Missing link in this invisible picnic whose leverage
Shrouds our sense of it.

"Reading Ashbery's text," Marjorie Perloff has written, "is thus rather like overhearing a conversation in which one catches an occasional word or phrase but cannot make out what the speakers are talking about. . . . And yet one does keep listening. For the special pleasure . . . is that disclosure of some special meaning seems perpetually imminent." This describes the motivation of the eavesdropper, the participant in gossip, or the casual reader-skimmer of the newspaper. All of us must answer for ourselves whether or not this accurately describes what we hope to experience by reading poetry.

It would be difficult for John Ashbery to answer this question. He makes a point of avoiding answers whenever possible. Based on the poems in the current volume, one might guess that his favorite word is *perhaps*. Ashbery plays to the word's suggestion of doubt and possibility, but the poems give no indication that their sensibility understands *consequence* in the word itself. Again, this is a problem of temperament as much as craft, and nothing calls our attention to it like the absence of notable characters. Even when Ashbery gives more than his usual glancing attention to narrative, he fails to develop such characters. His are instead all stereotypes, the sort of secondary people we expect to meet in some less-than-first-rate fiction. All of them resemble, in the snapshot glimpses of them we are allowed, the framed photo of the aged mother's banker son in "The Instruction Manual": ". . . a dark-skinned lad with pearly teeth grins out at us from the worn leather frame." The strategy of discontinuity prohibits any deeper insight.

In an essay written several years ago, Laurence Lieberman accurately observed that "Ashbery's career has vacillated between two poles, two opposite aesthetics—the rage to leave everything out, the rage to put everything back in." But this vacillation might be wholly intentional—a clever gambit by which the poet masks a fundamental dearth of subject matter. Interpreted in this way, Ashbery's work chillingly exemplifies Parmigianino's "life-obstructing task" in every line. As Ashbery himself put it, his goal has been to write "as though an argument were suddenly derailed and something that started out clearly suddenly becomes opaque. . . . What I am probably trying to do is to illustrate opacity and how it can suddenly descend over us, rather than trying to be willfully obscure."

The method is not difficult to analyze. Whereas a poet preoccupied with images will build his poem through a sequence of images to an earned generalization, Ashbery will reverse this movement; he begins with generalization, then rambles on until the *language of generality* (not to be confused with the language of philosophy) suggests an image. Consider these lines from "A Wave" (italics mine):

> . . . everything, in short,
> That makes this explicit earth what it appears
>   to be in our
> Classiest moments when a *canoe shoots*
>   *out from under some foliage*
> *Into the river* and finds its calm . . .

Occasionally, Ashbery drops the form of poetry altogether and attempts to write poetic prose philosophy. "The System" and "A wave" are prime examples, and in these poems he is most unashamedly himself, a writer for whom "our landscape" is always "partially out of focus, some of it too near." These pieces, generated by a vague desire to reconcile opposites, have less in common with a dream book than with a psychoanalytic daybook in which syntax is swept away by its own cuteness and hypothesis is overwhelmed by self-satisfaction.

It may be true that in the poetry of ideas the poetry pales as the ideas achieve an ever more suffocating lock on the poet's imagination. When this occurs, the poetry of ideas becomes the poetry of poses. In Ashbery's case, the poetry repeatedly sets us up; because nothing matters, it seldom delivers resolutions of consequence. Without the hope of consequence and threads running to it, there is no significant communication. The poet who denies consequence becomes the man absorbed in his crossword puzzle as his train pulls away, leaving him behind in the station.

If we embrace the discontinuous system of which Ashbery is so fond, seeing our lives as little more than random splotches of color, we merely play a passive part in replacing one system—the system reference—with an even less satisfying one that seeks to preserve the romanticized past. John Ashbery is no fool. He is as much a cultural naysayer as Allen Ginsberg, which is to say that he is no naysayer at all. Like Ginsberg, Ashbery is successful and comfortable, his success and comfort maintained by institutions of the very culture he purports in his poetry to despise. What in his youth was a legitimate critical-poetic attack against cultural conditions that begrudge change has become, in late middle age, mannered and inaccurate repetition. "Perhaps we ought to feel with more imagination," he writes. Perhaps we ought to imagine with more feeling, one might retort. John Ashbery's discontinuous experiments were all carried out by the middle of the last decade. Succeeding books confirm that they are played out. Now the Academy, with characteristic sluggishness, rises to honor and explain them. This complicated process has nothing to do with poetry.

Derek Walcott:
Poet of the New World

DAVID MASON

To Joseph Summers

Although Helen Vendler has called Derek Walcott a "Poet of Two Worlds"(1), it may be more accurate to call him a poet of the New World, a world which has absorbed the old and is still faced with its own lack of definition. His formal proclivities help him bridge old and new writing styles, and, increasingly, his work is shaped by a history of self-exile and divorce, a continuous breaking down of the structures in which complacency breeds. He is one of a handful of modern poets who root themselves in tradition, yet become reliable witnesses to modern life.

In the marketplace of Castries, the capital of St. Lucia, where Derek Walcott was born, the audible mixtures of English and patois remind one of the voices in Walcott's poems: the English and French with their Anglo-Saxon and Latin heritages, the vestiges of African dialects that survive in a few inflections or turns of phrase. Walcott has mastered the speech of former rulers and former slaves, which gives him a special right to speak of "The leprosy of Empire."(2) Like Ovid at the fringes of Roman domination, Walcott has observed imperial power, but he has also witnessed life in a New World of which Ovid never dreamed. As both poet and playwright, he has set himself an ambitious schedule of assimilation. His literary territory, which began as the Caribbean basin, has expanded to include North America and Europe (particularly England, Greece, Rome and, via Brodsky and Mandelstam, Russia). Perhaps because his vision is of Whitmanesque proportions, the work itself has been uneven. He has produced a few gems among his poems, and a great many rougher stones which still repay examination.

"The emotional attitudes of Walcott's early verse were authentic," Vendler writes, "but shallowly and melodramatically phrased."(3) It is true that a certain Latin grandiosity creeps into his style, creating moments of unjustified inflation. But Vendler also emphasizes Walcott's unique point of view:

> Walcott's agenda gradually shaped itself. He would not give up the paternal island patois; he would not give up patois to write only in formal English. He would not give up his topic—his geographical place, his historical time, and his mixed blood; neither would he give up aesthetic balance, "the rightness of placed things." He was in all things "a divided child," loyal to both "the stuffed dark nightingale of Keats" and "the virginal unpainted world" of the islands. . . .(4)

Unlike most poets, Walcott was born with a subject; he had something to say, in large part because he was born in a place that embodies so many diverse elements of the modern world, and he was gifted with an ear for its languages. These senses of subject and purpose, as well as his refusal to let either be diminished, are precisely what have always given Walcott the potential for a kind of greatness.

Inheritance and imitation, coupled with fresh experience, resulted in complex ambitions, illuminated by Walcott himself in his memoir, "What the Twilight Says":

> In that simple schizophrenic boyhood one could lead two lives: the interior life of poetry, the outward life of action and dialect. Yet the writers of my generation were natural assimilators. We knew the literature of Empires, Greek, Roman, British, through their essential classics; and both the patois of the street and the language of the classroom hid the elation of discovery. If there was nothing, there was everything to be made. With this prodigious ambition one began.(5)

It is ambition as great as Joyce's, as great as Whitman's, and even to identify it is quite an accomplishment. Although it is difficult to tell at this point whether Walcott's poetry will ever completely defeat the clamor of influences, he has made his own mature style supple enough to be recognizable in *vers libre* as well as closed forms and blank verse. There is practically no verse technique in which he has not, at some point, worked well.

Throughout his career, Walcott has "caught style from others like a cold,"(6) but this is not necessarily indicative of a dire condition. His very ambition and assimilation have demanded imitation of others, to which he has always added his own presence, more definable with each new volume. In *Selected Poems*, which gathers work completed earlier than 1964, Walcott's indebtedness to the seventeenth-century poets is evident on nearly every page. The title of his first significant volume (or at least the first published in the "imperial" capital, London) was *In a Green Night*, a phrase from Andrew Marvell's "Bermudas." In his title poem Walcott borrows Marvell's imagery, but recasts it into tetrameter quatrains that convey doubts of the poet's role in an Edenic landscape. Marvell's is not the only seventeenth-century influence found in *Selected Poems*. "Orient and Immortal Wheat" takes its title and epigraph from the Third Century of Thomas Traherne's *Centuries of Meditations*, and bits and quotations from other poets of the period are sprinkled throughout. *The Fortunate Traveller*, Walcott's sixth book of poems (depending on how you count), gets its title, playfully, from Thomas Nashe, who died at the opening of the seventeenth century.

The same volume illustrates Walcott's experimentation with a very different tradition, island patois, to evoke characters of Caribbean folk tradition. In the dialect poem, "The Spoiler's Return," Walcott, although lapsing into English poetic diction, produces long passages that work splendidly. None of his earlier attempts at dialect poetry works quite so well. With "The Spoiler's Return," Walcott is not so much creating the character of the Spoiler for us as he is playing with the voice to produce sophisticated local satire. Except for the poem's mock-dialect, it could be compared to many of the verse satires of the seventeenth-century, from Jonson to Suckling to Marvell, as well as their Augustan successors:

In all them project, all them Five-Year Plan,
what happen to the Brotherhood of Man?
Around the time I dead it wasn't so,
we sang the Commonwealth of Caiso,
we was in chains, but chains made us unite,
now who have, good for them, and who blight,
    blight;
my bread is bitterness, my wine is gall,
my chorus is the same: "I want to fall."

. . . as for the Creoles, check their house, and
    look,
you bust your brain before you find a book,
when Spoiler see all this, ain't he must bawl,
"area of darkness," with V.S. Nightfall?

The personal reference to Walcott's favorite whipping boy, V.S. Naipaul, is straight out of English satirical tradition, and perhaps, too, the tradition of the Calypso taunt. Clearly Walcott is having literary fun, and does not expect us to believe, in street-life terms, that his dialect is accurate.

Like Ben Jonson, Walcott can turn his "ventriloquism" (Vendler's word) to good use when it comes to paying compliments. His poem, "Beachhead," written for Anthony Hecht, suggests the imagery of war remembered in some of Hecht's best poems. Though its measure is shorter than that which Hecht has most often used, his voice is still suggested:

A sepia lagoon
bobbing with coconuts –
helmets from the platoon
of some Marine unit –

whose channel links those years
of boyhood photographs
in *Life* and *Collier's* to dim Pacific surf.

An earlier poem, "R.T.S.L.," written in memory of Robert Lowell, takes on Lowell's *Life Studies* voice convincingly:

. . . there was the startle of wings
breaking from the closing cage
of your body, your fist unclenching
these pigeons circling serenely
over the page. . . .

Walcott's own mature voice is most evident in poems like
"Hurucan," "The Hotel Normandie Pool," and in the momentary
transcendence of "The Season of Phantasmal Peace." "Hurucan"
derives its strength from description:

When the power station's blackout
grows frightening as amnesia,
and the luxury resorts
revert to the spear-tips of candles,
and the swimming pools in their marsh light
multiply with hysterical lilies
like the beaks of fledglings uttering your name,
when lightning fizzles out
in the wireless, we can see and hear
the streaming black locks of clouds.

The seventh line of this passage contains an image that isn't quite
clear, but the rest of it is stunning writing. In "The Hotel
Normandie Pool" Walcott takes up the familiar theme of exile. He
is not, like his friend, Joseph Brodsky, a political exile barred from
returning to his native country. Yet, for Walcott, the pain and
responsibilities of adulthood are themselves a kind of exile, and
childhood is a landscape to which he can never return; the Castries
of his childhood was long ago gutted by a fire. The personal and
political exile of other poets before him seems a haunting pres-
ence; Constantine Cavafy and George Seferis play important roles
in *The Fortunate Traveller*. Cavafy visited Athens only a few times;
Seferis lost his Smyrna early, and Greece itself during the German
occupation. "Suddenly you discover you'll spend your entire life in
disorder," Seferis wrote. "It's all that you have; you must learn to
live with it."(7) The same sense of moodiness infects Walcott's
"The Hotel Normandie Pool":

Then Ovid said, "When I was first exiled,
I missed my language as your tongue needs salt,
in every watery shape I saw my child,
no bench would tell my shadow, 'Here's your place';
bridges, canals, willow-fanned waterways
turned from my parting gaze like an insult,
till, on a tablet smooth as the pool's skin,
I made reflections that, in many ways,
were even stronger than their origin.

He begins with an image of the poet sitting down to write in what would seem a second-class hotel:

I choose one of nine
cast-iron umbrellas set in iron tables
for work and coffee. The first cigarette
triggers the usual fusillade of coughs.

The poet's solitude is exile, however self-willed, and in the end Ovid taunts him with his own activity: "Because to make my image flatters you." It is a graceful and moving poem about delusion and diligence, and its final note is struck with real precision.

As early as *Selected Poems* there are pieces that only Walcott could have written. In "A Sea-Chanty," he composes a good portion of his poem out of Caribbean place names and indigenous nouns. Like Adam or Whitman, he becomes the New World figure pointing and naming, a tendency he continued in his 1969 book, *The Gulf*:

I loved them all, the names
of shingled, rusting towns, whose dawn
touches like metal. . . .

He makes an effort not only to absorb his culture, but to define it for others. This goal explains why a novelist like V.S. Naipaul, who seems to hold no hope for the region, becomes emblematic of a despised pessimism. Naipaul may very well be the "winter-bitten novelist" of the poem, "Hic Jacet," who is "praised for his accuracy of phlegm" (*The Gulf*). In *Sea Grapes* (1976), a poem called "At Last," subtitled "To the exiled novelists," begins,

> You spit on your people,
> your people applaud,
> your former oppressors
> laurel you.

Walcott has his own dark, brooding side, his pessimism about the potential of black power movements, politicians, tourism, Rastafarianism; but usually he is less concerned with judgment than with vision and meaning. Naipaul's fastidiousness and tone of disgust—at least in *The Mimic Men* and *Guerrillas*—would be perceived by Walcott as unhelpful, out of place, and even ignorant. Walcott is more of a sensualist than Naipaul; he may dislike what corrupt governments do to human life in his "tourist archipelagoes,"(8) but he can still see positive vitality and culture in the population.

This social stance—an attitude of commitment which is the converse to his attitude in poems about self-exile and historical solitude—is best expressed in Walcott's plays. Like the poems, they are uneven. His musical, *O Babylon!*, is about the sufferings of a small band of Rastafarians in Jamaica. In his efforts to express the full range of Caribbean life, Walcott must have found the subculture of Rastafarianism fascinating.(9) He has adapted their unique language for the stage, trying to avoid the betrayal of a complete English translation. In the end he creates a celebration of reggae among motley shanties on a Jamaican beach.

Like America's hippies, Walcott's Rastas greet each other with, "Peace and Love," and like so many spiritual movements before them, the Rastafari have been pushed aside to make room for economic development. Thus, Walcott has found in his community a microcosm for the strange mutations of political oppression.

He probably founded the Trinidad Theatre Workshop (in 1959) with a great sense of idealistic purpose. His plays have been experimental, mythological and poetic—in fact, he must be one of the few successful writers of theatrical verse in this century (although his best play *Pantomime* is written in prose). Writing for the theater has sometimes allowed Walcott to be playful, less rigorous, and to liberate lines that might be difficult in a poem:

> Thy kingdom come, condominium −

But occasionally the poet overwhelms the dramatist, and actors are asked to deliver lines unthinkable for their characters, even given Walcott's elevated stage poetry.

Apparently Walcott's dreams of a catalytic theater responsible for social change or at least social identity have been disappointed, but his theatrical contribution has nevertheless been a substantial public service, developed from the same impulses that motivate his poetry:

> . . . my first poems and plays expressed this yearning to be adopted, as the bastard longs for his father's household. I saw myself legitimately prolonging the mighty line of Marlowe, or Milton, but my sense of inheritance was stronger because it came from estrangement.(10)

There is a question as to whether Walcott, in his recent work, has abandoned his social mission for a more personal art. His satirical pot-shots continue unabated, and he has apparently not abandoned the stage, where he may continue to have a brilliant career. But the scale of his work in both genres appears to be more personal and focused. That he learns and grows from every encounter—if his art is any indication—should be encouraging. One wonders how an island so small could have produced a poet so large, with the great knowledge and ambition of Derek Walcott. But of course it wasn't the smallness of the place that mattered so much as the language and his twin needs: to be adopted by the larger world and to speak of his origins. One is left with an image of Walcott on one of his visits south, perhaps to Trinidad, barefoot on the sand, gazing out at a "sail which leans on light," and uttering what may be the best pentameter line he has ever written:

The classics can console. But not enough.

1. Helen Vendler, "Poet of Two Worlds," *New York Review of Books* 4 (March 1982): 23-27.

2. Derek Walcott, *Selected Poems* (New York: Farrar, Straus, and Giroux, 1964), p. 5.

3. Vendler, 23.

4. Vendler, 23.

5. Walcott, *Dream on Monkey Mountain and Other Plays* (New York: Farrar, Straus, and Giroux,, 1970) 4.

6. Walcott, *Sea Grapes* (New York: Farrar, Straus, and Giroux,, 1976), p. 52.

7. George Seferis, *A Poet's Journal*, trans. Athan Anagnostopoulos (Cambridge: Belknap, 1974), p. 53.

8. Walcott, *The Star-Apple Kingdom* (New York: Farrar, Straus, and Giroux,, 1979), p. 40.

9. The Rasta lifestyle is a growing and, apparently, positive force in black culture, but its "true" members represent a way of life diametrically opposed to the white Englishman's and the white North American's. As English travel writer Patrick Leigh Fermor wrote in 1950, "What a curious, dreamy and lotus-eating life they lead! Their existence consists exclusively of dodging the police, singing songs in praise of a monarch who knows nothing about them, planning the downfall of the white world, drinking rum, throwing dice and smoking reefers." Rastafarians are a minority with strong and basically peaceful beliefs (violent Rasta crime is said to be committed only by those who are not "true believers") and their own language. For a more thorough discussion of Rastafarianism, see *The Caribbean Review* 14, no. 1.

10. Walcott, *Dream on Monkey Mountain*, 31.

Part Three:
The Poetic World

The Poet's Calling: On a New Model of Literary Apprenticeship

MARY KINZIE

In a response to one of my critical reviews, a letter writer some years ago made the remarkable claim—remarkable in the sense that a critic should be implicitly proscribed from speculating on the poet's psychology—that I used my "talent for analysis to spy on the author."(1) A good critic "spies" only so far as to detect whether the daemon has spoken through the writer. With Louise Bogan's injunction still in our ears, and with the searing imagining of death in Coetzee's work still palpable, arguments about the mediocre appear not only more petty but also more important to sort out according to the magisterial laws given in the greatest literature.

One of these laws is that the aesthetic mission is also a moral one. So when a defender of a novice's work calls me to task for educing false standards of moral criticism, which the writer went on to explain meant that I thought poetry "must be held politically accountable for the nature of its insights, [and] that 'perception' is not subject enough for a poem," I felt, and feel, obliged to transform the objections into the terms of a useful lesson. Yet while I took pains in my reply to remove the meaningless modifier "politically" from the sentence, I was less certain how to put in a positive light these accusations, which were all quite true. How to persuade someone who thinks it reprehensible even to hint at such issues that the poet and the poem alike must be held responsible for the nature of their insights, that the personality of the author as well as the flavor of the text come into play in producing a body of work, and that, indeed, "perception" with its readily plumbed empirical backdrop is hardly subject enough for a poem?

To complicate (yet also, as it turned out, to help me clarify the real differences), these objections were joined by those of another letter writer, who thought artists must be "allowed" their material, citing *Guernica* and *Howl*. One argument against unfettered exposure of the ghastly and depraved is that it depraves the exposer. I suggested that the audience was not constrained to accept the equation between dreadful and shocking matter, and aesthetic "power" (let alone aesthetic harmony). We can say: This is a decadent subject; this is a corrupt treatment; this is a marriage of the sentimental with the brutal (if these happen to be the case). We are not, in other words, sentenced to silence by the autonomy of the artist.

This view is eloquently argued in his autobiography by the poet Edwin Muir, disturbed by the perversions, castrations, and livid raging in the plays of Wedekind and Toller:

> It is curious how often the questionable is invoked
> by German writers when they set out with a moral
> purpose. The resolve to expose evil in its most
> squalid form may be enough to account for this;
> but almost invariably something sordidly inquisi-
> tive comes into the treatment as well, adding to
> the moral confusion. The result is that the spec-
> tator is not cleansed, but involved in the impuri-
> ties he is witnessing, and the moral intention is
> perverted into its opposite.(2)

Indeed, this corruption where cleansing is promised is precisely what concerns me in the poems of Adrienne Rich, Sharon Olds, and Jorie Graham. Their work, more and less artful depending on the occasion, is of the nature of such visionary pornography as in these lines:

> All the
> statistics, the century's
> burned and gang-raped
> turning, lifting, a blade catching the
> late
> light

> redeeming it, and us needing its
> wrongest beauty. . . .(3)

It is clear that such amassments of "the century's" victims are journalistic, despite the ornamental verbiage, and that the motive is a kind of civic prurience. But how to speak to the committed enthusiasts of such work? How to persuade of the wrongness of "wrongest" and of the flaccidity of "and us needing" and of the sentimentality that discovers the beautiful in the grotesque? Surely we are worlds distant from an art of which one might say that it finds the words for any situation.

I answered the letters as best I could,(4) but the feeling grew of talking to deaf ears. The problem was perhaps not one that could be resolved in a single exchange. Indeed, I began to realize that the problem was one of the gap between the typical contemporary poet's aspirations, and her intellectual and technical—especially narrative—means. I also began to believe that the solution would have to do with a new and fruitful approach to the writer's apprentice years.

Perhaps I am simplifying. For the problem is not that the contemporary poet's aspirations are excellent and the means wanting, but that the means are wanting to favor both execution and conception: Writers also need to discover in their apprenticeship some center of gravity for the taking-on of aspirations. Conceiving the mission of the poem and of poetry requires as deep a knowledge of technique and of human nature as does composing this hypothetically serious and innovative poem in response to such intentions.

Much of the poetry composed today is not merely stereotypic with regard to its style but clichéd with regard to its imaginative premise; and the clichés of feeling promote the stereotyping of the forms. This weakening codependency of clichéd feeling with, on, and against stiff execution in an empty idiom illustrates a principle the art critic Edgar Wind first articulated with respect to the mechanical reproduction of paintings in art catalogues, and the chemical cleaning of paintings to achieve what is thought by restorers to be the works' original vividness of hue. Because, says Wind, our eyes have been "sharpened to those aspects of painting and sculpture that are brought out effectively by a camera," we therefore tend to take more satisfaction in the primitive look of a painting when its colors have been "fixed" by the limitations of the photographic medium than we taken in the layered subtlety of the originals:

> Since the mechanics of stripping down a painting reverses the sequence in which it was built up, it is almost inevitable that processed pictures acquire a surface that looks machine-made, resembling the hard luminous gloss of mechanical reproductions, with brute colors in glaring juxtaposition. The satisfaction aroused by paintings reduced to that state may probably be ascribed to the fact that vision has increasingly been trained by derivative prints, which tend to over-define an image in one direction by fixing it to a mechanical scale.
> —Edgar Wind, *Art and Anarchy*, 68–69

What Wind describes with respect to the deterioration of the vision necessary to appreciate delicacy of color in painting could also be said of the deterioration both of the language and of the concepts necessary to appreciate the subtlety in feeling, idea, and analogy, and in the tension between the moral and sensuous gratification that enriched the poetry of the Renaissance and the eighteenth century, but which now seem obsolete if not abhorrent in the careers of contemporary poets.

At present, verse in English has, to adapt Edgar Wind's terms, been *overdefined* in the direction of perceptual and sensuous immediacy and uncensored directness, without any gradation in palette or graduation in time of response: Perception is an instantaneous good. One of the mechanisms that fix poetry to the scale of stunned immediacy is the syntax of nominalized verb and verbal adjectives, which announce great movements and perform none. Another of these mechanisms is the pursuit of colloquial presence. A poem proves authentic in proportion as it exhibits the rhetoric of a kind of unself-conscious experiential appetite. Above all the stereotyped poem of the present cultural moment—even the poem that professes to experiment with language and syntax—to the extent that it is based on clichés of feeling, traps its writers in a circle of redundancy. But the lure of the vivid, and even the garish, is strong; cliché is only the more deeply entrenched by the illusion of "sincerity."

Vladimir Nabokov well describes these clichés of feeling (he locates them in the German ego as well as the American); to them he gives the collective name *poshlust* (to suggest the unsavory core of such assumptions as, for example, that the nuclear family is made happy by purchasing goods for one another and that size is directly proportional to value—not to mention the insidious non-commercial clichés that insist on trusting in spontaneous reactions, sharing problems, valuing the attempt more than success, believing that the old regret not being young, that beauty is somehow more correct than ugliness, that appetite is finally natural or healthy, that a certain overstuffed rondure in the female figure is desirable, and so on), and he makes clear that these clichés are the basis of advertising, even for periods before that marketplace term or the practice was widespread.(5) Whereas the true writer, like Nabokov himself, will ever work against the grain of cliché, avoiding the word's denotation, a machine-stamped rigidity of associations, rather adjusting to the shifting light-and-shadow play of experience in time.

What can be called "literal symbols" are always specific before they take on larger and possibly archetypal (that is, extensively metaphorical) significance.(6) To imagine an implement like a knife, for example, one would, like Elizabeth Bishop in her magisterial poem "Crusoe in England," instinctively avoid the implication that knives are sharp, dangerous, and ominous:

> The knife there on the shelf—
> it reeked of meaning like a crucifix.
> It lived. How many years did I
> beg it, implore it, not to break?
> I knew each nick and scratch by heart,
> the bluish blade, the broken tip,
> the lines of wood-grain on the handle . . .
> —*Geography III*, 1976

The focus on the radiantly clear object (like Bishop's focus on the knife in "Crusoe in England") permits the poet to perform the writer's two tasks simultaneously—to describe the world, and to interpret it. And in order to show the general interpretation imbedded in what is literal and specific (including the literal and specific perceptual minutiae of elapsing time), it is necessary for the writer to render clearly what is near at hand. Such clarity of rendering in turn will require a sensibility that is anything but reduced to mere perceptual immediacy.

When one is in the presence of a genuinely "new" poem, one feels that it has achieved its precarious new status by adumbrating, even opening, an entire fresh volume of possible spiritual motions that are, nevertheless, recognizable, even unaccountably familiar (although the true innovation is not just the performance of a nice, familiar choreography). I believe that Eleanor Wilner's new poem "Bat Cave," 100 lines long, collected in *Reversing the Spell*,(7) speaks to the same ability as does Bishop's "Crusoe"—to tread the razor's edge between archetypal manifestation and literal flatness. The immediate objects in the poem are bats hanging in myriads above virtual stalagmites of guano in a cave on the island of Bali near Denpasar. But every time the poet comes close to this or that "phenomenon," perception eloigns itself. Even as Wilner assembles the clues that indicate the ostensible subject of the poem, meaning shifts key, for the walls of the cave, on closer inspection, as they

> slanted up into a dome   5
> were beating like a wild black lung—
> it was plastered and hung with
> the pulsing bodies of bats, the organ
> music of the body's deep
> interior, alive . . .   10

And where an organ plays in a thoracic cave already somehow "sacred," an "altar" is not far to fathom, particularly owing to the rock-hard piles of white excrement, a fine contrast to their origins in that leathery, breathing, quasi-fleshlike muscle of uncanny mammals, the contrast producing a hint of greater echoings to come from this solemn, and filthy, hollow space.

Wilner is, like Bishop's persona, often a "tourist," "superior with fear" (lines 25–26), hovering as it were (she says) on the street side of a bead curtain as it trembles before a shop's suspect, dim

interior (lines 27–30). Thus the voyeuristic impulse is acknowl-
edged—and the craving for mystery and awe of the exotic that
must have brought the tourists there. Accordingly, the traveling
couple "thought of the caves / of Marabar" where Mrs. Moore
encounters the horrible echo of cosmic emptiness in E. M.
Forster's novel *A Passage to India*, and where Adela Quested
believes she was raped (or almost) by the misguiding, floundering
friend-to-the English, Aziz. Interestingly, it is neither of the
women, but the author Forster whom Wilner imagines as wander-
ing the tunnel opened in the colonial soul:

> We thought of the caves   30
> of Marabar, of a man who entered
> and never quite emerged—
> the caves' echoing black
> emptiness a tunnel in the English
> soul, where he is wandering still.   35

Through the resonant and undeniably apt recollection of
another complex work of art, Wilner deepens her poem psycholog-
ically as well as historically. By comparing her own attitude to that
of Forster and his characters, she is enabled to "read" the English
soul—the soul of the well-meaning but protectionist colonizer,
interpreter, civilizer—even as the phenomenon is held in abeyance
(what *was* in the Caves of Marabar? Why/how do these tens of
thousands of bats in their cave haunt and accuse the spectator?).

The multiplex echoings of the Forster novel in Eleanor
Wilner's poem prepare us for a lesson that is, in a thoroughgoing
sense, cultural as well as personal. Before the outing to Marabar,
Forster had remarked of Adela Quested that she could not get
beyond the "echoing walls" of the Indian women's civility (again, a
surface assumed to be resistant and rigid transforms its substance
into resilient, mysterious flesh).(8) Eleanor Wilner has remarked
to me that she attempted to teach *A Passage to India* to Japanese
students during her two-year stint in the 1970s in Japan, and that
these students themselves appeared to her to present an echoing
wall of sweet civility to her Western probing. As in the experience
of teaching in Japan—like the experience, at one remove, of trying
to understand Adela, Fielding, and Forster in their bafflement with

India—so in the poem "Bat Cave" a clear parable of disturbance and of dissonance is in progress; the apparition of the bats in their cave can't entirely be "resolved" by the tourists' eyes—until they step across the cave's threshold (with all the nuances of transgression into an irreversible ban which that entry betokens).

Like new initiates into a frightening cult, the human couple feel "the radiant heat of pumping / veins" (lines 41-42) as they behold "the familiar / faces of this many-headed god, / benevolent" but also appetitive as the bats are released in a dark froth into the "starlit air," wheeling in "wild wide arcs / in search of fruit, the sweet bites / of mosquito" (lines 43–54). Thus far, the entry into the mystery is marked by little more than pleasant apprehension: These are warm-blooded creatures, after all, in many ways featured like us, like us possessed with thirst. Their liberated aerial soarings appeal, just as "sweet bites" and "starlit air" carry forward their practically unconscious commendatory connotations from the work of Keats and Shelley. But now, at the mid-point of the poem, we start to fall into a terrible visionary world—made more horrific by the fact that it is recent and real; I quote from the long penultimate stanza which we begin with the clatter of the bats' bony wings still audible after they start their nightly feeding exodus:

> while the great domes of our   55
> own kind slide open, the eye
> that watches, tracks the skies,
> and the huge doors roll slowly back
> on the hangars, the planes
> push out their noses of steel,   60
> their wings a bright alloy
> of aluminum and death, they roar
> down the runways, tear into
> the night, their heavy bodies fueled
> from sucking at the hidden   65
> veins of earth . . .

Following the emergence of the sleek phallus of fire from line 60, it takes no more than a few lines for the bombs to begin falling on Baghdad, whose children scream to awaken from a nightmare run on command. The poem's third act is what Nemerov calls perfectly dialectical, the metaphysical happiness of true saying shining from the chamber of the broken heart. The pacing of these middle lines, where the bright and heavy planes "push out" of their shadowy hulls, is at once full of lentor and solemnity, and electric with fascinated revulsion as the creatures of death take wing. But what is yet more remarkable to me is that Wilner refuses to let the poem close on her grand accusation.

Movement after movement, Eleanor Wilner's poem resists premature closure and easy moral positions. Just as the achieved and mysterious analogy between creaturely and colonial appetites, which Wilner builds in the first fifty lines of "Bat Cave," is prevented from reflecting (and subsiding) ruefully upon itself as her head looks up from the poem she is writing, so Wilner will not allow herself to relish, with a final stylistic trump, even the harrowing results, in military action, of material and global greed for the oil sucked by the aircraft out of the mother's veins (the earth). She returns to the bat cave. She vectors in upon the homing bats, attuned as all physics is to the shifting planets, but blind as all beings are to their own causative role in making things happen:

> the bats
> circle, the clouds wheel,
> the earth turns   85
> pulling the dome of stars
> among the spinning trees, blurring
> the sweet globes of fruit, shaped
> exactly to desire—dizzy, we swing
> back to the cave on our stiff dark   90
>   wings . . .

Thus in line 89, she makes us one with *them*. Rather than political selfloathing as citizens who don't demonstrate hard enough against our vicious militaristic oil-dependent governments, we are instead provoked to question our need to be siblings of appetite, warm in our cave, "the sweet juice of papaya / drying on our jaws" (lines 91–92), pulsing with our fellows under the cave roof where

> we can see what was once our world
> upside down as it is

and wonder whose altars
those are, white,
encrusted with shit.   100

Like the monuments to our aggressions (observatories; battle-
fields), the temple of the body also emits mental monsters from
one end, and from the other, no matter how you turn, shit. The
forthright word may not be the only one that would do, but it is the
one the poem throughout has striven to find a way to use. One
feels a turn of the screw as the word falls at line 100, neat, instant-
ly hard, symmetrical, impossible to ignore.

In my estimation, Eleanor Wilner's is a superior poem of
protest against all forms of (even perceptual) passivity. While lift-
ing blame against those in high places, "Bat Cave" also implicates
its speaker as a voyeur of the foreign and as a dilettante of exotic
pain, and by this mechanism of complicity with a fiction of her
own benightedness, the poet locates in her own habits of projec-
tion the very flaw that sentimentally sees any outpouring of the
local body as holy: Indeed, whose altars *are* these, encrusted with
dung? (None but ours.) She asks the question implicitly of the lit-
erary tradition as well. Who do we think we are, making and
bequeathing legacies? Poetry (when it becomes too encrusted with
its own wisdom—which is to say, its own ignorance) is like the
men's club of commerce. And the currency of commerce, as Freud
all too relentlessly reminds us, is excrement.

When I argue against prose in "The Rhapsodic Fallacy" I argue the
need for the poem like Eleanor Wilner's in which we see a new
variety of response and subtlety of layering in the making of poet-
ic works: The world grows more complex and solid, too—less a
mere occasion for cleverness. It turns out that such an argument
is necessarily a call for greater aesthetic honesty—a greater loyalty
to the love of beauty as truth (and truth-telling)—than the stereo-
typic poem of almost any age evinces. More variety and truth-to-
fact means greater inherent order in the writing of poetry and in
conceiving the goals and ends of poems. Paradoxically, greater
poetic unity demands greater complexity and openness of articula-
tion, not stiffer univocality. The essay expresses in part a hope for
a new prosodic and cognitive receptiveness to discourse in poetry

so that forms other than lyric can again be pursued. It is a common call. Marjorie Perloff makes it in an essay on the avant-garde in *Formations* (Fall 1984):

> Postmodernism in poetry, I would argue, begins in the urge to return the material so rigidly excluded—political, ethical, historical, philosophical—to the domain of poetry, which is to say that the Romantic lyric [can be made to give way] to a poetry that can, once again, accommodate narrative and didacticism, the serious and the comic, verse and prose.

Now, Perloff is hardly suggesting that we should attempt a return to the eighteenth century when satire flourished alongside comic and didactic impulses; neither am I suggesting such a return. Rather, I assume as basic the need to rediscover and reinculcate the enormous musical varieties of verse (which Perloff does not emphasize), along with the many rhetorical conventions that might be combined with those musics (which she does). For even the unprepossessing conversational voice requires conventions to render its middle ranges broad and interesting. And if formal conventions bear up the meaning, conditioning and enabling it, there is nothing the least mechanical about those forms. By the same token, even explosive, impromptu free-verse conventions are mere creaking machinery in the absence of a controlling imagination.

Using terms and categories much like Perloff's toward a different end, A. D. Hope has described the middle form of verse (in which the uses of poetry mesh so provocatively with those of prose) as a form that serves

> without pretension the purposes of narration, the essay, the letter, conversation, meditation, argument, exposition, description, satire or cheerful fun. It was in this middle field that *the poets learned the exercise and management of their craft*, the maintenance and modulation of tone.
> —"The Discursive Mode," 1965; my emphasis

The middle form is the area in which Hope's novice can experiment with his craft; it becomes the ground from which he can move higher if need be. Thus it differs from much of the poetry of the mid-1960s, based in what Hope calls a "profusion of startling images" (hence a poetry that obsessively soared to inflated heights); the middle mode is grounded in the same resources poetry shares with ordinary English prose "when used with inimitable aptness and animated by metre and rhyme." As Hope observes, some command of the discursive, middle style is essential for the art of modulation in any kind of poem: "On this depend proportion, harmony, connection, surprise, and the power to return without lapsing into dullness." No long poem can exist without recourse to these skills of variety and recombination.

Despite the two-and-a-half decades that have elapsed since Hope's essay, the lyric-imagistic profusions of poets writing in English have chugged along in much the same way, although a reduction and hardening have accompanied the profusion, making the convention of sensitive free verse more dingy and inelastic than before, at once touting and masking the rhapsodic elements. As a result the middle style Hope describes, with its animation by music and invigoration by discourse, will be more appealing than ever before if, despite its conformation to and echoing of prose, it can produce poetry (even poetry like Hope's own) far more vivid and responsive to nuance and idea than the poetry that I consider in my essay "The Rhapsodic Fallacy." Such is the case with Wilner's "Bat Cave," which achieves its harmony and surprise by the successive adoption of the arguments (some defensive) hinging on clearly defined point of view. So, too, Robert Pinsky's "At Pleasure Bay" moves beyond the mere surface of sadness by investing the lyric with historical as well as sacramental design. John Ashbery's "Fragment" takes on the appalling vantage of a figure who rejects the autonomic perceptions much the same way an insomniac resists sleep.

There is a long poem published by John Koethe in the *Gettysburg Review* (Winter 1989) that emerges from a clear background of literary indebtedness to Ashbery and to Wallace Stevens while embodying the virtues of rigorous independence. While "The Constructor" is evidently a poem about the toils of poetic inheritance, it also explores the charms that release the poet from any inherited way of thinking. In so doing, of course, it also recapitulates the revolutionary renunciations that are solidly in the romantic tradition—although Koethe's particular renunciations are tentative and exploratory. Aloofness in this poem has a curiously affectionate tinge or, rather, takes a curiously determined route through a series of self-examinations about the meaning of living in the present in which the ideas of love and responsible belonging are always prominent, even as the awareness of sentimental temptation is unremitting. In "The Constructor's" 209 lines of suspended animation before the mystery of objectless recollection, the possibility of reduction to the banal and in

complete comes to resemble that of rescue from these conditions:

> Mustn't there be something to
> This tenderness I feel encroaching on my mind,
>   these
> Quiet intimations of a generous, calm hour
>   insensibly
> Approaching day by day through outwardly
>   constricted
> Passages confused by light and air?   190

Writing of this high order has, in some ways, already resolved the romantic dilemma at the level of both feeling and word. Depth of self-knowledge brings transcendence within reach—if not for appropriation, at least for the purpose of scrutiny. Just as there is no irritable reaching after large phrases, so there is, for all the pathos of the longing, no fundamental dissatisfaction with feeling. Emotions are not disappointing. The poet here only experiences increasingly elementary waves of doubt—expressed, indeed, in wavelike language and long, efflorescing syntax—about the action of time upon his perception of the future. And even here, it is not some absolute operation he finds himself desiring through his "long, erotic sentences," but the return of the illusion of an open horizon of years:

> I thought I felt a moment opening like an
> unseen flower   125
> Only to close again, as though something

had called it,
Or as though, beneath the disaffected surface, something
Limpid and benevolent were moving at a level of
    awareness
I could not yet find; and so I let the moment slide
    away.

Koethe's most credible and moving achievements as a poet are those moments when he steps over the edge of the known into what he cannot entirely imagine—and "a different way of seeing" seems to shape itself. Intuiting an area or space in which his experience, by analogy, might be unfolding, he rope-dances over a precipice of uncertainty as to what exists behind the personality: "a part that all along had / Been too close to feel begins to breathe as it becomes / Increasingly transparent." When he reads literary works, he wonders why, the closer he comes, the blander and less permeable art's surfaces become. He tries to fasten on the image of a person, prepared even to accept that persistent ghost of the self as the sort of ordinary individual who once had hope of some higher endeavor, but then, when he readdresses the inchoate, blent, hovering disappearance of mind in body, that personal image full of "numinous desires" refuses to politely disappear:

There was this chorus of strange vapors, with a name
Something like mine, and someone trying to get free.
You start to see things almost mythically, in tropes   170
And figurations taken from the languages of art—to
See your soul as sliding out of chaos, changeable,
Twice blessed with vagueness and a heart, the feelings
Cumbersome and unrefined, the mood a truly human one
Of absolute bewilderment; and floating up from that 175
To an inanimate sublime, as though some angel said
Come with me, and you woke into a featureless and
Foolish paradise your life had gradually become; or
From a dense, discordant memory into a perfect world
As empty as an afterthought, and level as a line.   180

One model for the unfettered elevation of viewpoint in "The Constructor" is probably the montage—or rather, double exposure—method of the Russian modernist El Lissitzky, whose most frequently reproduced work, a self-portrait from 1924, bears this title. For this artist, unlike many of his avant-garde peers, preferred to "see through" the same photographic plate rather than to cut-and-paste images of different media. The images are soulful and haunting in a way that seems dependent on the successive intrusions of light through the prior, or continuous, surface: As metaphor and method for consciousness, luminous face and glinting cityscape come to the same upper plane almost simultaneously. Eye and avenue, post and figure, wet cobble and a steady moisture like tears settle out to the same depth, converging and confirming one another in a vision whose content is an ineffably poignant emptiness. Like the luminescent throngs of presences in El Lissitzky, the "sweet, hypnotic motions of a life" of connectedness with others of which John Koethe writes, with their "merely illusory" sense of weight and "consequence," sometimes inadvertently survive the knowledge that there is no comprehensible way for them to coexist with his awareness. Yet "[t]hey calm the days / With undirected passion," he writes at the poem's very close,

> and the nights with music,
> Hiding them at first, then gradually revealing them
> So differently—these things I thought I'd never   205
> Have—simply by vanishing together one by one, like
> Breaths, like intermittent glimpses of some incomplete,
> Imperfect gratitude. How could this quiet feeling
> Actually exist? Why do I feel so happy?

Once the personal god of overarching meanings, personal election, and stark romantic "recklessness" has departed, there remains the necessary angel of an ineradicable sense of blessedness, caught on the wing, unreasonable, unprovable, unarguable, and summoned in verse as rhetorically subtle, transparently honest, and melodious as there is to be found in any young poet now writing.

Still, of the poetry of the past three decades that attempts to reintegrate some of the virtues of prose with those of verse, for example

223

the work of the Wintersian school and of poets in middle age like C. K. Williams, Anne Winters, and Frank Bidart, I would be tempted to entertain Bonnie Costello's telling maxim: "Prosaism haunts poetry at *all* its entrances."(9) Although these are all poets I admire very much, I may still regret in their work the want of the enormous *range* of energies, where style is concerned, of such paragons of rhetorical poise and visionary sophistication as Eliot, Ovid, Kafka, and Dante. Indeed, it would appear that even in much fervent and accomplished descriptive, meditative, and conversational verse today, mental and imaginative constructs are hobbled by a limited knowledge of and attention to discursive and rhetorical devices (figures of speech) and tropes (figures of thought), not to mention a flattened prosody. This latter limitation is compounded by the fact that the lineation, typography, and use of white space to control rhythm and attention too often come down, at best, to a mildly appealing visual and cognitive pattern or, at worst, to a secret (*not shared*) compositional aid.

Actually, I can think of no poet today, with the possible exception of Charles O. Hartman, who comes remotely close to the blistering mastery of syntax, rhetoric, and diction characteristic of the pyrotechnical side of John Ashbery. Ashbery is a true and dedicated genius, an inheritor of the great symbolist experiment who dazzles the senses as well as the attentive mind. He has admirably extended what poetry is capable of saying. But his ironies, apt though they may be for the times, force him into endless closed circuits and lonely sunken labyrinths, like the minotaur's. In some respects, as I have hinted in an earlier essay on Ashbery, he is like the brilliant and idiosyncratic Marianne Moore, but more elusive and transparent; he is more a force unto himself. Imitating him gets many an imitator washed up, even if one or another of his stylistic tricks is accurately parodied. In this regard, I think John Koethe and Douglas Crase form a serious and innovative responsorial Ashbery school, but one that stresses the elegiac element in Ashbery's cognitive orchestration. Nevertheless, these adept and often poignant younger meditative writers show that, if imitation has any significance with regard to Ashbery, it means that his art can be imitated only from within, by following his ambiguities as well as his learning, reading voluminously and eclectically as he has read, hearkening to his mentors, looking at painting, thinking in French, brooding over the rhythms of the imagination and the drain of daily time, and taking it all so lightly there is never any hint of ponderosity.

But so one behaves with any model: One tries to reexperience the writer's sensibility, to think as and why he or she thinks. What I believe needs refreshment is the idea of such an apprenticeship. As part of a young poet's training, I would first of all encourage the apprentice to learn to discuss, which means practice in the skills that attach to the discursive mode as Hope delineates them so that a base can be learned from which to rise and range. To this end, I would also urge the study of logic, ethics, rhetoric, and metaphysics, and would highly recommend a good knowledge of European art and languages, not to mention extended periods of complete silence.

Whether or not conditions are now propitious for the recovery of such discipline as has clearly nourished the brilliant ruminations of a poet such as Koethe, surely the upholding of value in this way is preferable to the more or less explicit historical determinism of several of the respondents, a determinism most baldly stated by Charles Molesworth:

> Arguments like Kinzie's, with their . . . call for discursive poetry, the values of clear thought, and the responsibilities of a public rhetoric, are just whistlings in the dark. We get the sort of poems we deserve, and if what we all too often get is an exacerbated individual ego mired in alienation then it's because that's what history and society offer us at this juncture.

I myself am mistrustful of pieties about the social and historical conditions that legitimize the status quo. The positions taken by the extreme literary sociologists (whether the Marxist who looks back or the disciple-of-the-new who looks forward) are suspect to the extent that they posit "forces" and "waves" that bond styles to groups and periods rather than making any direct critical estimation of poetic content, its virtue or its truth. The reason "history and society offer us" the working of the ego and the tiny fireworks of perceptual romanticism instead of literature that engages on all levels is in part owing to the inertia of the institutionalized writer—what Molesworth earlier in his reply calls the "compromised professionalism" of writers' workshops (I think Bonnie Costello and Paul Breslin would both agree). The workshop syndrome—the kind of indulgent and ahistorical poetry produced by the various schools, as well as the debasement of critical discourse that comes from the system of what might be called protective reviewing of friend by friend—can with effort be corrected. For if the workshop is part of history, so are its critics. Speaking up may change the "sort of poems we deserve," so that, at last, we may deserve better. If work is done to improve not only the discernment with which poetry is read but also the subtlety and sophistication with which poets speak, we may see not just a smarter and finer generation of poets but even a more brilliant generation of readers to appreciate and cause them.

Several respondents suggest that one should not be harsh on mediocre writers. Stephen Yenser cautions against criticizing work to which one has not surrendered oneself, to which I can only reply that it is both dangerous and fruitless to surrender oneself to sentimentality and kitsch—while, at the same time, it is important to give reasons for calling kitsch kitsch. To critics who assert that it is indelicate and wrongheaded to censure, I would again suggest that what I censure is lack of discipline and not mature aesthetic choice. Naturally, one always takes a risk in making such an estimation; one critic's censure is another's celebration. But readers can learn to estimate critics, too, and to judge their arguments by the rules of evidence, as well as by the "rules" of empathy alongside rigor. Moreover, Auden's proscription against dwelling on overboiled cabbage to the exclusion of decent cuisine is only partially relevant to contemporary letters, inasmuch as there is such a widespread belief that overboiled cabbage is delectable. The education of the palate to better and more nourishing food inevitably involves the weaning of the human subject from the food that is so familiar, so unchallenging, and so addictive. There comes a time to take the dish away and, as Melville wrote of Jonah, to appall rather than please, to court dishonor, to preach the truth to the face of falsehood.

Marjorie Perloff has a similar argument: Art is always ninety percent watery roughage; why waste one's time chewing it over? Why not, instead, offer as corrective a variety of poetry at a still further remove from the tastes that have been so clearly weakened by current practices?—which for Perloff means dismissing lyric, along with rhyme and meter, and the notion of genre, and championing the work of experimental writers who have hitherto hunted in the twilight between poetry and theory. Although she is willing to estimate and dismiss the outmoded conventions of romanticism and modernism (symbolism and pure poetry—*not* the products of Williams, Pound, or Zukofsky), her favored "language poets" are not evaluatively discriminated from each other.

Now Harold Rosenberg also thought description and clear presentation were the primary task of the critic of the new, but he suggested that one must answer the question "'What is it?'—the question of identity . . . in such a way as to distinguish between a real novelty and a fake one," and that such an answer to the question of identity "*is itself an evaluation.*"(10) This a distinction that cannot be maintained, however when the *kind* of experiment is a recoil from standards, valued for itself, while the individual literary production is merely a helpful illustration of the preapproved class. And difference between a real and a fake novelty thus disappears. So I would argue also with Bonnie Costello's defense of "process" and freely emerging forms: In order to decide that something is good, to establish a standard (even a standard vis-à-vis process), one has to be prepared to identify what is less good, to rank, to place within a hierarchy. Otherwise the real novelty will have no force.

Paul Breslin's insightful defense of "My Weariness of Epic Proportions"(11) as a "mutant pastoral" brings up a related issue having to do with the way time transforms genres like an inexorable glacier. It is Breslin's claim that, although the Simic poem is nothing more than a minor *jeu*, it can nevertheless stand in the shadow of the great debate over "poetic kinds" precisely by mimicking the turn from epic and state attitudes to pastoral and personal ones. The point is well taken. The difficulty is that one cannot study Charles Simic to learn anything one does not already know—about the possibilities in pastoral, for example. One can only study genuine attempts to reincorporate pastoral elements and attitudes into new forms of composition (Auden and Ashbery abound in examples) to get a sense of what pastoral is and has been. Then, perhaps, with this knowledge in mind, one might return to the little Simic poem and diagnose its wan demeanor.

Simic and the other poets quoted in these exchanges have recoiled from established forms to such a degree that they have very little left in the way of reliable conventions to perceive the world *through*. Or, as Theodore Roethke wrote to Léonie Adams at Bennington (enclosing a syllabus for a course in which he would spend two weeks on the tetrameter couplet alone): " 'Form' is regarded not as a neat mould to be filled, but rather as a sieve to catch certain kinds of material."(12) The packinghouse poem (quoted by Charles Molesworth), although forcefully defended by Stephen Yenser, has no sieve to catch much meaning in, only a funnel that directs the flow the same way at the same rate all the time—a funnel of social consciousness and pity that may at best, for the careful observer like Yenser, be seen to yield a little rust when the water is acidic.

Whether fumbling toward the first recognitions of the tribe or exploring the derivative labyrinths of temporal dilation and sequence, too much of the energy in contemporary poetry (whether canonical or extramural) has been spent addressing language as something alien and inscrutable—like something unearthed from a tomb whose purpose the writer no longer recognizes. Thus a compass might be tried on a loaf of bread, while an ornamental comb might be taken for some kind of calendar.

There are not only better ways to cut bread and tell time: There are better uses for these rediscovered objects that, by placing them back in a continuous perspective with the past, would irradiate their true designs as well as helping distinguish ornamental flourishes from scientific, sacramental, and even aesthetic purposes. By the same token, there are better uses for language than the enforced naïveté or blind self-referential play. To assume that language is the only telling index of its own use is at once to sanctify its abstract qualities (syntax in germ but not in use) and to posit some stereotypical "normal user" whose little impulses are dwarfed by the immensity of the expressive medium, as if language ran on automatic pilot, sweeping its user away. Furthermore, as Santayana says, "the normal, too, is pathological when it is not referred to the ideal."

Although it may be tonic for us to recall Foucault's strictures against an overfondness for the author's personality, it is neither helpful nor true to assume that the author's personality, intentions, power, and will are fictions that are inert in governing the writing of texts. I think most artists would strenuously object to Foucault's claim that " 'profundity' or 'creative' power, [the author's] intentions or the original inspiration manifested in writing" are little more than "projections . . . of our ways of handling texts."(13) However different the religious beliefs and social ease and individual forwardness of artists in time, only one kind of individual—someone intimately possessed of personality, if not with the egoism that often comes with it—ever composes poems worth saving and rereading. I have in mind the way one instinctively averts the mind from such arguments about "handling texts" in reading over again lines like these:

> This ae nighte, this ae nighte,
>> Everie nighte and alle,
> Fire and sleete and candle lighte,
>> And Christe receive thy saule.

Or these:

> O lang, lang may the ladies stand
>> Wi' their gold kems in their hair,
> Waiting for their ain dear lords,
>> For they'll see them na mair.

Or these:

> Barely a twelvemonth after
> The seven days war that put the world to sleep,
> Late in the evening the strange horses came.(14)

Denis Dutton, editor of the journal *Philosophy and Literature*, believes that questions about intention will persist in importance. We must, he says, acknowledge the value of the works to the makers of the works: To do so is not to refuse to see "the extent to which traditions, and indeed language itself, help to 'make' texts," but it might, "contra Beardsley, find a legitimate place for authorial intention in criticism, and it might, contra Barthes, set some limits on what we find worthwhile to talk about in criticism."(15)

The novelist and philosopher Iris Murdoch, writing three

decades ago, put the situation in terms more dire. Inasmuch as the problem is one of a limited idea of personality, so its solution has to be more internally motivated than the adoption of new skills. She suggests that the idea of sensuous immediacy is (more than simply a trend in vitiated prose or verse) a phenomenon of the social and ethical realm. Immediacy, isolation, and sincerity alike have been dictated to the modern writer by the eighteenth-century philosophical heritage that puts a "lonely self-contained individual" at the moral and cognitive center of the universe. In place of flexible concepts, we the inheritors are given implacable images, such as that of "a brave naked will surrounded by an easily comprehended empirical world."(16) To counteract this reduction, rigidification, and flattening, Murdoch recommends that we allow the incomplete: "it is through an enriching and deepening of concepts that moral progress [and imaginative vision] take[] place"; rather than a fixed shape, our sense of reality must shift about, becoming a "rich receding background" for thought and attention (20). Neither aesthetic crystal nor vapid journalism, the work of the imaginative is contingent, unpredictable, expressive; it refuses the *mere* consolations of form, while recognizing that no art can shape itself without an armature of idea.

It is something like this expressive ideal to which Julia Randall's response reflexively turns. There is no doubt that Randall speaks for many great poets when she regrets the failure of subjective vision in the nineteenth century, just as she speaks with the generations of poets in mind when, with the long, comfortable perspective of someone at home in the tradition, she admonishes: "Without music poetry resigns all claim to give that pleasure which initially draws us into the magic circle of symbolic form." Julia Randall is correct: The aim is song. Contrary to Terence Diggory's careful and sympathetic response, I do not consider the mimetic attitude(17) the primordial or preoccupying one for us now, although its lessons should be learned *first* by the poets to come. In the same way, I think the pragmatic theorists' focus on the poem as something contrived with skill can guide the apprentice writer by forcing consideration of the local working, as well as the logical implication, of exempla, trope, and ornamentation. The objective theories of art as an antiscientific heterocosm or second nature that has its own weather and its own laws can serve to reflect how every poet in every poem acts "autotelically," changing the contours of language and of thought by compulsions intrinsic to the work, and hence giving knowledge of objective theory a pleasantly recollective function.

But at the deepest level, I am with Randall an upholder of the expressive theory of art. The program I have sketched with the help of A. D. Hope and others is designed to make poetry of the highest and most heart-piercing kind possible again, for one must learn to speak well and leisurely again before learning what kind of song there is to sing. As the true end and glory of art, I believe in the bias that animates the work of Spenser, Wordsworth, Yeats, Rilke, Stevens, Bogan, and Walcott, and of lesser-known contemporaries like William Hunt, John Koethe, and Julia Randall herself, that all poetry originates in beauty, music, and longing, and in something almost not namable by the waking intelligence:

The Last Hour

Joy of the one who turned back,
who will do all for the beloved,
in this plateau of intoxication and pain.
Envision only the moment of turning—
will the loved one gaze back at us,
eyes lift upward and welcome us,
even our soiled hands? Blood
filling our thoughts, clouding our minds?
Will that joy be welcomed in the last hour?

In this section from the poem still in manuscript by Chicago poet William Hunt, *One Hundred and Eleven Leaves*, which comes closer than that of any American poet to the uncompromising interiority of Paul Célan, the image of Orpheus and Eurydice is rewoven with the death that fills and clouds the forward-looking consciousness. It is a reimagining as hopeless and without redemption as anything by the name of joy can be. And yet the saying, the singing, is carried forth on lines of great purity. Hunt is suspended between a moment of genuine rhapsody from which song flows, and a moment of inconsequence, hiatus, bafflement, in which all a poet is authentically capable of telling belongs to the movements of brooding or quiet conversation in the shadow of a coming ordeal.

By such a fierce measure as that for the true rhapsode, which permits only a handful of poets to speak with absolute gravity and transparency of the business of the soul—by such a gauge many poets are excluded: In this light, W. H. Auden and the frequently touching Howard Nemerov become figures of sharp-edged dissenting demonic clarity rather to one side of the main procession of stricken souls like Paul Célan, Thomas Hardy, and Emily Dickinson, the holy cripples on the pilgrimage, and Edwin Muir, their luminous guardian with his uncanny angelic wholeness. All good lyric poets are at least slightly distorted by the task: One learns to take their queerness with their ravishing grace. What is more important is that the eloquence of the good lyric poet is to be judged only by and against the truth, in which judgment we recognize the highest function of mimesis.

I support the appeal of Murdoch to the young writers coming along, echoing the call with which Hope, Perloff, and others address the times:

> Literature can arm us against consolation and fantasy and can help us to recover from the ailments of Romanticism. If it can be said to have a task, now, that surely is its task. But if it is to perform it, prose must recover its former glory, eloquence and discourse must return. I would connect eloquence with the attempt to speak the truth.(18)

If for "prose" we could read "poetry"—after all the greater and more embracing art—Iris Murdoch's formulation of the task facing the writer is the most accurate and fiendishly demanding of them all. For this is the call for a recuperation of stamina, variety, and valor in the work of imagination. It is the poet's calling.

1. This exchange of letters appears in *American Poetry Review* (May/June 1984): 37–38.

2. Muir, *An Autobiography* (London: Hogarth Press, 1954), 221.

3. Jorie Graham, "Updraft," *Erosion*, 62. See also my "Rhapsodic Fallacy," in *The Cure of Poetry in an Age of Prose* (Chicago: University of Chicago Press, 1993), pp. 18–21. Considerations of Adrienne Rich and Sharon Olds appear in my essays, "Weeds in Tar" (*American Poetry Review* [May/June 1985]) and "Idiom and Error" (*American Poetry Review* [July/August 1984]), respectively.

4. *American Poetry Review* (May/June 1984).

5. See Nabokov's study, *Gogol* (New York: New Directions, 1944), pp. 63–74.

6. The phrase "literal symbol" was coined by Christine Brooke-Rose in *A Grammar of Metaphor*. Her examples are from Yeats—tower, stare's nest, ditch—objects that are themselves in a deeply localized way before (but as a precondition for) their emergence as archetypes of thought, transient effort, and the sordidness of human fate. See chaps. 1 and 2 on "Simple Replacement" metaphors, passim, pp. 29–30, 67, and 315–17.

7. Eleanor Wilner, "Bat Cave," in *Reversing the Spell: New and Selected Poems* (Port Townsend: Copper Canyon Press, 1997), pp. 94–97.

8. E. M. Forster, *A Passage to India* (New York: Harcourt, Brace & World, 1952).

9. Bonnie Costello's comment, along with responses by Marjorie Perloff, Julia Randall, Alan Shapiro, Paul Breslin, and Stephen Yenser to "The Rhapsodic Fallacy" as it originally appeared in *Salmagundi* (Fall 1984), appeared in *Salmagundi* (Summer 1985). Responses by Terrence Diggory and Charles Molesworth appeared in the Fall 1984 issue along with the essay.

10. Harold Rosenberg, Preface, *The Tradition of the New* (New York: McGraw-Hill, 1960).

11. By Charles Simic.

12. Ralph J. Mills, Jr., ed. *Selected Letters of Theodore Roethke* (Seattle: University of Washington Press., 1968), p. 104.

13. Michel Foucault, "What Is an Author?" [1969], in *Language, Counter-Memory, Practice: Selected Essays and Interviews*, by Michel Foucault, ed. D. F. Bouchard (Ithaca: Cornell University Press, 1977), p. 127.

14. The first two excerpts are from the anonymous ballads "This ae nighte" and "Sir Patrick Spens," and the third from "The Horses" (1956), by Edwin Muir.

15. Denis Dutton, "Why Intentionalism Won't Go Away," in *Literature and the Question of Philosophy*, ed. Anthony J. Cascardi (Baltimore: Johns Hopkins University Press, 1987), pp. 207–08.

16. Iris Murdoch, "Against Dryness: A Polemical Sketch," *Encounter 16* (1961): 18, 19.

17. See "The Rhapsodic Fallacy," *The Cure of Poetry in an Age of Prose*, p. 4; and the note on M. H. Abrams and the four theories of poetry, p. 67.

18. Murdoch, "Against Dryness," p. 20.

Word by Word, Page by Page

RACHEL HADAS

I

After my mother's death, I was glad to get letters of condolence. From many I learned things I had not known before; in some cases facts about my mother, in others about the writers of the letters. But being pleased to get such letters didn't keep me from being highly critical of what I read. It wasn't the sentiments expressed that I found fault with, generally; rather, the language in which these sentiments were expressed sometimes aroused my ire. I'm thinking of a letter in which the writer referred first to the "surcease" of my mother's pain and then the "amelioration" of our sorrow to which my family would now be able to look forward.

This letter fulfilled what may be a purpose of letters of condolence: It made me miss one of the many qualities in my mother I had taken for granted. So much leaps out at us after the death of a person we thought we knew and appreciated that it's hard to understand what we were doing for all the years they were alive. My mother, a Latin teacher for many years (but then so was the author of this letter), would never have perpetrated such pedantries. "Surcease" at least provided the fun of reminding me of the tongue twister from *Macbeth* ("if th'assassination/ Could trammel up the consequence, and catch/ With his surcease, success"). But "amelioration": Would our grief get better and better?

Fuss, fuss. I'm famous for it in our family. As my mother would have been the first to remind me, the letter was not only highly literate, it was kindly meant. "Don't edit people's letters," said my sister, an editor. I tried with some success to cease (surcease) and desist, to concentrate on people's kindly thoughts and feelings, as if these could be separated from their words.

Still, I felt vindicated when a few months later I came across a passage in *In Memoriam* in which that anatomist of bereavement Tennyson expresses exasperation with at least one of the letters of condolence he has received on the occasion of Arthur Hallam's death. Tennyson's impatience takes the characteristically poetic form of an irritated pouncing on the exact words his luckless correspondent has chosen.

> One writes that "other friends remain,"
>   That "loss is common to the race"—
> And common is the commonplace
>   And vacant chaff well meant for grain.
>
> That loss is common would not make
>   My own less bitter, rather more.
> Too common! Never morning wore
>   To evening, but some heart did break.

My first response to these lines was the relief of recognition. I wasn't alone! Another poet had had the gall to take umbrage at the "vacant chaff" he found in that most impossible of literary forms, the condolence letter.

Another reason I wasn't alone turned out to be that not only had Tennyson anticipated me, I had anticipated myself. A poem I wrote soon after my father's death gets no further than its second line before irritably quoting the advice of a friend not to write about my loss for six weeks—advice that clearly precipitated "Daddy," the poem in question.

> Stay off it for six weeks, one said. No. Only
> pulling at the past can bring me up to what is
> dead.

Even at the age of eighteen, bereaved poets are not good at taking advice.

But to return to *In Memoriam*: As I copied out Tennyson's line, my sense of recognition, of familiarity widened and deepened—not only because I knew just how the author felt but also because I had now detected an echo. Consciously or not, Tennyson, by virtue of taking issue with the word "common," is harking back to Hamlet's tense exchange with his mother.

> QUEEN: Thou know'st 'tis common, all that lives must die, Passing through nature to eternity.
> HAMLET: Ay, Madam, it is common.
> QUEEN: If it be, Why seems it so particular with thee?

Instead of answering this difficult question, Hamlet finds fault with the way his mother has posed it. Again he pounces on her choice of words, contemptuously echoing what she has just said.

> Seems, Madam! Nay, it is: I know not "seems."

In precisely the same way, Tennyson italicizes the "vacant chaff" of his hapless correspondent by putting it in quotation marks, scornfully echoing words that seem to him to show insufficient thought or feeling, that misconstrue his unique and terrible pain. Does this reaction mean that Tennyson would rather not have received this letter of condolence at all? On the contrary, such an omission would probably have irritated him even more. Bereaved poets are impossible people.

II

Perhaps it is because *Hamlet* is such a crucial text on the subject of mortality that these quotes kept popping up. Perhaps, as Philip Roth writes in *Patrimony*, there is something intrinsically limited in the ways we are able to think about and talk to our dead. It both proves Roth's point and confirms the centrality of *Hamlet* that Roth is unable to write about this subject without mentioning the play.

> I find that while visiting a grave one has thoughts that are more or less anybody's thoughts and, leaving aside the matter of eloquence, don't differ much from Hamlet's contemplating the skull of Yorick. There seems

little to be thought or said that isn't a variant of "he hath borne me on his back a thousand times." At a cemetery you are generally reminded of just how narrow and banal your thinking is on this subject.

Of course, leaving aside the matter of eloquence is just what good writers are reluctant to do. Roth's own description of his unplanned visit to his mother's grave, to which the above passage is a kind of aside, is extremely moving. His account of how impossible it is to think of anything fresh to say on such occasions is just right; I immediately recognized the truth of what Roth was saying. In the same way, both Hamlet's quicksilver speculations about Alexander's dust and Horatio's instinct to squelch such inappropriate flights of fancy ("'Twere to consider too curiously, to consider so") are recognizably true.

One would never want to disregard Shakespeare's language. Yet the resonance of that exchange at the graveyard goes far beyond felicities of phrasing or dramatic timing or even characterization. The scene expresses something so basic that once we have read it we can hardly begin to think about certain aspects of death without referring back to it.

Hamlet is, in the term developed from Biblical reading, the *type* of a mourner. When we think typologically, any particular text or character takes on a weather-beaten look, losing its sharpness of specificity but gaining the authority of the generic. I found in my bereavement what Tennyson and Philip Roth, to name only two of countless other bereaved people, had discovered before me. Hamlet is more than a convincing depiction of a person who has lost a loved one. He is a type, probably *the* type in our literature of such a person.

As a general rule in typological reading, the verbal surface or the details of plot are less importance than the essential situation. But *Hamlet* is a special case. It presents us with a crucial figure, in both senses of the word: both character and image of mourning and mortality. But the play also is, or maybe I should say also was, one of the great storehouses in English for verbal echoes and textual references. That these two facts coincide in one play is part of what makes *Hamlet* an astonishing masterpiece, but the coincidence should not make us confuse two very different functions. Verbal echoes are the opposite of typological references; what brings them into being is not the essential figure of the original text but its consummate wording. It's true that the verbal echo (the single word "common") in *In Memoriam* carries with it some of the wit, weight, and darkness of the whole play and not merely the scene between Hamlet and his mother. But many verbal echoes are frankly superficial. If you begin to look for quite frivolous echoes of *Hamlet*, you find them everywhere, though in my limited survey such echoes are most frequent in work written before the First World War.

Thus it's only because I'm a hopelessly old-fashioned writer that two of my poems have titles taken from lines in *Hamlet*—"Pale Cast" and "Less Than Kind." But neither of these poems gains a great deal of significance from the reference; and I think the same could be said of three passages I've happened upon in the last week. The first of these is from E. M. Forster's *Howards End*:

> The letter that she wrote Mrs. Wilcox glowed
> with the native hue of resolution. The pale
> cast of thought was with her a breath rather
> than a tarnish.

Second, Henry James writes in his essay on George Sand:

> In other words, she talks no scandal—a con-
> summation devoutly to be wished.

And finally, among the papers that came to me after my mother's death is a letter from my grandfather, then a graduate student in Germany, to his fiancée:

> How I wish I could take you to walk this
> spring. The spring is the best season here, but
> it is also the time when Halle seems flattest
> stalest and most unprofitable.

None of these references depends at all importantly on the plot of the play, though in the final example I suppose one could push the parallel that the writer of the letter is, as Hamlet once was, a student at a German university. But the point with verbal echoes of his kind is not to pursue such parallels, not to look for more significance than is meant.

The echo stays on the surface. But how did it get there, and what is it doing? Verbal echoes are not intended to show off the writer's knowledge of a text, nor are they meant to furnish irrelevant flourishes and squiggles of ornament. Echoes are (or again, were) almost automatic, almost a reflex, but no less mysterious for that. The familiar phrases were latent somewhere in Forster's mind, or James's, or Lewis Parke Chamberlayne's, or mine. Somehow they rose to the surface of our lips or the tips of our fingers at the apposite moment.

III

The difference between a beginner's and a more mature writer's use of other people's words is not quantitative. We never outgrow our dependency on what others have written; we're magpies all our lives. If anything, as we read more our appropriations increase in proportion, which may be part of what T. S. Eliot had in mind when he observed that bad poets imitate and good poets steal.

Borrowing persists, but styles change. The story of how one develops as a writer need not be a story of outgrowing one's sources and discarding them, like a rocket casting off its casing as it zooms into orbit. Nor need the process be one of gradual, discreet absorption until all one's sources are transformed into one's own triumphant style. On the contrary, I realize more and more (and write more and more about the realization) how much I still owe to everything I've ever read or been read.

To say one owes a lot to early influences can sometimes sound insincere or sentimental, like a quiz show winner thanking her family, friends, neighbors, classmates, and dog for her success. But the point is not that all the books I've read, like some down-home cheering section, encouraged me to fulfill my potential, to become what I am. They are what I am. If I take my poems apart, if I even examine a few of them closely, those early books are what I find. Eliot in "Tradition and the Individual Talent" has this unbeatable answer to young writers who think they know much more than earlier generations did: "Yes, and they are what we know."

My own poetry has found all sorts of ways to treat its sources. Sometimes I proclaim an important passage by quoting it verbatim; sometimes I disguise it; and sometimes I echo some other writer without realizing that I am echoing anything. As a general rule, the longer I write the more comfortable I seem to feel in presenting the words of what Wallace Stevens calls "a separate author, a different poet" as frankly *other*. A recent poem like "A Copy of *Ariel*" takes a literary source as its primary subject matter. My early poems, on the other hand, while relying at least as much on what I had read at the time, tend to refer to their sources only in very general terms.

"That Time, This Place," a poem I wrote in college, is a good example of a fairly thorough assimilation of its literary roots. The poem mourns my father's recent death through the filter of the Trojan War, which in my treatment has a generalized, typological feel:

> All terribly remembered towers of Troy,
> this too known house cries out for you.
>
> Priam gone the rest of the sons and daughters
> bickering in porticoes reciting
> anecdotes by now catalogues of failed
> glories slaughters or triumphs lost downtown.

The mythology and the characters I refer to don't have a specifically Homeric or Virgilian cast, just a generic plangency. My interest isn't in any particular text, translation, or passage; it's in mood. I use Troy as a scaffolding on which to drape my sadness— as a distancing and aggrandizing mechanism that makes it unnecessary for me to risk speaking in my own person. I wasn't even trying for my own voice. By interposing a layer of references like a pane of glass over the open wound of my father's death, the poem distances, disguises, and softens, while also expressing clearly enough the pain of that wound. What muffles the specific nature of my loss is the generic treatment of the Trojan War. A note of discomfort is certainly present, but I now think it's hard to detect in the poem the specific bewilderment of the adolescent who has suddenly lost a parent.

In "That Time, This Place" I used the Trojan War as a type, for the essential resonance of the reference is the powerful pathos that emanates from even the single word *Troy*. In order to feel this pathos, it isn't necessary to reread the *Iliad* or the *Aeneid*. We needn't even read these poems once; the idea of the Trojan War, the vaguest outline of the tale, is sufficient. In his essay "A Battle-field Playground," my grandfather recalls that a single line of a poem (not Homer) was enough to establish this type for him:

> I cannot remember a time when the [Civil] war was not a familiar thing to me, but I can remember exactly when I first read of the Tale of Troy. It was in Percy's *Reliques*, in the ballad of which I remember only one line, "And corn now grows where Troy town stood." Even then I remember the siege of Troy seemed to me a type of the war, and Hector only an earlier Lee.

Like my grandfather, in "That Time, This Place" I identify my side—specifically, my family—with the Trojans. Instead of Hector's being a prototype of General Lee, Priam is now a prototype of my lost father. But a line like the poem's opening, "Priam gone the rest of the sons and daughters" has a figural rather than a specific force. Priam the dead patriarch is the type of father whose loss has left the survivors adrift. As I've said earlier, a type need coincide only generally with what a particular text presents; and in my poem I wasn't sticking close to any known version of the tale of Troy. In the *Iliad*, Priam of course survives his son Hector. In the *Aeneid*, the death of Priam is one of a string of atrocities that attend the fall of Troy. In neither poem is Priam survived by a houseful of disaffected yet nostalgic grown children.

Thus this poem constructs my own variant on the type, combining for my personal purposes the familiar elements of the kind and wise Priam and of the children of the royal house trapped in the besieged city. If this reading tells more about me than it does about Troy, that too is a familiar characteristic of typology.

Not that I always swathed my personal concerns in classical drapery. An earlier poem, "Afterword," that speaks quite unadornedly, without literary references is, oddly enough, about books. After my father's death, some of his books were sold. As they were taken off the shelves, packed, and removed, I felt as if not only part of a daily scene of my childhood but also part of myself was being dismantled and taken away.

> Landscape across twenty years of suppers,
> mine because mine no longer. Probably
> my first ideas came out of what I saw there
> not looking. Now I look in them to find:
> now they are gone.
>
> Stirred by the cutting out from underneath
> of pieces of my making—call it blood
> that brims this way with rediscovered loss.
>
> I sit back out of sight, see through the window
> the now boxed books being hustled into a truck,
> headed for new careers on Staten Island.
> They lose their family and keep their life
> the way books do.

Had anyone tried to console me for the loss of these time-hallowed books, I would certainly have snapped back at the consoler in a manner that should be familiar by now. Very likely I would have written a poem having for its point d'appui the attempt to console me. Nevertheless, the strongest lines in the poem now seem to me to be those in which I try to console myself:

> They lose their family and keep their life
> the way books do.

"The way books do"—I venture here on a general statement unrelated to my intense and particular self-pity. That books keep their lives was a truer statement than I could have known at nineteen. In fact, losing their family and keeping their life isn't a bad description of the way literary echoes work.

At the time I wrote those lines, I was already the author of a handful of poems that were repositories, reliquaries for the very treasures whose disappearance I was so gloomily lamenting. Did I know subliminally that I would carry some of what was precious in these books with me? Did I know that what I was really mourning was simply change?

The change in the familiar facade of the book-lined dining room at 460 Riverside Drive was undoubtedly painful. But whether I knew it or not, I had already embarked on the laborious process of transferring the contents of those shelves into my head. James Merrill, writing of the posthumous publication of his friend Hans Lodeizen's book of poems, describes the way a writer gradually turns into his or her own books.

> Between these ounces of paper and leather
> and print he had become . . . and the person
> I'd known and loved lay all the difference in
> the world. I glimpsed . . . the degree to which
> I was consenting to the transformation my
> friend had already undergone . . . wouldn't I
> too turn, word by word, page by page, into
> books on a shelf?

It's possible, by the way, that Merrill is here echoing, consciously or otherwise, another passage from Tennyson's masterpiece of mourning, which refers to rereading Hallam's letters: "So word by word, and line by line, / The dead man touched me from the past." The resemblance could also, of course, be a coincidence.

By moving, as soon as I finished college, to a nearly bookless place, I was (consciously? unconsciously?) setting in motion a process opposite to what Merrill is describing. Word by word and page by page, the books on that rifled shelf were being turned into me. Or rather, they had been part of me all along, but now I would have a chance to find this out.

IV

When I lived on a Greek island in the early seventies, there were few people with whom I could speak English, but I read a lot of English poetry, particularly Tennyson and Wordsworth. A poem called "Island Noons," which I wrote near the end of the decade, begins by looking back on that experience.

All day there's nothing to do but sprawl in the sun
reading of fountains, meadows, hills, and groves.
Nothing to do but float in a blue
fluid through which forgotten
words shoot up like bubbles.

And there that day when the great light of heaven
Burned at his lowest in the rolling year,
On the waste sand by the waste sea they closed

my eyes as I lie on the beach
to block the glare. I will a cloud to come.

Almost as soon as it begins, my poem quotes—without quotation
marks—a phrase from near the conclusion of Wordsworth's *Ode:*
Intimations of Immortality:

And 0, ye Fountains, Meadows, Hills, and Groves,
Forbode not any severing of our loves!

"Island Noons" soon becomes more explicit about its sources. I
describe the experience of swimming on my back in the Aegean
and remembering—remembering is not the right term, of having
float or slide into my head a passage from "The Passing of Arthur"
in Tennyson's *Idylls of the King*. If in the last stanza of "The
Creations of Sound" one were to change *floor* to *ocean floor*
Stevens's lines would capture with complete accuracy the experi-
ences I had:

We say ourselves in syllables that rise
From the floor, rising in speech we do not speak.

Perhaps it was the weightlessness of floating myself that was con-
ducive to words floating into my mind. Perhaps it was the empti-
ness of that mind, at least its apparent, foreground emptiness, that
allowed the lines from Tennyson to sound so clearly instead of
being buried under other flotsam and jetsam.

Not that one can ever really call a mind empty. Empty minds
ask to be filled, and they are filled. Stevens's poem "The Well

Dressed Man with a Beard" concludes "It can never be satisfied, the mind, never." In his poem "And *Ut Pictura Poesis* Is Her Name," John Ashbery posits an "almost empty mind" as only one condition of poetic creation. Other conditions include not literary influence, as we might expect, but one's desire to communicate and the desire of others, or of one other, to understand.

> His head
> Locked into mind. We were a seesaw. Something
> Ought to be written about how this affects
> You when you write poetry:
> The extreme austerity of an almost empty mind
> Colliding with the lush Rousseau-like foliage
>   of its desire to communicate
> Something between breaths, if only for the sake
> Of others and their desire to understand you and
>   desert you
> For other centers of communication, so that under
>   standing
> May begin and in so doing be undone.

"Island Noons" could be read as a cry of homesickness, an expression of alienation. It could be condemned as revealing how important dead white male authors were for me, or how snobbishly I shrank from involving myself in the culture of the place where I found myself living. It could be read as an ironic allegory that depicts me striking out into deep water with my head full of English poetry, leaving Greece, youth, femininity, and the present stranded on the beach in the person of a little girl appropriately named Ariadne.

> A shadow on the sand
> makes me lift my head.
> Dizzily I squint
> at Ariadne. Knock-kneed, light behind her,
> shyly she smiles hello, tries on a flipper
> Her eyes are blue. I have no words to give her.
> I put the poet down and plunge away,

> the secret greenwood seared and quenched
> and hissing in salt water.

If I follow the thread of that last idea too far into the labyrinth of symbolism, will I turn out to be Theseus, who deserted Ariadne on an island in the Aegean? Once an exegesis takes on a life of its own, the fact that there really was a beautiful azure-eyed child named Ariadne will be no excuse.

Especially if one is looking back over one's shoulder, there are innumerable ways to read a poem. What chiefly interests me now in "Island Noons" is that it succinctly captures the fact that my homesickness was for language—my own language, which I didn't hear much of, but of which I turned out to have an unsuspected supply. Immersion (to use a suitably watery term) in Greek combined with a paucity of people with whom I could speak English to produce an unexpected result.

In Ashbery's terms, the extreme austerity of my almost empty mind made it easier to be aware of that mind's contents, however meager. In "Island Noons," the phrase from Wordsworth and the lines from Tennyson are speech I did not speak in the sense that they are other people's words, consciously incorporated by me into my own poem. But it can also happen that a writer thinks speech she is speaking (i.e., writing) is her own, only to discover later on that she was echoing someone else. Every poet, every writer will acknowledge the truth of Elizabeth Bowen's observation that "the imagination, which may appear to bear such individual fruit, is rooted in a compost of forgotten books." (This wise sentence, by the way, is quoted near the start of Thomas Mallon's witty, enlightening, and disquieting study of plagiarism, *Stolen Words*, recommended reading for plagiarists and nonplagiarists alike.)

Does the individual fruit of the imagination to which Bowen refers, or for that matter its compost bed, take the form of words or ideas? In Peter Ackroyd's *English Music*, a novel that (to pick Bowen's figure) might be compared to a garden run riot from being over fertilized from a welter of partly forgotten books, a Sherlock Holmes-like figure addresses the youthful hero. One of the many incarnations of literature peopling young Tim's dream visions, this nameless character talks about Locke's ideas on the confusing way language merges with thought.

> The mind, in all its thoughts and reasonings,
> has no other object than its own ideas. And
> yet a little before that he explains that there is
> so close a connection between ideas and
> words that they cannot be untangled.
> Everything is made up of words, therefore.

The tangled relationship between words and ideas becomes even more involved when one text comes into contact with another. The resulting web is often referred to these days as *intertextuality*, though the figure of weaving has almost faded out of the word *text*, leaving it a dead metaphor. It is part of the skill of a writer of Ackroyd's caliber that he restores its etymological force to the word by reminding us that the word *text* (like the word *web*, which I use above) refers to weaving.

> So may we use our books to form a barricade
> against the world, interweaving their words
> with our own to ward off the heat of the day.

In Tim's dream vision of Crusoe's island, to which the above passage alludes, both the barricade and the umbrella seem to be made of books. Books are made of other books. People themselves—bookish people, that is—seem to be made of books. No wonder Wallace Stevens has a poem entitled "Men Made of Words."

Poets like Stevens and Ashbery know that in such confusing territory, metaphor is indispensable. It's also unavoidable; haven't we already encountered, in the course of this quest to understand the workings of the imagination, figures as various as bubbles, web, barricade, dirty silence, and compost? I want to turn back to Elizabeth Bowen's horticultural figure—fruit, roots, compost—in scrutinizing a forgotten source for another poem I wrote a good many years ago.

"Marriage Rhapsody" is easy to date: It was written shortly after George Edwards and I were married, on July 21, 1978. The poem starts by setting the scene, purporting to describe the look of the summer day in Vermont.

> No one could paint how green July is here.
> Lollipops, shamrocks, trading stamps are
> wrong . . .
>
>   The freshly cut
>   grass glistened green as glass

In however trickily alliterative a fashion, wasn't I merely trying to depict the verdant lawn?

Presumably. But about six years later I found myself reading my young son a Golden Book that my mother reminded me had been an early favorite of mine. Sure enough! Looking at Margaret Wise Brown's *Color Kittens* after a gap of thirty years or more, I found I remembered the text and pictures perfectly. I still loved the story of the two kittens who set out to find the color green.

> O wonderful kittens! O Brush! O Hush!

> At last, almost by accident, the kittens
> poured a bucket of blue and a bucket of yel-
> low together, and it came to pass that they
> made a green as green as grass.

"As green as grass," not "as green as glass," Brown had written—I double-checked. Is the echo then merely coincidental? I can't prove it, but I'm almost positive that Brown's forgotten kittens were hiding in my head as soon as I opened the poem with a reference to painting and circled back to that childhood—bright green grass.

In James Merrill's Sandover trilogy, *No Accident* is a leitmotif of the lessons DJ and JM learn from the powers. I am not the first person to point out that the very idea of the Ouija board plays on the notions (the twin notions, Merrill might say) of the death of the author and of ghostwriting. Margaret Wise Brown hedges her bets a bit more when she describes the kittens' crowning achievement of finally coming up with green. Is this feat an artistic creation or does it just happen? "Almost by accident," writes Brown. Or, as Merrill might put it, yes and no.

V

"They lose their family and keep their life/the way books do," I'd written at nineteen, not knowing how much of that life was already in my custody. For poems like "Island Noons" could never have been written if certain texts had not been somehow encapsulated or incorporated in my own body or mind; if I had not unwittingly found in the course of some confused years of traveling my own version of Crusoe's island, where, as Ackroyd puts it, I used my "books to form a barricade against the world, interweaving their words with [my] own to ward off the heat of the day."

I might have been reassured, too, by the paradoxical truth (explored in an essay I was to come across years later) that books can be neither preserved nor destroyed for the reason that they are incorporeal. One of the best ways to preserve a book's contents, then, is through memory:

> The primary fact about the nature of libraries—and the one most often ignored—is that libraries do not house works of literature or other verbal works. Language is intangible; works that use language as their medium are inevitably intangible also; and one cannot preserve something that is intangible in a physical space. All arts in which the products have duration—with dimensions in time rather than in space—employ intangible media; and if works of this kind are to be experienced more than once, the instructions for their reception must be committed to memory or to a tangible surface like paper. Such sets of instructions constitute "texts," but these texts are not the works themselves. . . . But because works of language can be performed within the mind as well as orally and because readers sitting in libraries are actually experiencing such works, many people have been misled into thinking that literature exists between the covers of books.

I wonder whether Thomas Tanselle, the author of this passage, knows he was anticipated in ancient times. Among the forgotten books, in Bowen's phrase, that go to make up the compost for Tanselle's passage I can identify two writers. Not surprisingly, both are Stoics in the sense both of the ancient philosophical school and in the modern sense of their matter-of-fact attitude toward death and change. In *The Consolation of Philosophy*, Boethius gives the figure of Philosophy these comforting words:

> It is not the walls of your library, decked with ivory and glass, that I need, but rather the resting place in your heart, wherein I have not stored books, but I have of old put that which gives value to books, a store of thoughts from books of mine.

And Tacitus ends *Agricola*, his biography of his father-in-law, with a moving eulogy that includes the following sentence:

> Images of men's faces, like the faces themselves, are empty and mortal, but the form of the mind is eternal, and you cannot capture that shape in bronze or marble but only in yourself, by the way you live.

The Boethius passage I discovered for myself. But the Tacitus has been a favorite ever since my mother, in a gesture profoundly characteristic of my family, sent it to me in college not long after my father's death. I kept the quote near my desk and in 1974 used it as the epigraph to my first book of poems, which was entitled, unsurprisingly, *Starting from Troy*.

A third passage that dovetails with Tanselle's argument cannot be among his sources but is worth quoting all the same. The paradox that literature cannot be preserved in physical form shades into a corresponding paradox: It is precisely the passionate lovers of books who come to see that books cannot be lost. Even in losing them, we keep them. The passage is from Ackroyd's *English Music*: Tim is remembering his life as a child in lodgings shared with his father:

All the life he and I shared had been taken
away; it was as if someone had gathered it up,
packed it into a box, sealed it, and then
thrown it into an abyss. But could the atmos-
phere of a life, the meaning of a past, be
removed as easily as the furniture and rugs?
Even then I sensed that this was not so, that
a harder and somehow more impersonal
residue was left behind. The mornings of
study, the evenings by the fire, the conversa-
tions, the silent companionship—all of these
things had gone, but the room itself had been
changed by them forever.

"If works of this kind (that is, works of literature with tempo-
ral rather than spatial dimensions) are to be experienced more than
once," writes Tanselle, "the instructions for their reception must
be committed to memory." And I wrote in "Island Noons,"

No book but what I'd brought or once had read—
like Tennyson—still floating in my head.

But I was indulging in a bit of poetic hyperbole. I did acquire a
few new books in English during the years I was living in Samos.
One of these, ordered from Blackwell's, was a copy of Sylvia Plath's
Ariel.

Thinking back to 1971 or '72, I realize that, aside from a cou-
ple of articles in the Harvard *Advocate* and perhaps Elizabeth
Hardwick's memorable piece (or did I read that later?) in the *New
York Review of Books*, this was my introduction to Plath's work. The
little Faber paperback was a true first edition as Proust would
(rightly) have us understand the term:

[I]f I had been tempted to become a biblio-
phile . . . I should have been one in my own
peculiar fashion. . . . The first edition of a
work would have been more precious in my
eyes than any other, but by this term I should
have understood the edition in which I read it

for the first time. I should seek out original
editions, those, that is to say, in which I once
received an original impression of a book . . .
even though I must make way for the "I" that
I then was if that "I" summons the thing that
it once knew and that the "I" of today does
not know.

My poem about this book, "A Copy of *Ariel*," was written around
1990. Perhaps twenty years had to elapse before I was ready to
"make way for the 'I' that I then was." As Combray emerges intact
from the madeleine and tea, so, I found, the person I was in the early
seventies, and the world in which that person was situated, could
unfold from the pungent pages of a battered little book of poems.
Twenty years later, that book was—is—still in my possession. But
Tanselle, Boethius, and my own experience agree in telling me that
even if my copy of *Ariel* had been lost in its transit through the years,
the book would retain its strength for me all the same.

A Copy of Ariel

Not only is the same bookmark in "Poppies
    in July"
But I can smell the mildew still—a seamold's
Rich and acrid pale-brown sour tang.
Or is it that the book enfolds a world
Bleary but flowering with possibilities?
Each morning I gazed at the milky sea
And it was always morning.

Who is the young woman in this poem, and what is she doing?
She is the same person who might float in the sea and find herself
remembering Tennyson, but other activities have to fill her long days
too. Perhaps six months or more have passed since the symptomatic
day on the beach recorded in "Island Noons." Perhaps it's now
autumn or winter—too cold to swim, at least in the morning. What
to do? Her Greek is getting better and better—at least her spoken
Greek. Here at hand is a book of astonishing poems, one of which
refers to a flower ubiquitous on this island. (Is it spring after all?) So

253

Why not translate "Poppies in July"
Into Greek?

Rereading "A Copy of *Ariel*," I wonder momentarily why the undertaking of translating one of Plath's poems into Greek seemed like an "effort to efface/ The person I had always been." Translating, after all, wasn't an alien notion. A few years before, in college, I had translated some Roman elegies. Translating, unlike most of the other activities I was engaged in at this time, was at least literary.

Significantly, the poems I later wrote about these years say little about my daily doings. They observe the beauty of the place and track some of my feelings. But what about the gardening, cooking, swimming? What about helping with the olive press? The truth is that these strenuous and (at the time) absorbing matters have vanished into brightly colored snapshots of someone else. The villagers knew better than I did where my attention really lay—on the book in my lap. "*Kserei ta grammata*" ("she knows letters"), they'd say. And yet, as I record in the second half of "Island Noons," I

> must have seemed enough a local woman
> after a while for them to ask, "You haven't
> forgotten your first language yet? You will!"

Not as long as I read and wrote in English, I wouldn't. But that may have been precisely why trying to translate a poem *out of* English went against the grain of my inmost self.

Whatever the reason, my translation of "Poppies in July" never got beyond a first draft that has long since disappeared. I do remember that getting across Plath's indescribably menacing tone ("Do you do no harm?") posed an insoluble problem. And as for a poem of my own in Greek that I contemplated writing at the same time, "It never got beyond the first two lines."

"A Copy of *Ariel*" moves from a failed translation to a failed poem of my own. As long as my life and motives were illegible, no wonder I could find nothing to say— couldn't even find the right language in which to say it. I was evidently ready to move beyond the voices of Tennyson or Wordsworth—Plath was a step in that direction. But I could let her into the life I was living only by trying to transform her, taking a single poem, relatively minor though characteristically savage, and trying to squeeze it into a different language, context, tradition. No wonder I couldn't see the enterprise through.

Before I began to be able to write with any authority (the root of this word is "author": exactly so) about the years in Samos, it was necessary to perform the act Proust describes with such precision, even though he apparently referred to reading rather than writing. (But then John Hollander has reminded us that writing is simply a more strenuous form of reading.) The trick, in Proust's words, is to

> make way for the "I" that I then was if that "I"
> summons the thing that it once knew and
> that the "I" of today does not know.

I had to find the words to acknowledge the alarming blankness by which I felt surrounded—the illegibilities, the opacity, the lack of reflection. Remembered lines from Tennyson might pulse through my brain for five seconds, but there were twenty-four hours in the day. Near the end of "Island Noons" I exhort myself to get past the prettiness of the sunny seascape:

> As if to tear a pastel sketch in two,
> pierce it through
> this shine and ruffle of the sun on water,
> and touch the bedrock of ineffable
> truth that is waiting in an ill-lit corner
> or would be if—no, here there is no dimness.

I had to create my own working conditions, my own dimness, my own distancing. I had to undazzle my own eyes, and the process took years.

VI

When I was younger, I snatched poems from experience before it could get away from me, scorning the gingerly counsel to "stay off it for six weeks." Later on, I began to compose poems long after the fact, piecing together fragments of experiences that I had recorded at the time but that were too painful to combine into a single picture until years had passed.

Not only has my way of writing kept changing, but so has my sense of who I'm writing for. Growing older enables you, if it doesn't absolutely force you, to assume the position of someone giving things to others—handing knowledge down, passing it on. Yet through these changes the essential subject matter remained the same. What I was handing on, in my poems about motherhood or teaching, was what I had always carried with me: language, books. I was continuing the process of transforming life, word by word and page by page, into books.

I have written of this process elsewhere; indeed, I wonder whether I have ever written about anything else. Every passing year confirms the truth of Oscar Wilde's statement, the kind of thing that seems deliciously world-weary to a teenager but turns out to be a simple fact: "It is impossible to change one's life; one merely wanders round and round the circle of one's own personality." A few years ago it became clear to me that my youth was in the past; now it sometimes seems that my present is, too.

Any experience can be written about, but surely not all experiences involve reading? Increasingly, for me, they seem to do just that. Nursing my baby, I sang him lullabies or read myself to sleep while he sucked. (My friend Lydia Davis had given me a copy of Basho's "The Royal Road to the North" before Jonathan's birth for this express purpose. She had found it good nursing reading herself.) Visiting my mother in the hospital, I corrected galleys while she dozed, then read the new biography of Stephen Crane, for which I'd been asked to write a blurb. The blurb never appeared, but I had a couple of pleasant conversations about *The Red Badge of Courage* with a friendly man on the hospital sun-porch who, I learned, was a Civil War buff. Visiting Charlie after he had lost his vision, I began, as per our plan, to read him *Emma*.

The way life flattens out into language, the same medium in which it will presently be preserved, is never more striking than when someone we love dies. As if to drive this point home, when my mother and Charlie died, each of them left me a large number of books. Since I didn't have room to keep the majority of these books, I donated many of them to the library of the Newark campus of Rutgers University, where I teach.

I wish this donation showed how far I have advanced from my nineteen-old sadness at seeing the familiar wall of books dismantled. Maybe donating books could even be seen as a reciprocal act; though the shelves weren't the same, I was putting books back.

Alas, not much has really changed; Oscar Wilde's circle is unbroken. For one thing, donating books hasn't exempted me from just as much sadness as I felt at nineteen. For another, even after my father's death more than half my life ago, I had already sensed that books do not die:

> They lose their family and keep their life
> the way books do.

Furthermore, the precept that books can be passed on without their essence being lost is not one that I put into practice out of innate generosity. Death, two deaths, forced my hand.

Nevertheless, it is a relief to find that the precept put into practice does work. My mother and Charlie are no less present to me now that some of what they gave me has passed out of my keeping. How could they be less present? I loved them and they loved me. "You are inside my heart," Charlie wrote to me two years before his death. He is inside mine. My mother is imprinted on me everywhere—my face, my feeling for words right down to my ability to spell, and, increasingly, my temperament, which I used to think was so different from hers.

Twice in these pages I have quoted the words of my mother's father, Lewis Parke Chamberlayne. These are words I have only recently acquired the opportunity to read. On the table beside me as I write are letters, poems, translations, an essay, and a book review by the grandfather I never met. Sadly, he was also the father my mother could not remember; he died suddenly in 1917, before she was three years old. Even had she been able to remember him, she is gone now too. But he has come alive for me since I have been able to read what he wrote. Some of the pages are manuscript, written in a beautiful hand with a pen that sometimes sputtered on pages now yellow and crumbling.

My grandfather was thirty-eight years old when he died. My friend Charlie was just short of thirty-six. A meaningless coincidence or "No Accident"? The resemblance between the two of them is very real to me. Both men died decades before they should have. Both were writers—poets, essayists, critics, correspondents—not only of versatility and charm but of honesty, power, and immense promise. Both were people who unmistakably endeared themselves to those around them. Above all, both had a striking desire to communicate their experiences and memories, their thoughts and feelings. The questions of why they were expressing all this, and to whom, can only be answered in a circular fashion: Both were born writers. Muriel Spark has said "It's possible that an artist is *made* by an absolute personal need to communicate." It's because both these men were writers that death has not been able to take them away from me.

Thinking of the books my mother and Charlie left me, I wrote,

> Two lives I loved are now compressed
> into this whiteness, paper-thin
> but mercifully written on.

But why shouldn't the written-on paper refer to unpublished papers, letters for example, as well as books? If this is the case, then my grandfather makes a third life preserved on paper; shouldn't I have written "three lives I loved," not two? And my father, whose loss shook me so deeply: doesn't he make a fourth?

I can easily rewrite "The Double Legacy," the poem that commemorates my donation of the books. Poems, after all, can sustain endless revision. If, as Tanselle suggests, we think of texts as sets of instructions, they need not be engraved in stone:

> If the marks on paper do not constitute verbal
> works themselves, but only instructions for
> the reconstruction of these works, then they
> must always be open to question, since at any
> point instructions can be erroneous; and
> every element in the presentation of these
> instructions is thus potentially significant as a
> clue for interpreting and evaluating them.

I could revise my poem forever. Any number of beloved dead can be accommodated once we move out of space and into time.

Affection's double legacy
provisionally passed to me;
I pass it on now to this library.

But comforting as it would be to end on this note of passage, the trust is just as double as the legacy. All our careful and endless revisions, expansions, and annotations in the text of experience are counterbalanced by the undeniable tendency of both books and life to be forgotten, denied, effaced. Art Spiegelman, the creator of *Maus*, has said of his father's recollections of the Holocaust what can be said of all human experience:

> Loss is inevitable. What my father articulated is less than what he went through. And . . . what I can understand is less than what he articulated. What I can articulate is less than what I can understand. And what readers understand is less than what I can articulate.

As stoically as Boethius, Spiegelman is telling an opposing truth. We do not always provide resting places in our hearts for what others pass on to us. We do fail to understand; we do forget.

Moreover, the inevitability of loss, and its universality, do not diminish its pain. At this point I hear Tennyson chiming in in agreement:

> That loss is common would not make
> My own less bitter, rather more.

Hamlet too has something to say on the subject. As these meditations end, on the double note of loss and restoration, silence and speech, others pick up the conversation where I leave off.

Talk Show:
The Rise of the Literary Interview

BRUCE BAWER

"Yet from none of these men, in conversation,
did I learn a critical thing."
—Donald Hall, *Remembering Poets*

My first interview took place when I was twenty-four, a graduate teaching assistant in English. I had the most tenuous possible claim to fame: I'd just published a newspaper op-ed piece—a modest forerunner to E. D. Hirsch's *Cultural Literacy*—in which I'd complained about how ignorant my undergraduate composition students were of even the most fundamental facts of history, geography, and the like. Somehow, the news director of the university radio station got wind of this article and decided to interview me on the air. "Controversial topic," he growled at me over the phone. "Hard-hitting." "Should I prepare anything?" I asked, in obsequious grad-student fashion. "Hell, no!" he barked. "Last thing we want is something prepared. Just talk off the cuff." When I showed up for the taping session, his only words of advice were, "Act natural."

Well, I acted natural, and I suppose it went well enough; my interviewer told me afterwards that I had come across as "very relaxed, very natural," and apparently this—along with the fact that my topic had been "controversial" and my approach "hard-hitting"—was all that mattered. Whether I had actually said anything worth listening to seemed to be relatively unimportant. In any event, once it was over, there were two things I knew for certain: first, that so far as I had managed to sound relaxed and natural, I'd been guilty of manufacturing an illusion; and second, that although most of what I'd said during the interview had indeed come off the top of my head, in those moments when I'd spoken to the point most clearly and succinctly there had been no spontaneity on my part whatsoever. On the contrary, I'd been working from a script—reciting from memory, that is, the words of my op-ed piece. This realization made me wonder why on earth radio listeners should be asked (and why, for that matter, they should be willing) to spend half an hour of their lives listening to an extemporaneous conversation on the subject of college students' ignorance—an interview that by the very nature of its form was bound to be characterized by inexact diction and needless repetition, among other infelicities—when they could instead, in the space of two minutes, read my article, in which I'd said everything I had to say on the subject in the best words I could find? In the twenty-eight minutes that the audience saved by reading the essay instead of listening to the interview, they could read half-a-dozen Wallace Stevens poems they'd never had time for, or listen to a recording of the Waldstein Sonata, or study a map of Eurasia or a diagram of the Krebs cycle or, for that matter, make love. Who was I to take up their valuable time with my unpremeditated yammering?

This was, I now realize, a foolish question. For it has become clear to me in the intervening years that, in these peculiar times, unpremeditated yammering—whether it is recorded on audiotape, videotape, or good oldfashioned paper—is one of those things of which we Americans simply cannot get enough. Interviews, in short, are hot. To glance at the television listings is to recognize that it is possible to spend upwards of ten hours a day watching almost nothing else. On a typical weekday in the New York metropolitan area, for instance, you can follow two hours of chatter on "Good Morning America," say, with an hour of "Geraldo" or of something called "The Morning Show," a halfhour of "Best Talk in Town," an hour of "Hour Magazine," an hour with either Phil Donahue or Oprah Winfrey (or both, if you choose to tape one for later viewing), and an hour of "Live at Five." In the evening, there's an endless stream of interview programs to choose from, including "Nightline" and "The Tonight Show"; for late-late television viewers, there are four straight hours of "CBS News Nightwatch"; and on the weekend, there's an endless stream of political interview programs, both national and local, along the lines of "Meet the Press." Although their titles may suggest that they consist principally of news or some sort of entertainment, these shows are mostly composed of interviews, one after another—interviews with TV stars and Vegas headliners, with public officials and opinion makers, with psychiatrists, sociologists, educators, clergymen, "experts" of every kind. And even, here and there, a few interviews with writers.

It doesn't seem much of an exaggeration, indeed, to say that, in America right now, the interview is an even hotter form than the music video. This is no less the case in the pages of the literary magazines than it is on the television screen. Forty years ago, in the heyday of the *Partisan* and *Kenyon* reviews, literary interviews were all but unheard of in the pages of serious journals; then, in 1953, George Plimpton founded the *Paris Review*, and nothing has been quite the same since. The second half of its title notwithstanding, from the very beginning the *Paris Review*'s editors held to a policy of not publishing critical essays or reviews. Instead, they ran literary interviews—a brilliant way to get the names of gigantically famous writers on the cover without having to pay gigantic fees for their work. And famous writers were, as it turned out, more than willing to cooperate. The interviews gave them an opportunity to promote their work, to settle old scores, to get their opinions into print without having to write about them. The interviews let them talk about themselves—and what could appeal more strongly to the average writer's ego? The first issue of the *Paris Review* contained an interview with E.M. Forster; another early number featured the now-famous conversation with Ernest Hemingway. These and other such interviews, published (usually) two to an issue, brought the magazine considerable early recognition at relatively little expense. In fact, they brought it a degree of fame that one cannot imagine it having attained on the basis of the poetry and fiction that have appeared in its pages. Other small-magazine editors took note, and during the sixties and seventies the *Paris Review*'s emphasis on literary interviews rather than critical essays was imitated widely.

Though scores of literary magazines nowadays routinely publish interviews with writers, the *Paris Review*'s contributions continue to be markedly more admirable than most. Part of the reason for this, I think, is that the *Paris Review* does something that might be considered cheating: it treats the interview transcript not as a sacred document to be presented verbatim, but as a piece of copy which, like everything else that goes into the magazine, is open to editing, tightening, revision. In addition to doing their own blue-penciling, moreover, the editors allow the writer being interviewed to make changes. The interview text itself, unlike most published literary magazine interviews, often represents more than one encounter between the parties; in many instances, if an interview is deemed too thin, the interviewer is dispatched a second time, and perhaps even a third, to post further questions.

The *Paris Review*, in other words, does not go in for what a friend of mine refers to as the "interview vérité." That's the sort of interview in which not only the subject's every word is dutifully transcribed, but also his sneezes, coughs, laughs, um's, and ah's are reverently recorded for the enlightenment of future generations. This sort of interview came into vogue in the sixties, thrived in the seventies, and has faded a bit in the eighties and nineties, though ludicrous examples of it may still be found here and there. Take, for example, this excerpt from an interview that the poet Tim Dlugos conducted with the poet Michael Lally for a 1980 issue of a magazine called *Little Caesar*:

> *TD: . . . What's your favorite color?*
> ML: It's um, uh . . . I'm looking for a new one.
> *TD: (Laughs)*
> ML: It's obviously been blue. For a number of years. I remember in the Fifties, it was red and black. Then it was pink and grey. Then it was grey and black, with a little olive drab. Then it became blue, and it's been blue ever since.
> *TD: What's your favorite T.V. show?*
> ML: That's a good question. Old movies. But, obviously, they don't qualify as T.V. shows, let me think a second. (long pause) I don't have a favorite at the moment, except now it's just specials.
> *TD: What's your favorite food?*
> ML: It's always been chicken. That's easy to answer.
> *TD: Okay (laughs)*
> ML: What's my favorite gender? (laughs) What's

my favorite. . . uh. . . . (laughs)

TD: That's a good question. What's your favorite gender? (long pause) Well, which do you like better, going to bed with men or going to bed with women?

ML: (pause) Women . . . (pause) in terms of the whole procedure. (pause) In my fantasies, it's mixed . . . now. Although up until my thirties it was always predominantly, almost exclusively women. I find women easier in some ways to approach and get along with and I find the whole sexual encounter with them more familiar and more acceptable to my style and so on. I have difficulties with that too though, I mean I went to bed with a woman the other night who's about as straight a woman as I've been to bed with in a long time . . . "been to bed with" . . . I hate that expression, but I don't know how else to put it. . . .

Interviews vérités seem more often to involve poets than fiction writers. Wendell Berry, in an astute essay on contemporary poetry for the *Hudson Review*, makes a few observations that, though not explicitly concerned with the interview vérité, nonetheless help explain the popularity of this subgenre among poets and their interviewers. To Berry's mind, the "sudden rise and growth" of the literary interview "suggests, as a sort of implied premise, that poets are of a different kind from other people; hence the interest in what they say as opposed to what they write." Berry speaks of "a class of what might be called poet watchers," whose purpose in watching poets is not to hear what they have to say about poetry but to "examine the poet, to study as unobtrusively as possible whatever privacies may be disclosed by the inadvertencies of conversation." The interview vérité is plainly a symptom of this sort of writer-worship gone berserk; and the writer-worship is in turn symptomatic of that perverse post-Beat Generation mentality that views the poet less as an artist—a human being using his craft, intelligence, and talent to create an ordered, controlled work of art—than as a prophet, a visionary, a seer, whose every act and utterance is taken to be of nearly scriptural significance. It's a mentality that doesn't understand how enormous the difference is between writing and talking—a mentality that doesn't appreciate the thought, the rewriting, the shaping that go into a coherent, unified literary composition.

Some of the best *Paris Review* interviews are so far removed from the verbatim transcripts of the *Little Caesar* type that they might not even be considered "interviews" at all, in the strictest sense. Though, in the most recent edition of *Writers at Work: The Paris Review Interviews*, the majority of conversations are conventional in format—May Sarton, Eugene Ionesco, Elizabeth Hardwick, Arthur Koestler, and William Maxwell were each apparently interviewed in one sitting, and Malcolm Cowley was interviewed twice—there are a number of departures from this standard operating procedure. John Ashbery, for instance, was interviewed once, with "a few additional questions . . . asked and answered" on later occasions and "incorporated into the whole." John Barth was interviewed on television by Plimpton, and the transcript of this exchange, being deemed "a bit short by the usual standards of the magazine," especially given that Barth was such a "master of the prolix"(!), was forwarded to Barth with additional questions to answer (although instead of complying, Barth shortened the text he'd been sent). Milan Kundera met with his interviewer, Christian Salmon, several times; but, as Salmon informs readers in his brief introduction, "instead of a tape recorder, we used a typewriter, scissors, and glue. Gradually, amid discarded scraps of paper and after several revisions, this text emerged." The interview with Raymond Carver was conducted partly by mail, and—most radical of all—the one with Philip Larkin entirely by mail.

What these last few incarnations of the *Paris Review* demonstrate is that a literary interview can come into being in any number of ways, so long as the end result reads like a conversation—preferably a spontaneous, informal conversation—between the author being scrutinized and the interviewer. Whether such a conversation ever took place is immaterial. Though there is something to be said, I suppose, for a strict constructionist's view of this modus operandi—for the argument, in other words, that a literary interview that is not the record of a real, live, face-to-face interview is not a bona fide interview at all—what's interesting to me is that, of all the above-mentioned interviews, the one that I consider by far the best is the one whose subject never even so much as met his interviewer. I refer to the interview with Philip Larkin, which Robert Phillips conducted by mail in 1981-82, and which contains this memorable exchange:

> INTERVIEWER: How did you arrive upon the image of a toad for work or labor?
> LARKIN: Sheer genius.

To say that such-and-such an interview is the best in the book, however, is to be confronted immediately with a not-so-easy question—namely, by what criteria do I deem this interview to be the best? Or, to put it more broadly, what critical standards should be brought to bear upon any literary interview? It's a fair question, for no one seems ever to have answered, in anything even remotely approaching a definitive manner, the intimately related and equally difficult question of just what a literary interview is. Is the literary interview, for example, itself a literary form? Can it be art? (An interesting distinction; in the epigraph to his book *Conversations with Capote*, a compilation of interviews with the late writer-celebrity, Lawrence Grobel asks, "Do you think that remarks can be literature?" Capote responds, "No, but they can be art.") Or is the literary interview at best only an entertaining hodgepodge of personality, public relations, and primary source material? Why do we read such things, anyway? Why *should* we read them—or should we perhaps take a cue from the editors of the very best literary magazines, such as *Poetry* and the *Hudson Review*, and not bother with them in the first place?

All of these complex questions can be summarized in one simple question: how seriously should we take the literary interview? Certainly the participants in many an interview take the form very seriously indeed. Again, this seems to be especially true of poets. Forty years ago, a poet with something to say about a poem, another poet, or poetry in general would write an essay; since the 1960s, however, it has become increasingly common for poets to air their literary opinions and theories not in essays but in interviews. With a few notable exceptions, poets don't *write* anymore. If you find it difficult to believe this, look at some of the books in the University of Michigan's "Poets on Poetry" series, the purpose of which is to present literary criticism by notable American poets. In one volume after another of this series, the interviews outnumber the essays; even extremely distinguished poets who have been publishing poetry for decades—some of whom I, for one, admire enormously—prove on inspection to have produced a shockingly small body of critical prose.

Frequently, in such para-critical (as one might call them) interviews, the questioner is also a poet, no less well known than his subject, and hardly any less talkative; sometimes no distinction at all is made between interviewer and interviewee, and the text is described not as an interview but as a "dialogue." Although these interviews may concern philosophical and aesthetic issues, one cannot get away from the fact that they are interviews, not essays; one is manifestly expected to excuse the repetitions, non sequiturs, logical inconsistencies, lapses in diction, and argumentative weaknesses because this isn't somebody writing but rather a transcript of two people talking.

Yet how profound these interview-happy poets try to sound! It's peculiar that the most brilliant and learned poet-critics of mid-century—people like Randall Jarrell and Delmore Schwartz—wrote essays on poetry that were lucid, engaging, and unpretentious; but many a third-rate poet of the present day seems unable to so much as talk about his art without pouring forth the most astounding banalities, couched in the most breathtakingly pretentious terms. Often the poet's purpose in these interviews seems to be not to convey an opinion or insight but to impress the reader with his vocabulary, learning, and ability to string together grandiose abstractions like beads on a string. Perhaps the most remarkable examples of the form are the ones in which both interviewer and interviewee go the pompous, verbose route. Take, for example, an interview that appeared in the fall 1986 issue of the *Seneca Review*. The interviewer is a poet named David Wojahn; the subject is David St. John, another poet. Let's join them *in medias res*:

> DS: . . . I think every poem has to be alert to history, both the history of literature and the history of the world. Every poem has to be conscious of the culture in which it is framed, though that doesn't mean that every poem need exhibit an

argument about topical matters. It seems to me the most interesting poetry is poetry that investigates the way the human mind performs and responds to history and experience.

DW: One of my reasons for asking that question is a sense I have in your work that artifice is seen as the force that defines our universe, that mitigates our existence, and that prevents our experience from being tragic and overwhelming, and I sometimes feel that that very kind of needful embrace of artifice is what allows you to achieve success with strategies and stylistic techniques that in the work of other poets might seem strained or mannered.

DS: Well, I hope that's true.

This sort of thing is not literary discourse—it's two poets showing off, pure and simple.

Every so often, to be sure, one comes across a literary interview that seems genuinely valuable—an interview that, if one were teaching an undergraduate course about the writer, one might well add to the reading list. A fine example is a brief interview that David Stern conducted with Robert Fitzgerald for *Sequoia* in 1976. It is a no-nonsense conversation in which Stern asks about Fitzgerald's method of translating Homer, about the development of the verse form used in his translations, about his opinion of other translations, and about the possible influences upon him of Pound and Stevens. Stern poses such questions as "What are the most important things to try to keep from the original Greek in an English translation?" Fitzgerald's answers are clear, taut, straightforward, carefully worded, and fitted out, where necessary, with well-chosen examples:

> D.S.: What kind of liberties did you feel you were allowed to take in your translations and what kind of liberties did you feel that you could not take?
> R.F.: Translating is finding equivalents. When I was at work on the *Odyssey*, I had to find them. For example, I had been puzzled, as everyone had

for centuries, by the epithet given to Nestor—"Lord of Pylos, Warden of Achaeans." In what sense he was warden of Achaeans puzzled everyone. I found among the palace tablets a list of categories of people employed by the palace. When I saw that among these categories were coast watchers, I knew I had found the answer. Pylos was on the west coast of the Peloponnesus and we knew that sea raiders were very common in those centuries among those waters. What was more natural that there should be coast watchers detailed in the keeping of the palace? This was something for which a modern equivalent might be found. I found it in the list of titles of the commanding admirals in the Second World War. In England there was a whole command of destroyers and destroyer escorts operating out of their West Coast to spot German submarines in the sea lanes leading to the British Isles. The name of that command was "The Lord of the Western Approaches." So Nestor became "The Lord of the Western Approaches to Achaea," and I knew I had my equivalent for him.

Few literary interviews, alas, are this serious and useful. Far from providing reliable information, most subjects of literary interviews are congenitally foggy about names, dates, titles, and such. In a *Paris Review* interview, for instance, Tennessee Williams declares that William Inge wrote "an enormously brilliant work"—but Williams can't remember the title: "*Natural Affection*, or something like that." Errors of transcription are also common. Thus, in the Tennessee Williams interview, Hemingway's story "A Simple Enquiry" becomes "A Simple Inquiry," Sheilah Graham becomes Sheila, and Elinor Wylie becomes Eleanor. Of course, errors of this variety may be found in critical essays too; but they seem to occur more frequently in literary interviews and to be taken far less seriously by all concerned. Indeed, there seems to be an unspoken understanding among interviewers, editors, and readers that literary interviews should not be held to the same standards of accuracy as, say, literary essays. Even if an interview subject misrepresents the truth, his questioner will almost certainly not contradict him. Why not? Because he couldn't care less about the truth. What literary interviewers are after is not truth but sheer portraiture. So what, their logic seems to run, if the interview subject gets his facts wrong, contradicts himself, or fails to support an argument adequately? That's *him*—and to try to correct his facts, or to ask him to rethink his argument, would only be to stifle his individuality, to muck up the character portrait.

In many an editorial office, in fact, a writer's value as an interview subject seems to be directly proportionate to the outrageousness, immoderation, and irresponsibility of his remarks. So at least it would appear from the publication, in recent years, of two grotesque compilations: Lawrence Grobel's *Conversations with Capote* (1985) and Robert J. Stanton and Gore Vidal's *Views from a Window: Conversations with Gore Vidal* (1980). Whatever one might think of Capote's and Vidal's fiction, it is obvious that they were made the subjects of such books not because their writings tower over those of their contemporaries but because both of them are notorious for saying sensational things. Even more than most writers, Capote and Vidal relish the interview as an opportunity to brag, to show off, to settle old scores and trash the competition with some *ad hominem* name-calling. The "literary criticism" in these two interview books, accordingly, is for the most part of the crudest variety (which is a marked contrast, one should add, to Vidal's often highly accomplished literary essays). In a chapter called "Contemporaries," for instance, Capote shoots spitballs at one after another of his fellow novelists: Kesey is "dead," Kerouac "was a joke," Bellow "is a nothing writer," Malamud is "unreadable." Updike? "I hate him." As for Joyce Carol Oates,

> She's a joke monster who ought to be beheaded in
> a public auditorium or in Shea or in a field with
> hundreds of thousands. (Laughs.) She does all the
> graffiti in the men's room and the women's room in
> every public toilet from here to California and back,
> stopping in Seattle on her way! (*Laughs.*) To me,
> she's the most loathsome creature in America . . .
> *Has she ever said or written anything about you to*

deserve such vituperation?

Yes, she's written me a fan letter. She's written me
extreme fan letters. But that's the kind of hoax she
is. I bet there's not a writer in America that's ever
had their name in print that she hasn't written a
fan letter to. I think she's that kind of person . . .
or creature . . . or whatever. She's so . . . oooogh!
(*Shudders.*)

So long as one is not on Capote's list of victims, this sort of
thing makes for entertaining reading. But after a while the utter
lack of substance wears one down, and Capote's cattiness seems
merely depressing. Can this really, one wonders, be the testament
of a major American writer? What is wrong with a literary scene
capable of producing such a document? What warped set of values
in America's editorial offices could possible have resulted in the
placing of such nonsense between hard covers?

Cattiness, it should be noted, is not the exclusive province of
American writers. Nearly all literary interviewees, foreign and
domestic, have something to say about their fellows, and whereas
young and ambitious writers tend to dole out more politic praise
than tough criticism, many older writers specialize in snappy put-
downs. In the course of her *Paris Review* interview, for instance,
Rebecca West makes mention of Somerset Maugham, who "could-
n't write for toffee, bless his heart"; of Leonard Woolf, who "had a
tiresome mind" ("But he was certainly good to Virginia"); of Arnold
Bennett, who "was a horrible mean-spirited hateful man"; and of
George Bernard Shaw, who possessed "a poor mind, I think." As for
Yeats,

He wasn't a bit impressive and he wasn't my sort
of person at all. He boomed at you like a foghorn.
He was there one time when Philip Guedalla and
two or three of us were all very young, and were
talking nonsense about murderers in Shakespeare
and whether a third murderer ever became a first
murderer by working hard or were they, sort of,
hereditary slots? Were they like Japanese special-
ists and one did one kind of murder, another did

another? It was really awfully funny. Philip was very funny to be with. Then we started talking about something on the Western isles but Yeats wouldn't join in, until we fussed round and were nice to him. But we were all wrong. What he liked was solemnity and, if you were big enough, heavy enough, and strong enough, he loved you. He loved great big women. He would have been mad about Vanessa Redgrave.

So much for the greatest poet of the century. This passage is of course vintage cantankerous, dotty old English literary lady, but in a sense it is a classic literary interview excerpt: one part valuable (the modest addition to the trove of Yeatsiana), one part ridiculous (the remark about how much less fun Yeats was to be with than Philip Guedalla), one part entertaining (the joke about murderers in Shakespeare), and one part utterly bizarre (the mention of Miss Redgrave).

It is rather refreshing to remember that for every know-it-all, like Capote or West, there is a *faux-naïf* like Larkin:

> INTERVIEWER: Is Jorge Luis Borges the only other contemporary poet of note who is also a librarian, by the way? Are you aware of any others?
> LARKIN: Who is Jorge Luis Borges?

To read an interview with a writer like Larkin is to appreciate the literary interview as a legitimate means of getting a glimpse of an extremely unusual personality—in this case, a personality that is crabbed yet somehow charming. Elizabeth Bishop is likewise an appealing interview subject, sensible and ladylike and truly modest: "There's nothing more embarrassing than being a poet, really." Isaac Bashevis Singer is also delightful, in the manner of a grouchy grandfather:

> INTERVIEWER: Sin is more interesting than virtue. That's what George Bernard Shaw said.
> SINGER: We didn't need George Bernard Shaw to say it.

William Goyen is gentlemanly and reflective, as demonstrated by this pensée, a part of his memory of his friend Carson McCullers's writing block:

> It was a murderous thing, a death blow, that block. She said she just didn't have anything to write. And really, it was as though she had never written. This happens to writers when there are dead spells. We die sometimes. And it's as though we're in a tomb; it's a death. That's what we all fear, and that's why so many of us become alcoholics or suicides or insane or just no-good philanderers.

William Maxwell, too, is a gentleman, just as sensitive, mild-mannered, and unpretentious as his wonderful novel *The Folded Leaf* might lead one to expect; one immediately likes him as much as one likes his work. But Maxwell is an exception; usually there's surprisingly little correlation between one's opinion of a writer's oeuvre and one's reaction to his personality as it comes across in a literary interview. However exquisite much of Capote's fiction may be, it is difficult to like him as a person; on the other hand, Stephen Spender is so genially candid about the weaknesses of his own work ("Auden was much better than I") that it's hard to dislike him. One can take the humble act too far, though: Kurt Vonnegut tries so hard to come off as a regular guy—telling dumb jokes, calling himself a "hack," and describing writing ostentatiously as a "trade"—that it seems a bit too much like slumming. But then one of the pleasures of literary interviews is watching writers (not all, but some) straining desperately to come off a certain way.

The foremost reason most writers agree so readily to grant interviews, of course, is that literary interviews are a splendid way to promote themselves. Many a big literary gun—the names of Vidal and Philip Roth, to mention two, spring instantly to mind—has developed this variety of media exploitation to a high art. (It might be convincingly argued, in fact, that it is in the fine art of publicity that such celebrity writers as these demonstrate their greatest gifts.) Far from merely using the literary interview, as movie stars use the television talk show, to plug their latest products, "name" writers like Vidal and Roth are out to establish the terms in which these products will be discussed by critics, to determine the criteria by which they will be judged. For example, when in the June 1987 *Interview* magazine Vidal discourses upon *Empire*, his historical novel set in America during the Theodore Roosevelt era—he seems eager to ensure that reviewers will dwell not upon its fictional artistry (or lack thereof) but rather upon its value as a history lesson. "I am the history teacher of the country," Vidal claims, adding that, in the series of novels of which *Empire* is a part, "I've redreamed the entire history of the Republic."

Not all interview subjects are as effective as Vidal at stage-managing their conversations. As often as not, interviewers retain the upper hand. Which topics they choose to dwell upon varies from one to the other. Some interviewers want to delve into what it means to be a woman writer, a black writer, an English writer, a homosexual writer. Daniel Stern asks Bernard Malamud: "Does this idea or theme, as you call it, come out of your experience as a Jew?" (And later: "Are you a Jewish writer?" Malamud: "What is the question asking?") Rebecca West's interviewer keeps asking questions that contain the word *woman* (and no wonder, because when one turns to the interviewer's biographical note, one discovers that she is the author of feminist studies of the Virgin Mary and Joan of Arc, and "is currently working on a study of female form in allegory"). More often than not, the interviewer is more interested than the interviewee in discussing such matters and tends to press on (as West's interviewer does) long after the author has clearly grown tired of the topic.

This is, needless to say, a mark of bad interviewing. One of the things a good interviewer must be able to sense is that it's time to move on. He must have good instincts, too, about the next turn the interview should take, must have the sensitivity and savvy to follow his subject's line of thought, and must be able to ask intelligent follow-up questions when the occasion arises. A good interviewer must know as much as possible about his subject, but must not wear that knowledge on his sleeve. He must have enough in common with his subject to make possible a meeting of the minds, but must be different enough to get something interesting going; he must balance sophistication with curiosity, respect with skepticism.

And he must ask the right questions. Naturally, most interview questions are familiar ones. Probably ninety percent of the conversations in ninety percent of literary interviews revolve around the same handful of topics: writing habits (What time of day do you write? How many drafts? Is it hard? Is it fun? Do you use a pencil, typewriter, or computer?); personal history (What was your childhood like? How autobiographical is your work?); other writers (What do you think of them? Which ones have influenced you?) and literature in general. And then there is that broad category of questions about the subject's social, political, ethical, and philosophical ideas. Usually, these are the questions that separate the men from the boys. Some distinguished authors, when they talk about non-literary ideas, are quite impressive; others are so blinkered, narcissistic, and just plain fatuous that they remind one of starlets holding forth on *The Tonight Show*. When Tennessee Williams praises Fidel Castro's regime, for example, it's plain that he's doing so mainly because, when he went to Cuba, Castro knew who he was, treated him with respect, and "introduced me to the Cuban cabinet . . . . When he introduced us, he turned to me and said, 'Oh, that cat!' and winked. He meant *Cat on a Hot Tin Roof*, of course. I found that very engaging." As for President Carter, the major fault Williams found with him was that he ran a dry White House: "We were only allowed to have one very small glass of what was purported to be a California chablis." And here just to show Williams, in his *Paris Review* interview, attempting to develop a serious critical thought—is the complete text of a section of the interview entitled "The State of the Culture":

> Literature has taken a back seat to the television, don't you think? It really has. We don't have a culture anymore that favors the creation of writers, or supports them very well. I mean, serious artists. On Broadway, what they want are cheap comedies and musicals and revivals. It's nearly impossible to get serious work even produced, and then it's lucky to have a run of a week. They knocked Albee's *Lolita* down horribly. I've never read such cruel reviews. But I felt it was a mistake for Albee to do adaptations. He's brilliant doing his own

original work. But even so, I think there's a way of expressing one's critical displeasures with a play without being quite so hard, quite so cruel. The critics are literally killing writers.

The principal emotion that one experiences when reading a passage such as this is embarrassment—embarrassment for Williams, for American drama, for literature. Would such silly, incoherent observations as these ever be allowed into print in any other context than a literary interview?

Complain as we may, the form continues to increase in prominence. In the past two decades, whole volumes of literary interviews have proliferated. In 1984, Alfred A. Knopf published Charles Ruas's *Conversations with American Writers* (among the subjects, unsurprisingly, are Capote, Vidal, Mailer, and Williams); in 1987, the University of Illinois Press issued *Alive and Writing: Interviews with American Authors of the 1980s*. (Editing volumes of literary interviews is apparently developing into a favorite, and respectable, scholarly pursuit; one of the two editors of Alive and Writing is a Professor Larry McCaffery of San Diego State University, who has also coedited *Anything Can Happen: Interviews with Contemporary American Novelists*.) The already-mentioned books of interviews with Vidal and Capote have been joined by an entire series of book-length "literary conversations" with individual writers (including Flannery O'Connor and Katherine Anne Porter) published by the University of Mississippi Press. A form of literary interview that became especially popular in the 1980s was the sort in which the subject himself was not interviewed—or, at least, was only one of many persons interviewed. I am speaking of the "oral biography," in which the biographical subject is portrayed not by a single biographer, who has sifted through the primary sources and formed a coherent vision of one person's life and character, but by a number of people who knew the subject; on such projects it is the job of the "biographer" (if such a word can even be used) to record, transcribe, edit, and put into some order these people's taped remarks about the subject. Peter Brazeau's *Parts of a World: Wallace Stevens Remembered* (1983) is one example thereof; Peter Manso's *Mailer: His Life and Times* (1985) is another. Just as the interview form has, then, in the past couple of decades, taken the place of the critical essay in the oeuvres of many poets, it has like-wise, in recent years, begun to move in on the territory of the lit-erary biography. Taken together, all of these developments—anthologies of interviews, book-length interviews, and oral biogra-phies—are an ominous sign that now, even when the topic at hand is literature, real writing is increasingly giving way to talking dis-guised as writing.

In his introduction to volume four of *Writers at Work* (1976), Wilfrid Sheed notes that, in a review of volume two, he had com-plained "that the information contained therein was neither better nor worse than Hollywood gossip." But the complaint, he confess-es, was "dishonest . . . in that I artfully concealed how much I enjoyed the volume—which meant it had some kind of value, if not the kind I was looking for. It was also an ingenuous piece because I did not yet realize that gossip is the very stuff of literature, the *materia prima* of which both books and their authors are made." (Note also Truman Capote in *Conversations With Capote*: "All lit-erature . . . is gossip.") Sheed goes on to say that a literary inter-view is worthwhile because it affords us a glimpse of the author in the act of "self-creation," of fashioning his own image; and he claims that what distinguishes writers from Hollywood movie actors—and what therefore makes literary interviews, despite their preoccupation with trivial details, more valuable than interviews with movie actors—is that an author "knows, as movie actors do not, that such details can immortalize a character." This argument seems to me extraordinarily misguided: if there's anything that movie actors do know about, it is the manufacturing of images and the fixing of characters in the public consciousness.

As for Sheed's point that all literature is gossip, I suppose in the broadest sense this could be said to be true; but one must dis-tinguish between the high gossip of Hamlet and the low gossip of Liz Smith's column, and one must recognize that the literary inter-view is closer to the latter than to the former. Whereas reading almost anything "literary" requires a certain level of concentration, reading literary interviews is mostly very much like reading Liz Smith, or for that matter watching television.

Yet Sheed does have a point. Literary interviews can be fun to read, and it would be dishonest not to admit, even while one is decrying the form for its vulgarities and pretensions, that one has been much entertained by them. And there's nothing *wrong* with being entertained by them. The important thing is to admit that most of the time, one is merely being entertained and not edified—to acknowledge that the majority of literary interviews fall squarely into the same category as movie-star biographies, literary party gossip, talk radio, and "Entertainment Tonight." And to recognize, even as one is enjoying oneself, that one's time would really be much better spent reading the fiction, poetry, or plays for which these people are famous than poring over a published transcript of their extemporaneous chatter.

Can Poetry Matter?

Dana Gioia

American poetry now belongs to a subculture. No longer part of the mainstream of artistic and intellectual life, it has become the specialized occupation of a relatively small and isolated group. Little of the frenetic activity it generates ever reaches outside that closed group. As a class, poets are not without cultural status. Like priests in a town of agnostics, they still command a certain residual prestige. But as individual artists they are almost invisible.

What makes the situation of contemporary poetry particularly surprising is that it comes at a moment of unprecedented expansion for the art. There have never before been so many new books of poetry published, so many anthologies or literary magazines. Never has it been so easy to earn a living as a poet. There are now several thousand college-level jobs in teaching creative writing, and many more at the primary and secondary levels. Congress has even instituted the position of poet laureate, as have twenty-five states. One also finds a complex network of public subvention for poets, funded by federal, state, and local agencies, augmented by private support in the form of foundation fellowships, prizes, and subsidized retreats. There has also never before been so much published criticism about contemporary poetry; it fills dozens of literary newsletters and scholarly journals.

The proliferation of new poetry and poetry programs is astounding by any historical measure. Just under a thousand new collections of verse are published each year, in addition to a myriad of new poems printed in magazines both small and large. No one knows how many poetry readings take place each year, but surely the total must run into the tens of thousands. And there are now about 200 graduate creative-writing programs in the United States, and more than a thousand undergraduate ones. With an average of ten poetry students in each graduate section, these programs alone will produce about 20,000 accredited professional poets over the next decade. From such statistics an observer might easily conclude that we live in the golden age of American poetry.

But the poetry boom has been a distressingly confined phenomenon. Decades of public and private funding have created a large professional class for the production and reception of new poetry, comprising legions of teachers, graduate students, editors, publishers, and administrators. Based mostly in universities, these groups have gradually become the primary audience for contemporary verse. Consequently, the energy of American poetry, which was once directed outward, is now increasingly focused inward. Reputations are made and rewards distributed within the poetry subculture. To adapt Russell Jacoby's definition of contemporary academic renown from *The Last Intellectuals,* a "famous" poet now means someone famous only to other poets. But there are enough poets to make that local fame relatively meaningful. Not long ago, "only poets read poetry" was meant as damning criticism. Now it is a proven marketing strategy.

The situation has become a paradox, a Zen riddle of cultural sociology. Over the past half century, as American poetry's specialist audience has steadily expanded, its general readership has declined. Moreover, the engines that have driven poetry's institutional success—the explosion of academic writing programs, the proliferation of subsidized magazines and presses, the emergence of a creative-writing career track, and the migration of American literary culture to the university—have unwittingly contributed to its disappearance from public view.

To the average reader, the proposition that poetry's audience has declined may seem self-evident. It is symptomatic of the art's current isolation that within the subculture such notions are often rejected. Like chamber-of-commerce representatives from Parnassus, poetry boosters offer impressive recitations of the numerical growth of publications, programs, and professorships. Given the bullish statistics on poetry's material expansion, how does one demonstrate that its intellectual and spiritual influence has eroded? One cannot easily marshal numbers, but to any candid observer the evidence throughout the world of ideas and letters seems inescapable.

Daily newspapers no longer review poetry. There is, in fact, little coverage of poetry or poets in the general press. From 1984 until 1992 the National Book Awards dropped poetry as a category. Leading critics rarely review it. In fact, virtually no one reviews it except other poets. Almost no popular collections of contemporary poetry are available except those, like the *Norton Anthology,* targeting an academic audience. It seems, in short, as if the large audience that still exists for quality fiction hardly notices poetry. A reader familiar with the novels of Joyce Carol Oates, John Updike, or John Barth may not even recognize the names of Gwendolyn Brooks, Gary Snyder, or W. D. Snodgrass.

One can see a microcosm of poetry's current position by studying its coverage in the *New York Times.* Virtually never reviewed in the daily edition, new poetry is intermittently discussed in the Sunday *Book Review,* but almost always in group reviews where three books are briefly considered together. Whereas a new novel or biography is reviewed on or around its publication date, a new collection by an important poet like Donald Hall or David Ignatow might wait up to a year for a notice. Or it might never be reviewed at all. Henry Taylor's *Flying Change* was reviewed only after it had won the Pulitzer Prize. Rodney Jones's *Transparent Gestures* was reviewed months after it had won the National Book Critics Circle Award. Rita Dove's Pulitzer Prize-winning *Thomas and Beulah* was not reviewed by the *Times* at all.

Poetry reviewing is no better anywhere else, and generally it is much worse. The *New York Times* only reflects the opinion that although there is a great deal of poetry around, none of it matters very much to readers, publishers, or advertisers—to anyone, that is, except other poets. For most newspapers and magazines, poetry has become a literary commodity intended less to be read than to be noted with approval. Most editors run poems and poetry reviews the way a prosperous Montana rancher might keep a few buffalo around—not to eat the endangered creatures but to display them for tradition's sake.

Arguments about the decline of poetry's cultural importance are not new. In American letters they date back to the nineteenth century. But the modern debate might be said to have begun in 1934, when Edmund Wilson published the first version of his controversial essay "Is Verse a Dying Technique?" Surveying literary history, Wilson noted that verse's role had grown increasingly narrow since the eighteenth century. In particular, Romanticism's emphasis on intensity made poetry seem so "fleeting and quintessential" that eventually it dwindled into a mainly lyric medium. As verse—which had previously been a popular medium for narrative, satire, drama, even history and scientific speculation—retreated into lyric, prose usurped much of its cultural territory. Truly ambitious writers eventually had no choice but to write in prose. The future of great literature, Wilson speculated, belonged almost entirely to prose.

Wilson was a capable analyst of literary trends. His skeptical assessment of poetry's place in modern letters has been frequently attacked and qualified over the past half century, but it has never been convincingly dismissed. His argument set the ground rules for all subsequent defenders of contemporary poetry. It also provided the starting point for later iconoclasts, such as Delmore Schwartz, Leslie Fiedler, and Christopher Clausen. The most recent and celebrated of these revisionists is Joseph Epstein, whose mordant 1988 critique "Who Killed Poetry?" first appeared in *Commentary* and was reprinted in an extravagantly acrimonious symposium in *AWP Chronicle* (the journal of the Associated Writing Programs). Not coincidentally, Epstein's title pays a double homage to Wilson's essay—first by mimicking the interrogative form of the original title, second by employing its metaphor of death.

Epstein essentially updated Wilson's argument, but with important differences. Whereas Wilson looked on the decline of poetry's cultural position as a gradual process spanning three centuries, Epstein focused on the past few decades. He contrasted the major achievements of the modernists—the generation of Eliot and Stevens, which led poetry from moribund Romanticism into the twentieth century—with what he felt were the minor accomplishments of the present practitioners. The modernists, Epstein maintained, were artists who worked from a broad cultural vision. Contemporary writers were "poetry professionals," who operated within the closed world of the university. Wilson blamed poetry's plight on historical forces; Epstein indicted the poets themselves and the institutions they had helped create, especially creative-writing programs. A brilliant polemicist, Epstein intended his essay to be incendiary, and it did ignite an explosion of criticism. No recent essay on American poetry has generated so many immediate responses in literary journals. And certainly none has drawn so much violently negative criticism from poets themselves. To date at least thirty writers have responded in print. Henry Taylor published two rebuttals.

Poets are justifiably sensitive to arguments that poetry has declined in cultural importance, because journalists and reviewers have used such arguments simplistically to declare all contemporary verse irrelevant. Usually the less a critic knows about verse the more readily he or she dismisses it. It is no coincidence, I think, that the two most persuasive essays on poetry's presumed demise were written by outstanding critics of fiction, neither of whom has written extensively about contemporary poetry. It is too soon to judge the accuracy of Epstein's essay, but a literary historian would find Wilson's timing ironic. As Wilson finished his famous essay, Robert Frost, Wallace Stevens, T. S. Eliot, Ezra Pound, Marianne Moore, e. e. cummings, Robinson Jeffers, H. D. (Hilda Doolittle), Robert Graves, W. H. Auden, Archibald MacLeish, Basil Bunting, and others were writing some of their finest poems, which, encompassing history, politics, economics, religion, and philosophy, are among the most culturally inclusive in the history of the language. At the same time, a new generation, which would include Robert Lowell, Elizabeth Bishop, Philip Larkin, Randall Jarrell, Dylan Thomas, A. D. Hope, and others, was just breaking into print. Wilson himself later admitted that the emergence of a versatile and ambitious poet like Auden contradicted several points of his argument. But if Wilson's prophecies were sometimes inaccurate, his sense of poetry's overall situation was depressingly astute. Even if great poetry continues to be written, it has retreated from the center of literary life. Though supported by a loyal coterie, poetry has lost the confidence that it speaks to and for the general culture.

One sees evidence of poetry's diminished stature even within the thriving subculture. The established rituals of the poetry world— the readings, small magazines, workshops, and conferences—

exhibit a surprising number of self-imposed limitations. Why, for example, does poetry mix so seldom with music, dance, or theater? At most readings the program consists of verse only—and usually only verse by that night's author. Forty years ago, when Dylan Thomas read, he spent half the program reciting other poets' work. Hardly a self-effacing man, he was nevertheless humble before his art. Today most readings are celebrations less of poetry than of the author's ego. No wonder the audience for such events usually consists entirely of poets, would-be poets, and friends of the author.

Several dozen journals now exist that print only verse. They don't publish literary reviews, just page after page of freshly minted poems. The heart sinks to see so many poems crammed so tightly together, like downcast immigrants in steerage. One can easily miss a radiant poem amid the many lackluster ones. It takes tremendous effort to read these small magazines with openness and attention. Few people bother, generally not even the magazines' contributors. The indifference to poetry in the mass media has created a monster of the opposite kind—journals that love poetry not wisely but too well.

Until about thirty years ago most poetry appeared in magazines that addressed a nonspecialist audience on a range of subjects. Poetry vied for the reader's interest along with political journalism, humor, fiction, and reviews—a competition that proved healthy for all the genres. A poem that didn't command the reader's attention wasn't considered much of a poem. Editors chose verse that they felt would appeal to their particular audiences, and the diversity of magazines assured that a variety of poetry appeared. The early *Kenyon Review* published Robert Lowell's poems next to critical essays and literary reviews. The old *New Yorker* showcased Ogden Nash between cartoons and short stories.

A few general-interest magazines, such as the *New Republic* and the *New Yorker,* still publish poetry in every issue, but, significantly, none except the *Nation* still reviews it regularly. Some poetry appears in the handful of small magazines and quarterlies that consistently discuss a broad cultural agenda with nonspecialist readers, such as the *Threepenny Review,* the *New Criterion,* and the *Hudson Review.* But most poetry is published in journals that address an insular audience of literary professionals, mainly teachers of creative writing and their students. A few of these, such as

American Poetry Review and the *AWP Chronicle*, have moderately large circulations. Many more have negligible readerships. But size is not the problem. The problem is their complacency or resignation about existing only in and for a subculture.

What are the characteristics of a poetry-subculture publication? First, the one subject it addresses is current American literature (supplemented perhaps by a few translations of poets who have already been widely translated). Second, if it prints anything other than poetry, that anything is usually short fiction. Third, if it runs discursive prose, the essays and reviews are overwhelmingly positive. If it publishes an interview, the tone will be unabashedly reverent toward the author. For these journals critical prose exists not to provide a disinterested perspective on new books but to publicize them. Quite often there are manifest personal connections between the reviewers and the authors they discuss. If occasionally a negative review is published, it will be openly sectarian, rejecting an aesthetic that the magazine has already condemned. The unspoken editorial rule seems to be "never to surprise or annoy the readers"; they are, after all, mainly our friends and colleagues.

By abandoning the hard work of evaluation, the poetry subculture demeans its own art. Since there are too many new poetry collections appearing each year for anyone to evaluate, the reader must rely on the candor and discernment of reviewers to recommend the best books. But the general press has largely abandoned this task, and the specialized press has grown so overprotective of poetry that it is reluctant to make harsh judgments. In his book *American Poetry: Wildness and Domesticity*, Robert Bly has accurately described the corrosive effect of this critical boosterism:

> We have an odd situation: although more bad poetry is being published now than ever before in American history, most of the reviews are positive. Critics say, "I never attack what is bad, all that will take care of itself," . . . but the country is full of young poets and readers who are confused by seeing mediocre poetry praised, or never attacked, and who end up doubting their own critical perceptions.

A clubby feeling also typifies most recent anthologies of contemporary poetry. Although these collections represent themselves as trustworthy guides to the best new poetry, they are not compiled for readers outside the academy. More than one editor has discovered that the best way to get an anthology assigned is to include work by the poets who teach the courses. Compiled in the spirit of congenial opportunism, many of these anthologies give the impression that literary quality is a concept that neither an editor nor a reader should take too seriously.

The 1985 *Morrow Anthology of Younger American Poets,* for example, is not so much a selective literary collection as a comprehensive directory of creative-writing teachers (it even offers a photo of each author). Running nearly 800 pages, the volume presents no fewer than 104 important young poets, virtually all of whom teach creative writing. The editorial principle governing selection seems to have been the fear of leaving out some influential colleague. The book does contain a few strong and original poems, but they are surrounded by so many undistinguished exercises that one wonders if the good work got there by design or simply by random sampling. In the drearier patches one suspects that perhaps the book was never truly meant to be read, only assigned.

And that is the real issue. The poetry subculture no longer assumes that all published poems will be read. Like their colleagues in other academic departments, poetry professionals must publish, for purposes of both job security and career advancement. The more they publish, the faster they progress. If they do not publish, or wait too long, their economic futures are in grave jeopardy.

In art, of course, everyone agrees that quality and not quantity matters. Some authors survive on the basis of a single unforgettable poem—Edmund Waller's "Go, lovely rose," for example, or Edwin Markham's "Man With the Hoe," which was made famous by being reprinted in hundreds of newspapers—an unthinkable occurrence today. But bureaucracies, by their very nature, have difficulty measuring something as intangible as literary quality. When institutions evaluate creative artists for employment or promotion, they still must find some seemingly objective means to do so. As the critic Bruce Bawer has observed,

A poem is, after all, a fragile thing, and its intrinsic worth, or lack thereof, is a frighteningly subjective consideration; but fellowships, grants, degrees, appointments, and publications are objective facts. They are quantifiable; they can be listed on a résumé.

Poets serious about making careers in institutions understand that the criteria for success are primarily quantitative. They must publish as much as possible as quickly as possible. The slow maturation of genuine creativity looks like laziness to a committee. Wallace Stevens was forty-three when his first book appeared. Robert Frost was thirty-nine. Today these sluggards would be unemployable.

The proliferation of literary journals and presses over the past thirty years has been a response less to an increased appetite for poetry among the public than to the desperate need of writing teachers for professional validation. Like subsidized farming that grows food no one wants, a poetry industry has been created to serve the interests of the producers and not the consumers. And in the process the integrity of the art has been betrayed. Of course, no poet is allowed to admit this in public. The cultural credibility of the professional poetry establishment depends on maintaining a polite hypocrisy. Millions of dollars in public and private funding are at stake. Luckily, no one outside the subculture cares enough to press the point very far. No Woodward and Bernstein will ever investigate a cover-up by members of the Associated Writing Programs.

The new poet makes a living not by publishing literary work but by providing specialized educational services. Most likely he or she either works for or aspires to work for a large institution—usually a state-run enterprise, such as a school district, a college, or a university (or lately even a hospital or prison)—teaching others how to write poetry or, at the highest levels, how to teach others how to write poetry.

To look at the issue in strictly economic terms, most contemporary poets have been alienated from their original cultural function. As Marx maintained and few economists have disputed, changes in a class's economic function eventually transform its values and behavior. In poetry's case, the socioeconomic changes have led to a divided literary culture: the superabundance of poetry within a small class and the impoverishment outside it. One might even say that outside the classroom—where society demands that the two groups interact—poets and the common reader are no longer on speaking terms.

The divorce of poetry from the educated reader has had another, more pernicious result. Seeing so much mediocre verse not only published but praised, slogging through so many dull anthologies and small magazines, most readers—even sophisticated ones like Joseph Epstein—now assume that no significant new poetry is being written. This public skepticism represents the final isolation of verse as an art form in contemporary society.

The irony is that this skepticism comes in a period of genuine achievement. Gresham's Law, that bad coinage drives out good, only half applies to current poetry. The sheer mass of mediocrity may have frightened away most readers, but it has not yet driven talented writers from the field. Anyone patient enough to weed through the tangle of contemporary work finds an impressive and diverse range of new poetry. Adrienne Rich, for example, despite her often overbearing polemics, is a major poet by any standard. The best work of Donald Justice, Anthony Hecht, Donald Hall, James Merrill, Louis Simpson, William Stafford, and Richard Wilbur—to mention only writers of the older generation—can hold its own against anything in the national literature. One might also add Sylvia Plath and James Wright, two strong poets of the same generation who died early. America is also a country rich in émigré poetry, as major writers like Czeslaw Milosz, Nina Cassian, Derek Walcott, Joseph Brodsky, and Thom Gunn demonstrate.

Without a role in the broader culture, however, talented poets lack the confidence to create public speech. Occasionally a writer links up rewardingly to a social or political movement. Rich, for example, has used feminism to expand the vision of her work. Robert Bly wrote his finest poetry to protest the Vietnam War. His sense of addressing a large and diverse audience added humor, breadth, and humanity to his previously minimalist verse. But it is a difficult task to marry the Muse happily to politics. Consequently, most contemporary poets, knowing that they are virtually invisible in the larger culture, focus on the more intimate forms of lyric and meditative verse. (And a few loners, like X. J. Kennedy and John Updike, turn their genius to the critically disreputable demimonde of light verse and children's poetry.) Therefore, although current American poetry has not often excelled in public forms like political or satiric verse, it has nonetheless produced personal poems of unsurpassed beauty and power. Despite its manifest excellence, this new work has not found a public beyond the poetry subculture, because the traditional machinery of transmission—the reliable reviewing, honest criticism, and selective anthologies—has broken down. The audience that once made Frost and Eliot, cummings and Millay, part of its cultural vision remains out of reach. Today Walt Whitman's challenge "To have great poets, there must be great audiences, too" reads like an indictment.

To maintain their activities, subcultures usually require institutions, since the general society does not share their interests. Nudists flock to "nature camps" to express their unfettered lifestyle. Monks remain in monasteries to protect their austere ideals. As long as poets belonged to a broader class of artists and intellectuals, they centered their lives in urban bohemias, where they maintained a distrustful independence from institutions. Once poets began moving into universities, they abandoned the working-class heterogeneity of Greenwich Village and North Beach for the professional homogeneity of academia.

At first they existed on the fringes of English departments, which was probably healthy. Without advanced degrees or formal career paths, poets were recognized as special creatures. They were allowed—like aboriginal chieftains visiting an anthropologist's campsite—to behave according to their own laws. But as the demand for creative writing grew, the poet's job expanded from merely literary to administrative duties. At the university's urging, these self-trained writers designed history's first institutional curricula for young poets. Creative writing evolved from occasional courses taught within the English department into its own undergraduate major or graduate-degree program. Writers fashioned their academic specialty in the image of other university studies. As the new writing departments multiplied, the new professionals patterned their infrastructure—job titles, journals, annual conventions, organizations—according to the standards not of urban bohemia but of educational institutions. Out of the professional networks this educational expansion created, the subculture of poetry was born.

Initially, the multiplication of creative-writing programs must have been a dizzyingly happy affair. Poets who had scraped by in bohemia or had spent their early adulthood fighting the Second World War suddenly secured stable, well-paying jobs. Writers who had never earned much public attention found themselves surrounded by eager students. Poets who had been too poor to travel flew from campus to campus and from conference to conference, to speak before audiences of their peers. As Wilfrid Sheed once described a moment in John Berryman's career, "Through the burgeoning university network, it was suddenly possible to think of oneself as a national poet, even if the nation turned out to consist entirely of English Departments." The bright postwar world promised a renaissance for American poetry.

In material terms that promise has been fulfilled beyond the dreams of anyone in Berryman's Depression-scarred generation. Poets now occupy niches at every level of academia, from a few sumptuously endowed chairs with six-figure salaries to the more numerous part-time stints that pay roughly the same as Burger King. But even at minimum wage, teaching poetry earns more than writing it ever did. Before the creative-writing boom, being a poet usually meant living in genteel poverty or worse. While the sacrifices poetry demanded caused much individual suffering, the rigors of serving Milton's "thankless Muse" also delivered the collective cultural benefit of frightening away all but committed artists.

Today poetry is a modestly upwardly mobile, middle-class profession—not as lucrative as waste management or dermatology but several big steps above the squalor of bohemia. Only a philistine would romanticize the blissfully banished artistic poverty of yesteryear. But a clear-eyed observer must also recognize that by opening the poet's trade to all applicants and by employing writers to do something other than write, institutions have changed the social and economic identity of the poet from artist to educator. In social terms the identification of poet with teacher is now complete. The first question one poet now asks another upon being introduced is "Where do you teach?" The problem is not that poets teach. The campus is not a bad place for a poet to work. It's just a bad place for all poets to work. Society suffers by losing the imagination and vitality that poets brought to public culture. Poetry suffers when literary standards are forced to conform to institutional ones.

Even within the university contemporary poetry now exists as a subculture. The teaching poet finds that he or she has little in common with academic colleagues. The academic study of literature over the past twenty-five years has veered off in a theoretical direction with which most imaginative writers have little sympathy or familiarity. Thirty years ago detractors of creative-writing programs predicted that poets in universities would become enmeshed in literary criticism and scholarship. This prophecy has proved spectacularly wrong. Poets have created enclaves in the academy almost entirely separate from their critical colleagues. They write less criticism than they did before entering the academy. Pressed to keep up with the plethora of new poetry, small magazines, professional journals, and anthologies, they are frequently also less well read in the literature of the past. Their peers in the English department generally read less contemporary poetry and more literary theory. In many departments writers and literary theorists are openly at war. Bringing the two groups under one roof has paradoxically made each more territorial. Isolated even within the university, the poet, whose true subject is the whole of human existence, has reluctantly become an educational specialist.

To understand how radically the social situation of the American poet has changed, one need only compare today with sixty years ago. In 1940, with the notable exception of Robert Frost, few poets were working in colleges unless, like Mark Van Doren and Yvor Winters, they taught traditional academic subjects. The only creative-writing program was an experiment begun a few years earlier at the University of Iowa. The modernists exemplified the options that poets had for making a living. They could enter middle-class professions, as had T.S. Eliot (a banker turned publisher), Wallace Stevens (a corporate insurance lawyer), and William Carlos Williams (a pediatrician). Or they could live in bohemia supporting themselves as artists, as, in different ways, did Ezra Pound, e.e. cummings, and Marianne Moore. If the city proved unattractive, they could, like Robinson Jeffers, scrape by in a rural arts colony like Carmel, California. Or they might become farmers, like the young Robert Frost.

Most often poets supported themselves as editors or reviewers, actively taking part in the artistic and intellectual life of their time. Archibald MacLeish was an editor and writer at *Fortune*. James Agee reviewed movies for *Time* and the *Nation*, and eventually wrote screenplays for Hollywood. Randall Jarrell reviewed books. Weldon Kees wrote about jazz and modern art. Delmore Schwartz reviewed everything. Even poets who eventually took up academic careers spent intellectually broadening apprenticeships in literary journalism. The young Robert Hayden covered music and theater for Michigan's black press. R. P. Blackmur, who never completed high school, reviewed books for *Hound & Horn* before teaching at Princeton. Occasionally a poet might supplement his or her income by giving a reading or lecture, but these occasions were rare. Robinson Jeffers, for example, was fifty-four when he gave his first public reading. For most poets, the sustaining medium was not the classroom or the podium but the written word.

If poets supported themselves by writing, it was mainly by writing prose. Paying outlets for poetry were limited. Beyond a few national magazines, which generally preferred light verse or political satire, there were at any one time only a few dozen journals that published a significant amount of poetry. The emergence of a serious new quarterly like *Partisan Review* or *Furioso* was an event of real importance, and a small but dedicated audience eagerly looked forward to each issue. If people could not afford to buy copies, they borrowed them or visited public libraries. As for books of poetry, if one excludes vanity-press editions, fewer than a hundred new titles were published each year. But the books that did appear were reviewed in daily newspapers as well as magazines and quarterlies. A focused monthly like *Poetry* could cover virtually the entire field.

Reviewers sixty years ago were by today's standards extraordinarily tough. They said exactly what they thought, even about their most influential contemporaries. Listen, for example, to Randall Jarrell's description of a book by the famous anthologist Oscar Williams: it "gave the impression of having been written on a typewriter by a typewriter." That remark kept Jarrell out of subsequent Williams anthologies, but he did not hesitate to publish it. Or consider Jarrell's assessment of Archibald MacLeish's public poem

America Was Promises: it "might have been devised by a YMCA secretary at a home for the mentally deficient." Or read Weldon Kees's one-sentence review of Muriel Rukeyser's *Wake Island*—"There's one thing you can say about Muriel: she's not lazy." But these same reviewers could write generously about poets they admired, as Jarrell did about Elizabeth Bishop, and Kees about Wallace Stevens. Their praise mattered, because readers knew it did not come lightly.

The reviewers of sixty years ago knew that their primary loyalty must lie not with their fellow poets or publishers but with the reader. Consequently they reported their reactions with scrupulous honesty, even when their opinions might lose them literary allies and writing assignments. In discussing new poetry they addressed a wide community of educated readers. Without talking down to their audience, they cultivated a public idiom. Prizing clarity and accessibility, they avoided specialist jargon and pedantic displays of scholarship. They also tried, as serious intellectuals should but specialists often do not, to relate what was happening in poetry to social, political, and artistic trends. They charged modern poetry with cultural importance and made it the focal point of their intellectual discourse.

Ill-paid, overworked, and underappreciated, this argumentative group of "practical" critics, all of them poets, accomplished remarkable things. They defined the canon of modernist poetry, established methods to analyze verse of extraordinary difficulty, and identified the new mid-century generation of American poets (Lowell, Roethke, Bishop, Berryman, and others) that still dominates our literary consciousness. Whatever one thinks of their literary canon or critical principles, one must admire the intellectual energy and sheer determination of these critics, who developed as writers without grants or permanent faculty positions, often while working precariously on free-lance assignments. They represent a high point in American intellectual life. Even sixty years later their names still command more authority than those of all but a few contemporary critics. A short roll call would include John Berryman, R. P. Blackmur, Louise Bogan, John Ciardi, Horace Gregory, Langston Hughes, Randall Jarrell, Weldon Kees, Kenneth Rexroth, Delmore Schwartz, Karl Shapiro, Allen Tate, and Yvor Winters. Although contemporary poetry has its boosters and publicists, it has no group of comparable dedication and talent able to address the general literary community.

Like all genuine intellectuals, these critics were visionary. They believed that if modern poets did not have an audience, they could create one. And gradually they did. It was not a mass audience; few American poets of any period have enjoyed a direct relationship with the general public. It was a cross-section of artists and intellectuals, including scientists, clergymen, educators, lawyers, and, of course, writers. This group constituted a literary intelligentsia, made up mainly of nonspecialists, who took poetry as seriously as fiction and drama. Recently Donald Hall and other critics have questioned the size of this audience by citing the low average sales of a volume of new verse by an established poet during the period (usually under a thousand copies). But these skeptics do not understand how poetry was read then.

America was a smaller, less affluent country in 1940, with about half its current population and one sixth its current real GNP. In those pre-paperback days of the late Depression neither readers nor libraries could afford to buy as many books as they do today. Nor was there a large captive audience of creative-writing students who bought books of contemporary poetry for classroom use. Readers usually bought poetry in two forms—in an occasional *Collected Poems* by a leading author, or in anthologies. The comprehensive collections of writers like Frost, Eliot, Auden, Jeffers, Wylie, and Millay sold very well, were frequently reprinted, and stayed perpetually in print. (Today most *Collected Poems* disappear after one printing.) Occasionally a book of new poems would capture the public's fancy. Edwin Arlington Robinson's *Tristram* (1927) became a Literary Guild selection. Frost's *A Further Range* sold 50,000 copies as a 1936 Book-of-the-Month Club selection. But people knew poetry mainly from anthologies, which they not only bought but also read, with curiosity and attention.

Louis Untermeyer's *Modern American Poetry*, first published in 1919, was frequently revised to keep it up to date and was a perennial best-seller. My 1942 edition, for example, had been reprinted five times by 1945. My edition of Oscar Williams's *A Pocket Book of Modern Poetry* had been reprinted nineteen times in fourteen years. Untermeyer and Williams prided themselves on keeping their anthologies broad-based and timely. They tried to represent the best of what was being published. Each edition added new poems and poets and dropped older ones. The public appreciated their efforts. Poetry anthologies were an indispensable part of any serious reader's library. Random House's popular Modern Library series, for example, included not one but two anthologies—Selden Rodman's *New Anthology of Modern Poetry* and Conrad Aiken's *Twentieth-Century American Poetry*. All these collections were read and reread by a diverse public. Favorite poems were memorized. Difficult authors like Eliot and Thomas were actively discussed and debated. Poetry mattered outside the classroom.

Today these general readers constitute the audience that poetry has lost. United by intelligence and curiosity, this heterogeneous group cuts across lines of race, class, age, and occupation. Representing our cultural intelligentsia, they are the people who support the arts—who buy classical and jazz records; who attend foreign films, serious theater, opera, symphony, and dance; who read quality fiction and biographies; who listen to public radio and subscribe to the best journals. (They are also often the parents who read poetry to their children and remember, once upon a time in college or high school or kindergarten, liking it themselves.) No one knows the size of this community, but even if one accepts the conservative estimate that it accounts for only two percent of the U.S. population, it still represents a potential audience of almost five million readers. However healthy poetry may appear within its professional subculture, it has lost this larger audience, who represent poetry's bridge to the general culture.

But why should anyone but a poet care about the problems of American poetry? What possible relevance does this archaic art form have to contemporary society? In a better world, poetry would need no justification beyond the sheer splendor of its own existence. As Wallace Stevens once observed, "The purpose of poetry is to contribute to man's happiness." Children know this essential truth when they ask to hear their favorite nursery rhymes again and again. Aesthetic pleasure needs no justification, because a life without such pleasure is one not worth living.

But the rest of society has mostly forgotten the value of poetry. To the general reader, discussions about the state of poetry sound like the debating of foreign politics by émigrés in a seedy café. Or, as Cyril Connolly more bitterly described it, "Poets arguing about modern poetry: jackals snarling over a dried-up well." Anyone who hopes to broaden poetry's audience—critic, teacher, librarian, poet, or lonely literary amateur—faces a daunting challenge. How does one persuade justly skeptical readers, in terms they can understand and appreciate, that poetry still matters?

A passage in William Carlos Williams's "Asphodel, That Greeny Flower" provides a possible starting point. Written toward the end of the author's life, after he had been partly paralyzed by a stroke, the lines sum up the hard lessons about poetry and audience that Williams had learned over years of dedication to both poetry and medicine. He wrote,

> My heart rouses
>   thinking to bring you news
>   of something
> that concerns you
>   and concerns many men. Look at
>   what passes for the new.
> You will not find it there but in
>   despised poems.
>   It is difficult
> to get the news from poems
>   yet men die miserably every day
>   for lack
> of what is found there.

Williams understood poetry's human value but had no illusions about the difficulties his contemporaries faced in trying to engage the audience that needed the art most desperately. To regain poetry's readership one must begin by meeting Williams's challenge to find what "concerns many men," not simply what concerns poets.

There are at least two reasons why the situation of poetry matters to the entire intellectual community. The first involves the role of language in a free society. Poetry is the art of using words charged with their utmost meaning. A society whose intellectual leaders lose the skill to shape, appreciate, and understand the power of language will become the slaves of those who retain it—be they politicians, preachers, copywriters, or newscasters. The public responsibility of poetry has been pointed out repeatedly by modern writers. Even the arch-symbolist Stéphane Mallarmé praised the poet's central mission to "purify the words of the tribe." And Ezra Pound warned that

> Good writers are those who keep the language efficient. That is to say, keep it accurate, keep it clear. It doesn't matter whether a good writer wants to be useful or whether the bad writer wants to do harm. . . . .
>
> If a nation's literature declines, the nation atrophies and decays.

Or, as George Orwell wrote after the Second World War, "One ought to recognize that the present political chaos is connected with the decay of language. . . ." Poetry is not the entire solution to keeping the nation's language clear and honest, but one is hard pressed to imagine a country's citizens improving the health of its language while abandoning poetry.

The second reason why the situation of poetry matters to all intellectuals is that poetry is not alone among the arts in its marginal position. If the audience for poetry has declined into a subculture of specialists, so too have the audiences for most contemporary art forms, from serious drama to jazz. The unprecedented fragmentation of American high culture during the past half century has left most arts in isolation from one another as well as from the general audience. Contemporary classical music scarcely exists as a living art outside university departments and conservatories. Jazz, which once commanded a broad popular audience, has become the semiprivate domain of aficionados and musicians. (Today even influential jazz innovators cannot find places to perform in many metropolitan centers—and for an improvisatory art the inability to perform is a crippling liability.) Much serious drama is now confined to the margins of American theater, where it is seen only by actors, aspiring actors, playwrights, and a few diehard fans. Only the visual arts, perhaps because of their financial glamour and upper-class support, have largely escaped the decline in public attention.

The most serious question for the future of American culture is whether the arts will continue to exist in isolation and decline into subsidized academic specialties or whether some possibility of rapprochement with the educated public remains. Each of the arts must face the challenge separately, and no art faces more towering obstacles than poetry. Given the decline of literacy, the proliferation of other media, the crisis in humanities education, the collapse of critical standards, and the sheer weight of past failures, how can poets possibly succeed in being heard? Wouldn't it take a miracle?

Toward the end of her life Marianne Moore wrote a short poem called "O To Be a Dragon." This poem recalled the biblical dream in which the Lord appeared to King Solomon and said, "Ask what I shall give thee." Solomon wished for a wise and understanding heart. Moore's wish is harder to summarize. Her poem reads,

> If I, like Solomon, . . .
> could have my wish –
>
> my wish—O to be a dragon,
> a symbol of the power of Heaven—
> of silkworm
> size or immense; at times invisible.
> Felicitous phenomenon!

Moore got her wish. She became, as all genuine poets do, "a symbol of the power of Heaven." She succeeded in what Robert Frost called "the utmost of ambition"—namely, "to lodge a few poems where they will be hard to get rid of." She is permanently part of the "felicitous phenomenon" of American literature.

So wishes can come true—even extravagant ones. If I, like Marianne Moore, could have my wish, and I, like Solomon, could have the self-control not to wish for myself, I would wish that poetry could again become a part of American public culture. I don't think this is impossible. All it would require is that poets and poetry teachers take more responsibility for bringing their art to the public. I will close with six modest proposals for how this dream might come true.

1. *When poets give public readings, they should spend part of every program reciting other people's work*—preferably poems they admire by writers they do not know personally. Readings should be celebrations of poetry in general, not merely of the featured author's work.

2. *When arts administrators plan public readings, they should avoid the standard subculture format of poetry only.* Mix poetry with the other arts, especially music. Plan evenings honoring dead or foreign writers. Combine short critical lectures with poetry performances. Such combinations would attract an audience from beyond the poetry world without compromising quality.

3. *Poets need to write prose about poetry more often, more candidly, and more effectively.* Poets must recapture the attention of the broader intellectual community by writing for nonspecialist publications. They must also avoid the jargon of contemporary academic criticism and write in a public idiom. Finally, poets must regain the reader's trust by candidly admitting what they don't like as well as promoting what they like. Professional courtesy has no place in literary journalism.

4. *Poets who compile anthologies—or even reading lists—should be scrupulously honest in including only poems they genuinely admire.* Anthologies are poetry's gateway to the general culture. They should not be used as pork barrels for the creative-writing trade. An art expands its audience by presenting masterpieces, not mediocrity. Anthologies should be compiled to move, delight, and instruct readers, not to flatter the writing teachers who assign books. Poet-anthologists must never trade the Muse's property for professional favors.

5. *Poetry teachers, especially at the high-school and undergraduate levels, should spend less time on analysis and more on performance.* Poetry needs to be liberated from literary criticism. Poems should be memorized, recited, and performed. The sheer joy of the art must be emphasized. The pleasure of performance is what first attracts children to poetry, the sensual excitement of speaking and hearing the words of the poem. Performance was also the teaching technique that kept poetry vital for centuries. Maybe it also holds the key to poetry's future.

6. *Finally, poets and arts administrators should use radio to expand the art's audience.* Poetry is an aural medium, and thus ideally

suited to radio. A little imaginative programming at the hundreds of college and public-supported radio stations could bring poetry to millions of listeners. Some programming exists, but it is stuck mostly in the standard subculture format of living poets' reading their own work. Mixing poetry with music on classical and jazz stations or creating innovative talk-radio formats could reestablish a direct relationship between poetry and the general audience.

The history of art tells the same story over and over. As art forms develop, they establish conventions that guide creation, performance, instruction, even analysis. But eventually these conventions grow stale. They begin to stand between the art and its audience. Although much wonderful poetry is being written, the American poetry establishment is locked into a series of exhausted conventions—outmoded ways of presenting, discussing, editing, and teaching poetry. Educational institutions have codified them into a stifling bureaucratic etiquette that enervates the art. These conventions may once have made sense, but today they imprison poetry in an intellectual ghetto.

It is time to experiment, time to leave the well-ordered but stuffy classroom, time to restore a vulgar vitality to poetry and unleash the energy now trapped in the subculture. There is nothing to lose. Society has already told us that poetry is dead. Let's build a funeral pyre out of the desiccated conventions piled around us and watch the ancient, spangle-feathered, unkillable phoenix rise from the ashes.

American Poetry and American Life

ROBERT PINSKY

When American poetry tries to include American manners it ends by questioning, or trying to assert, its own social place. This questioning, critical and self-critical pull may be one force that drove the modernist flowering of American poetry in the early twentieth century, making our modern poetry one of the great historical bursts of poetry in English. If the truest political component of poetry is the sense of whom the poem belongs to—the sense of what social manners, assumptions and tastes the poem imagines—modern American poetry has been uniquely situated, between the old, aristocratic authority of the form and against that authority a powerful, shifting social reality. In my own generation, the same force—attention to American life swerving toward attention to the poem's role in that life—seems to impel some of the most valuable work, poems that seem to aim somewhere beyond the sets of mind that imply a settled knowledge of what poetry is and where it belongs: beyond a genial middlebrow tolerance or a bohemian following, an Anglophile mandarin elite or an avant-garde coterie.

If there is any truth in this idea, despite exceptions and qualifications, it can help show what disparate American poems and poets share. For instance, the minor William Carlos Williams poem "Tract," which used to be Williams's main entry in anthologies and textbooks—

> I will teach you my townspeople
> how to perform a funeral—
> for you have it over a troop
> of artists—

unless one should scour the world—
you have the ground sense necessary.
See! the hearse leads.
I begin with a design for a hearse.
For Christ's sake not black—
nor white either—and not polished!
Let it be weathered—like a farm wagon—
with gilt wheels (this could be
applied fresh at small expense)
or no wheels at all:
a rough dray to drag over the ground.

This is not advice, but mock-advice, dramatizing a role the poet
does not have. A similar characterization applies to Frank O'Hara's
"Ave Maria" ("Mothers of America / let your kids go to the movies!
/ get them out of the house so they won't know what you're up to"),
with its scandalous, unpalatable "they may even be grateful to you
/ for their first sexual experience / which only cost you a quarter /
and didn't upset the peaceful home." In both poems, the point is
less the advice than the preposterous quality of the advice, the vac-
uum that flexes when the poem assumes not only a relation with a
communal audience, but the perhaps equally unlikely existence of
that audience—as if "my townspeople" or "Mothers of America"
had an objective existence as a group, like a feudal manor or the
Kiwanis International. Both poems are slight within their author's
canons because of this similar, perhaps too self-permissive come-
dy, the license of a voice that does not matter too much, address-
ing a phantom gathering.

Here is a brief poem of a nearly opposite kind, one that has
given many readers pleasure:

Autumn Begins in Martins Ferry, Ohio

In the Shreve High football stadium,
I think of Polacks nursing long beers in Tiltonsville,
And gray faces of Negroes in the blast furnaces at
            Benwood,
And the ruptured night watchman of Wheeling Steel,
Dreaming of heroes.

All the proud fathers are ashamed to go home.
Their women cluck like starved pullets,
Dying for love.

Therefore,
Their sons grow suicidally beautiful
At the beginning of October,
And gallop terribly against each other's bodies.

James Wright's poem does not pretend to be addressed to any particular American audience. The convention is not oratorical or mock oratorical, but the lyrical present of "I think." Within that frame, Wright presents the values and strivings of a specific American community, without simply condescending to those values on the one side or giving in to them entirely on the other. With the phrases that end each stanza, he also puts the striving into the context of the epic, European past: "Dreaming of heroes," "Dying for love," "gallop terribly against each other's bodies." Many contemporary poems (and novels and movies) try to include such elements as the place names, the football, the disparity between American working-class life and the idea of freedom.

All this is held together successfully in Wright's poem by the sense of who has made it, who says "I think." The heroic or high language of each stanza's last line is in the first two stanzas partly ironic, because a little limp and bald, the participial fluidity of dreaming of heroes and dying for love. In the last stanza, the qualification is explicit, not ironically implicit: the beautiful young men gallop terribly, and against one another. Who speaks these words? Someone who in the second line "thinks," and with the one appearance of the word "I" uses the low, sometimes offensive expression "Polacks," and who chooses through a grammatical ambiguity to be more or less dreaming of heroes along with the night watchman, and those in the bars and blast furnaces.

The poem's placing of its own utterance takes another turn with the word "therefore," a discursive logical pointer almost parodically different socially from the stadium, bar, steelworks revery of the first movement, and from the declaration of the middle stanza. This rhetorical pointer introduces the third stanza's more heartfelt, successful linking of the local and the heroic—Martins Ferry and the *Iliad*—a linking only yearned-after vaguely by dreams of heroes and dying for love. Linking the local and the heroic is the theme of European poems, too—such as Yeats's "Easter 1916," echoed by "beautiful" and "terribly"; the American element in Wright's poem is embodied by the playing-off of "Polacks" against "therefore," "Tiltonsville" against "heroes" and perhaps even more in the buried, all but lost cultural resonances of American names and phrases. I mean not only the faint ghosts of meaning that vibrate between "Shreve" and "High," but the contest between the Germanic and Latin words in the ordinary phrase "football stadium." The very weakness of Classical languages in the American sense of English can give a special overtone to such infinitesimal matters of pitch. And it is matters of pitch that give emotion and meaning to the movement from long beers and blast furnaces to the Homeric image at the end.

In a way, Wright's poem is a meditation on what he has to celebrate, or on the relation between the celebration of poetry and the available glory in American life. What use have the football players or the generations that glory in them for the adverbs and "therefores," the Homeric or chivalric images, of the poet? The variation of idiom, as it threads through poetry's formal demands, puts this question. The play between Latin and Norman roots on one side and Anglo-Saxon roots on the other culminates in the last line's elegant French *galloped*, its normative Latin *terribly*, and blunt Germanic *bodies*. The young men take on both the unconscious beauty of horses and the brutal gallantry of knights. The social criticism that links suicidal beauty and sexual unfulfillment to the drabness and harshness of economic and social conditions may be vague, for some readers even sentimental. But the poem's drama of an authorial "I" who compares his response to this local desire and glory with the old bardic models is precise, clear and beautifully modulated. The poem is opposite in kind to "Tract" and "Ave Maria" because they address patently imaginary audiences disposed to heed poetry, whereas Wright, letting the explicit "I" drop away after his second line, imagines the actual vacuum between the poetry he knows and the America he knows.

The contrast between Latinate and Germanic roots seems to me a characteristically American trope. This is a technical matter that becomes more than a technical matter in the context of an

amazing polyglot culture, where high and low, native and import-
ed, lose their old meanings. When Landor exploits this way of vary-
ing texture by describing fallen orange blossoms as "crisp" and
"unevolved" the contrast appeals to a nineteenth-century British
audience that has studied enough Latin in school to hear "evolve"
both in its abstract, temporal sense and also in the physical sense
of "unroll" or "uncurl." An intuitive, unschooled sense of the dif-
ference in texture may miss some of that kind of meaning, but be
still more sensitive to others. I mean the intuitive or athletic sense
of language that hears the two sources arranged chiastically—
home-abroad-abroad-home, or native-Roman-Norman-native—in
Jefferson's "Life, Liberty and the Pursuit of Happiness." In that
instance, the plain domestic roots "life" and "hap," with their
Germanic hominess, bracket the Latin and French overtones of
"liberty" and "pursuit" with their flavors of law, the hunt, and
books. The rhetoric of the list thus bases the direct, simple needs
of "life" and "happiness," beginning and end, in the justifying
social atmosphere of monks and lawyers, hunters and knights.

Wallace Stevens may be the American poet who uses this kind
of American contrast between "native" and Latin or exotic roots
most loudly and overtly—not least by entertaining the idea of
French and English as a single language, since each component
language would offer more opportunity for contrast, as do his bar-
baric noises. The noises are a kind of meta-Germanic root, more
un-French and therefore more demotic than mere words of any
kind could be:

> Poet, be seated at the piano.
> Play the present, its hoo-hoo-hoo,
> Its shoo-shoo-shoo, its ric-a-nic,
> Its envious cachinnation.
>
> If they throw stones upon the roof
> While you practice arpeggios,
> It is because they carry down the stairs
> A body in rags.
> Be seated at the piano.
> ("Mozart, 1935")

Arpeggios, stones upon the roof, shoo-shoo-shoo, cachinnation, ric-a-nic and rags: this comic music of widely diverse origins is one music of an American modern that embraces past and present, Mozart and 1935, and all possible languages—embraces their disparity. The goal of the poet in these lines is the same as in Stevens's "The American Sublime": to "confront the mockers, / The mickey mockers"—words which make a similar native music out of the Latinate verb *confront* and the English object *mockers*, the verb corresponding to the poet and the object to the mocking laughter—the derisory cachinnation—of his fellow Americans.

Some other examples: The title of "An Ordinary Evening in New Haven" uses in the first word after the article an exotic root (with echoes of church government) to denote the idea of routine, echoed by the Germanic second word with its similar meaning—"making things even"—so that these two words together may perhaps by contrast awaken just a little of the sense of freshness and hazard sleeping in the last two: new, haven. "A single voice," as the poem itself says more clangorously, using the verbal noises, the exotic word, the contrasted roots, to make a diverse music, held together by a comic unity in discord: past and present, exotic and domestic, Europe and America, all joined in what the poet chooses to say:

> A celestial mode is paramount,
> If only in the branches sweeping in the rain:
> The two romanzas, the distant and the near,
> Are a single voice in the boo-ha of the wind.

When Stevens reaches toward the eclectic sounds of American names, which are not American in their parts but only in the process of their making—"Mrs. Alfred Uruguay," "Cortège for Rosenbloom"—the effect is to locate his imagination between a foreign element and a less foreign, the distant and the near, the poet more than a little on guard defining his own place by incorporating the widest possible range of contrasts. The comic beauty of disproportionate parts gives a role to the poet who combines them. By incorporating the vulgar laughter, by calling it "cachinnation," he asserts his place in relation to it.

This is not anyone's favorite side of Stevens. It reminds us of his limitations; it has the quality of snobbery, the pathos and fear-fulness that mickey mockers will find in his music only a laughable dandyism. On the other hand, the energy that enables his great poems seems to come partly from this need to question and adjust his place, to confront the comedy of that quest by exaggeration. And however mannered or arch, his collisions and noises reflect an American eclecticism of culture, the not-quite melting pot of imports and appropriations. By exaggerating the strangeness and odd yokings in the national language, he dramatizes the strange and yet oddly indigenous nature of his work.

Here is an example of a somewhat similar effect from an extremely dissimilar direction, the opening stanzas of Jean Toomer's "Georgia Dusk":

> The sky, lazily disdaining to pursue
>> The setting sun, too indolent to hold
>> A lengthened tournament for flashing gold,
> Passively darkens for night's barbecue,
>
> A feast of moon and men and barking hounds,
>> An orgy for some genius of the South
>> With blood-hot eyes and cane-lipped scented mouth,
> Surprised in making folksongs from soul sounds.
>
> The sawmill blows its whistle, buzz-saws stop,
>> And silence breaks the bud of knoll and hill,
>> Soft settling pollen where plowed lands fulfill
> Their early promise of a bumper crop.
>
> Smoke from the pyramidal sawdust pile
>> Curls up, blue ghosts of trees, tarrying low
>> Where only chips and stumps are left to show
> The solid proof of former domicile.

Toomer's sunset lets the Tennysonian "lengthened tournament for flashing gold" clang against the deeply native word *barbecue* (an Indian word taken into Spanish and French). The idiom of the poem associates that contrast between old richness and new, European and American, exotic and plain, with the contrast between kinds of root, the alternated "lazily" and "disdaining," "indolent" and "hold," "passively" and "darkens," all complicated and folded back by exotic "barbecue" coming from Indian through Romance languages to play against plain Germanic "night." The effect is less like Stevens than like Hart Crane, the richness of old pentameter eloquence made richer by the untamed, cane-lipped genius of the specific American place, the sexual, heavily atmospheric silence that settles, in a brilliant image, like pollen. It is an atmosphere that teases and questions the poet's own voice: who says "barbecue" in the rhythms of Tennysonian quatrains and sunsets, against that sexual Georgia silence? By implication, the poem wonders what human voice or voices can put "bumper crop" and "domicile" together in this place where landscape and human life both seem to evade the poet's terms.

The poem's rhythms, the closed pentameter quatrains, seem to slow and stall as the pollen of fading light and quieted machinery settles over it: "Surprised in making folksongs from soul sounds." The spondaic phrase of "soul sounds" and the term "folksongs" stall and drawl in a kind of loving self-mockery. The rest of the poem converts the implicit comparison of song and poem into explicit action:

> Meanwhile, the men, with vestiges of pomp,
> Race memories of king and caravan,
> High-priests, an ostrich, and a juju-man,
> Go singing through the footpaths of the swamp.
>
> Their voices rise . . the pine trees are guitars,
> Strumming, pine-needles fall like sheets
> of rain . .
> Their voices rise . . the chorus of the cane
> Is caroling a vesper to the stars . .
>
> O singers, resinous and soft your songs
> Above the sacred whisper of the pines,
> Give virgin lips to cornfield concubines,
> Bring dreams of Christ to dusky cane-lipped throngs.

With this vivid, culturally mixed, many-rooted procession the simple alternation of roots breaks into a multiple fracturing and reblending of linguistic elements—Arabic and Latin, African and English, *juju-man* and *king*, *swamp* and *caravan*, *pine* and *guitar*, *strummings* and *vespers* of the *cane*.

These singing voices have an assurance and unity unlike that of the poem that describes them; the singers give no sign that they find their pomp "vestigial," nor does their singing seem to encompass anything like the tension between pentameter stanzas and high diction on one hand and juju-man, barbecue and landscape on the other. On the contrary: "Their voices rise . . the chorus of the cane." Witnessing the singers, Toomer by implication compares his work to theirs, a comparison marked by a return, in the final stanza, from the multiple roots that evoke the procession back to the alternating pattern of Latin and Germanic: *resinous* and *soft*, *sacred* and *whisper*; and in the perfect chiasmus of the next-to-last line:

Give virgin lips to cornfield concubines,

where the opposed Latin conceptual terms for the female body frame the earthbound *lips* and *cornfield*. As if bursting out of this intellectual bracketing, the monosyllabic, physical terms win out in the final line's imperative: "Bring dreams of Christ" and "dusky cane-lipped throngs" jamming the movement to a Hopkins-like retard, echoing the earlier "making folksongs from soul sounds." Whether this imperative is based on the actual weaving of Christian hymns into a partly African ritual, or imagines it, the poem's final plea or prayer is to have its own contradictory roots and intentions made coherent. The bringing together of Christianity and the culture visible in the cornfield is no more or less fantastic than the bringing together of this American scene with what the poet brings to the scene. The poem, reaching for a mystic eloquence similar to that which Crane was fashioning at the same time, ends by calling up a paradoxical, visionary idea of coherence.

This American version of "The Solitary Reaper," in other words, expresses its action partly through a kind of formal inclusion of many actual and potential voices. The somewhat cumbersome technical term might be formal heteroglossia. Each moment of idiom and rhythm asks what tongue should speak next—what language, what person, in what cadence? (From this perspective, the Black poets of the nineteenth and early twentieth century are not fringe elements in the record of our poetry, but characteristic, even quintessential, insofar as the clash between means and experience may require an American poet to forge imaginatively his own place in what he sees.)

The questioning demanded by our heterogeneous life finds its expression in heteroglossia. American poetry's exploitation of the English language's immense and bastardized vocabulary, including the abstraction and formality tied to Latinate words, the physicality and plainness of Germanic words, is only one example of such sensitive mixing and blending. The American poet's relation to levels of syntax, or to kinds of lore and learning, breaking and rearranging ideas of high and low, might offer other examples. This way of looking at style is another way to see the association between modernism and American art. The rapid, shifting play between formality and informality; movement between traditional rhythm and its breaking, and back; levels of syntax speeding ambiguously up and down and through "spoken" constructions and "written" ones; syntax racing or drifting through resemblance to innumerable kinds of speech, kinds of writing—these and all of the other kinds of flexibility and speed one might call "modernist" are also responses to American social reality, especially if one thinks of that reality as one where poetry itself may be an alien or unrealized presence.

As I have tried to suggest by looking at Toomer's poem and some lines of Stevens, such mixing and testing—"formal heteroglossia"—characterizes our poetry over a wide range of different concerns and styles. For instance, an athletic sureness in finding an idiom and form adequate to such thrilling, shifting ground characterizes both Robert Frost and William Carlos Williams, a quality they share under their differences. Whether it is sentences shooting with unexpected grace and knots through iambic channels, or the syncopation of free verse, what we admire in both poets is a formal resourcefulness in defining one's place on shifting ground. Their work brings the speech and behavior of their American social setting into an energetic, self-calibrating struggle with all that poetry was, just before they came to it. In comparison, no matter how active and jagged the imagination of W. H. Auden may be, the enclosing idiom and form that indicate the social frame of his work seem relatively fixed and solid.

Another kind of contrast with the work of Frost and Williams might be a mere regionalism: place as an end rather than a means, the imaginative re-creation, contrary to fact, of stable ground: New Jersey or New England presented as if without the contradiction and movement embodied by their very names. And yet the contradiction and movement of national life as a whole can in some ways be responded to only through a region or place, New Haven or Georgia, the particular names and features flashing by in their change and ambiguity like the distance markers in a car race. There is a comic relish to this process, ebulliently invoking a place almost to doubt its moral reality or permanence, as in Philip Levine's poem "An Ordinary Morning," which begins, "A man is singing on the bus / coming in from Toledo." The man and the bus driver sing to one another, like bizarrely transformed shepherds out of Spenser or Sidney, about love and about the new day, as the passengers wake up, watery-eyed. Levine's closing lines characteristically mix notes and keys—high and low, comic and exalted, local and global, ironic and heartfelt:

> The sun enters from a cloud
> and shatters the wide windshield
> into seventeen distinct shades
> of yellow and fire, the brakes
> gasp and take hold, and we are
> the living, newly arrived
> in Detroit, city of dreams,
> each on his own black throne.

To take just a few examples: "the sun enters" is both a comic stage direction, and a heroic substitute for the ordinary "the sun comes out." The literal shattering of the windshield in one line is revealed in the next as figurative, and that line in turn with its "seventeen" shades is both extravagantly descriptive and slangy. The enjambed lines imitate this same changing or combining of tones, lifting or dropping: "shades" turned by "of yellow and fire" toward violence and energy; "brakes" turned by "gasp" toward human wonder and back from the mundane; "the living" widening the range of "we are" while maybe dropping its tone back toward the mundane; "newly arrived," which suggests new birth after "the living," drops back comically with "in Detroit." And "the living, newly arrived / in Detroit, city of dreams" is not entirely ironic. The history of Detroit as a place where whites and blacks went from the rural South to work in automobile plants is certainly a history of dreams, a history as ambiguous as the final image of the poet and other bus riders, "each on his own black throne." One could exemplify this fluidity of tone, including the inseparable blend of comic and ecstatic, formal and vulgar, in an enormous range of American poets, John Ashbery and Elizabeth Bishop, George Oppen and James Merrill, Allen Ginsberg and Marianne Moore. (I think that the stylistic trait I mean also characterizes poems that do not explicitly take up American cultural material such as bus rides or movies.)

I have been trying to describe modern American poetry's capacity for formal surprise, a sense of mystery about how a thing will be uttered. Beginning with the first modernist generation, the social aspect of this surprise and indeterminacy has been accompanied by another, philosophical aspect, a preoccupation with the unreliability or rigidity of language itself. In my own generation, these elements have taken on new configurations, in works that criticism has hardly begun to catch up with or identify. I mean, for instance, the fluidity of the transitions in James McMichael's *Four Good Things*, a book-length poem set in Pasadena, where Cal Tech was first founded as a crafts school in the spirit of William Morris: the way McMichael moves from his stamp collection through an analysis of the styles of British and German imperialism, through the wind tunnel and the first experiments with television and the beams of cathode-ray electrons, synchronized each thirtieth of a second ("successively, in league, they looked like something")—the whole movement of twenty or thirty lines alluding to countless levels of speech, as it drifts toward, and then far away from, iambic pentameter. The range of McMichael's book, and its formal fluidity, embody an art that defies any trite social correlatives of form, the conservative sestina or liberated free verse. Every line he writes includes some formal twist, or some surprising, rapid verbal turn, that confounds such categories.

I'll try to show what I mean by looking in some detail at another recent poem. Here are the first four stanzas of Anne Winters's "Night Wash":

> All seas are seas in the moon to these
> lonely and full of light.
> High above laundries and rooftops
> the pinstriped silhouettes speak nightmare
> as do the faces full of fire and orange peel.
> Every citizen knows what's the trouble: *America's longest*
> *river is—New York: that's what they say, and I say so.*
>
> Wonderful thing, electricity,
> all these neons and nylons spun dry by a dime
> in the Fifth Street Laundromat. The city
> must be flying a thousand kites tonight
> with its thousands of different keys.
> —Sir, excuse me, *sir?*
> Excuse me interfering, but you don't want
> to put that in—it's got a rubber backing, see? Oh, not at
> all . . .
>
> Piles of workshirts, piles of leopard underthings,
> it's like fishing upside down all night long, and then the
>   moon rises
> like armfuls of thready sleeves. Her voice
> rising and falling, her boys folded sideways asleep on the
>   bench:
> —Listen, that old West Indian cleaning lady?
> Ask anyone here, she never has change.
> Come on, she's too wise . . .
>
> Down in the Tombs
> the prisoner's knuckles climb like stripes
> of paint in the light. He dreams he hears
> the voice of a pig he used to slop for his uncles.
> It pokes its head
> through the bars and says
> "Have you brought any beet greens?"

315

One interesting thing about the passage is its mixture of the literary and the colloquial, or rather several kinds and degrees of the literary and the colloquial. These are innumerable: the formal, rather dense and elevated first sentence, the written language of poetry; the plainer, more spoken poetry of the sentence about neons and nylons; the italicized, spoken but rather formal sentence about New York as our longest river; the somewhat stiff speech, possibly the poet's, in the actual dialogue, "Excuse me interfering"; the other voice that talks about the cleaning woman; the omniscient sentence that knows what the prisoners dream in the Tombs; the more limited sentence that sees the children folded sideways like laundry; the slight primness of saying "underthings"; the voice that dreams; the voice of the pig. . . . The chorus of silent and uttered and dreamed sentences, formed and unformed voices, is the sound of the long river that is the city. Someone has uncles; someone makes the fanciful simile about fishing upside down all night long; someone makes an allusion to Benjamin Franklin's experiment with electricity; and it is not the fragmentation but the flow, the dreamy and resistless movement from part to part, moment to moment, that carries much of the developing emotion.

Without the sense of motion and merging, the details might seem merely rich, imaginatively conceived or recorded. Instead, they suggest a restless demand, a congeries of needs floating and drowning, and so prepare for the next movement of the poem with its images of water:

> —You can never leave them alone at night. Like today
> the stitching overseer says to me
> If you can't keep the rhythm missus . . .
> I says to him fire
> me all you want, I don't take that shit
> off anybody. That was a scare though—
> you can't always get back on a day shift.
>
> In the moonlight
> the city rides serenely enough, its thousand light moorings
> the hunted news in their eyes. Even the rivers
> are tidal, as sailors and bankers know.
> The glass bank of the Chase Manhattan stands dark

over the Harbor. One last
light slowly moving around the top floor.

The bizarre wit that sees the building of the financial bank as a
harbor bank floats almost innocuously and tonelessly in its sur-
roundings; the light moves like a boat around the bank above the
capitalized microcosm of the Harbor. Then this dream world yields
to the focus of dialogue or monologue again, and the conclusion:

>—No washing machines in the basement, that's
>what's the trouble. The laundry would dry
>   overnight
>on the roof, in the wind. Well a month ago
>you know, some big boys took this twelveyearold
>little Spanish girl up there. Then they killed her,
>   they
>threw her, six stories down. Listen, the stone age
>   or something
>running around on those roofs. So this cop said to
>   me
>*Your street is the bottom,* he actually
>said that to me. So what could I say—that it's
>   great?

>On the folding table the same
>gestures repeat, smoothing and folding
>the same ancient shirt. Or the old West Indian
>   cleaning lady
>pretending to finger her pockets for change. At
>   midnight she'll prop
>her gray spaghetti mop and glide toward you
>in her black cotton trousers, her black
>lavender face tilted up. Very clearly
>she says to the world in dream-language
>*I mean to live.*

"They killed her" and "they threw her" have the more force because
of the sleepy sentence fragments like "One last / light slowly mov-
ing around the top floor" and "No washing machines in the base-

ment, that's / what's the trouble." Characteristically, one of these two fragments is in the framing narrative voice while the other is spoken by a character, a character whose remarks have a skewed moral conviction: "that's / what's the trouble," "he actually / said that to me." The fragments and the certainty bob in the aqueous world of the poem along with the muted ordinary street comedy of "stone age or something," "the bottom," "it's great."

Fragments, two of them, begin the last stanza as well, followed by the peculiar sequence of tenses, future ("At midnight she'll prop") then present ("she says"). This is the sequence of prophecy or vision, but then again one of my favorite notes in the last stanza is the way the homely phrase "spaghetti mop" comes in, heightening the drugged or dream quality, with its odd rhyme on "prop." "Ancient" and "stone age" belong here along with the mop, and along with the last recurrence of the prim or stiff diction, on "trousers." My terms—note, voice—are the best I can do in tracing the open, uncentered but clear movement that places the horror of the child's death in its true, placeless or flowing locale. The poem's last phrase, the italicized "*I mean to live*," spoken in a language that the poem identifies as no language of this waking earth, also sounds like the language of a definite person in a place, so that we can believe the authorial "very clearly." The two senses of the verb *mean* as "I intend to live" and "I signify living" come together very clearly, in the final phrase that confirms and summarizes the poem's movement. That movement, the way each moment in the poem's course means to live, conveys its emotion, where a lesser poem might try merely to deplore or exploit. I think that Winters's mastery of an extreme, packed formal alertness is part of a characteristically American response to shifting, undetermined manners, forms and idioms, to heroic structures and appalling lives and deaths.

To put it differently, I like the visible speed and intelligence of Anne Winters's poem. These qualities don't necessarily depend upon the direct treatment of social details and materials—I don't intend anything as quixotic or odious as prescribing a subject matter, or proscribing one. Rather, the point is that a certain kind of fluidity, a formal and moral quality, seems to have been demanded of American poets by their circumstance: in some ways, having to do with expectation and need, poets are at the center of national life, where Whitman would have them; in other ways they are at the fringes, supplanted by the overwhelming variety and power of a reckless national culture.

Fluidity and rapidity have a lot to do with what I like about poetry itself. The mind in it glides and whirls like an ice skater over its medium; prose often wades. Some of the effortful straining of experimental fiction seems to struggle for poetry's freedom to dart from narrative to meditation to exposition and back, inserting a self-reflexive undermining of narrative illusion and then restoring narrative again, without visible seams or audible creaks. It seems possible that such motion is redoubled in the modern American context. Philosophical worrying at the nature of language itself, which has characterized modernism from its beginnings, becomes ever more conventional, an historical gesture. The open question of America's use for poetry refreshes that gesture, gives it a per-petually renewed meaning. Winters's laundromat with its "*I mean to live*" seems simultaneously to challenge and embarrass poetic language, and to incorporate it: to defy poetic form, and to demand it. Language itself may be untrustworthy; the language we use here is also immense, strangely broken, unforeseeable.

I have tried to suggest that American poetry's critical response to American life has been inherently a self-criticism as well: the disparate, mutually revising phrases "I don't take that shit / off any-body" and the "thousand light moorings" take their place in the endless debate between pairs like Toomer's "barbecue" and "pyramidal" or Stevens's "arpeggio" and "shoo-shoo-shoo," each pair with its dreamy aspiration and its saving vulgarity. This con-flict is a special, American version of the old contest between all of established rhetoric on one side and the fresh growths of culture and personal experience on the other. To paraphrase Yeats's dis-tinction between poetry and rhetoric, it is American poetry's ongo-ing argument with itself. Literary criticism has hardly begun to trace the sinuous course of that debate, and the formal means that embody it, in American poetry since the modernist generation.

This self-examination is not necessarily a dour, embattled process. I have in mind something more like the closing lines of Frank O'Hara's "Naphtha," with its brilliant collage of the Eiffel Tower, where Jean Dubuffet did his military service as a meteorol-ogist; New York's Iroquois construction workers "unflinching-foot-ed" on steel girders high over the city; Duke Ellington; the

American Century's technological nightmares, wars and works of art. At the end O'Hara says: "I am ashamed of my century / for being so entertaining / but I have to smile." By finishing off his eclectic and eccentric catalogue with a happy, nearly apologetic reflection on his own response, the poet acknowledges his unsettled role. It is a moment that reminds me, in its sudden, cheerful confession of a not-yet-settled subjectivity, of Williams spiralling from "The pure products of America" to "some doctor's family, some Elsie." On the one hand, the poet is alone and must be one; on the other hand, the many-voiced mode, the poem implying more voices than we can see or hear, let alone identify, seems the only means suited for such vast quantities and qualities of shame and entertainment. The question of who speaks or writes and the question of what kind of many-voiced place that one speaker or writer inhabits become one question.

Bruce Bawer

Bruce Bawer is a freelance writer and editor. His degrees were earned at State University of New York, Stony Brook: BA (1978), MA (1982), PhD (1983). Poetry publications include *Innocence: Eight Poems* (Aralia, 1988), *And So You Bid Me Go* (Aralia, 1989), *Confirmation* (Aralia, 1990), and *Coast to Coast* (Story Line, 1993). His critical studies include *The Middle Generation: The Lives and Poetry of Delmore Schwartz, Randall Jarrell, John Berryman, and Robert Lowell* (Archon, 1986), *Diminishing Fictions: Essays on the Modern American Novel and Its Critics* (Graywolf, 1988), *A Place at the Table: The Gay Individual in American Society* (Poseidon, 1993), *The Aspect of Eternity: Essays* (Graywolf, 1993), *Prophets and Professors: Essays on the Lives and Works of Modern Poets* (Story Line, 1995), and *Stealing Jesus: How Fundamentalism Betrays Christianity* (Crown, 1997). Honors include a *Choice* magazine Outstanding Academic Book award (1987) for *The Middle Generation* and a Reviewer's Citation from the National Book Critics Circle (1987). He lives and works in New York City.

Rita Dove

Rita Dove is Commonwealth Professor of English at the University of Virginia. She served as Poet Laureate and Consultant in Poetry to the Library of Congress from 1993 to 1995. She was reappointed Special Consultant in Poetry for 1999 to 2000. A 1970 Presidential Scholar, she received her BA *summa cum laude* from Miami University of Ohio (1973) and her MFA from the University of Iowa (1977). She also held a Fulbright scholarship at Universität Tübingen in Germany (1974-1975). She has received numerous literary and academic honors, among them the 1987 Pulitzer Prize in Poetry and, most recently, the 1996 Heinz Award in the Arts and Humanities, the 1996 National Medal in the Humanities, the 1997 Sara Lee Frontrunner Award, the 1997 Barnes & Noble Writers for Writers Award, and the 1998 Levinson Prize from *Poetry* Magazine. Dove's poetry collections include *The Yellow House on the Corner* (Carnegie-Mellon, 1980), *Museum* (Carnegie-Mellon, 1983), *Thomas and Beulah* (Carnegie-Mellon,

1986), *Grace Notes* (Norton, 1989), *Selected Poems* (Pantheon, 1993), *Mother Love* (Norton, 1995), and *On the Bus with Rosa Parks* (Norton, 1999). A book of short stories, *Fifth Sunday* (Virginia, 1990), the novel *Through the Ivory Gate* (Pantheon, 1992), and the essay collection *The Poet's World* (Library of Congress, 1995) are among her published prose works. Dove's play *The Darker Face of the Earth*, (Story Line, 1996), which had its world premiere in 1996 at the Oregon Shakespeare Festival, was subsequently produced at the Kennedy Center in Washington, DC. She lives with her husband, the German writer Fred Viebahn, and their daughter Aviva in Charlottesville, Virginia.

Dana Gioia

Dana Gioia worked as a businessman for fifteen years, eventually becoming a vice president at General Foods. In 1992 he left to become a fulltime writer. Gioia has also taught as a visiting writer at Colorado College, Johns Hopkins University, Sarah Lawrence College, Mercer University, and Wesleyan University. He received a BA from Stanford University, and before returning to Stanford to earn and MBA, he completed an MA in Comparative Literature at Harvard University, where he studied with poets Robert Fitzgerald and Elizabeth Bishop. Gioia's poems, translations, essays, and reviews have appeared in many magazines, including the *New Yorker*, the *Atlantic*, the *Washington Book World*, the *New York Times Book Review*, the *Nation*, *Slate*, and the *Hudson Review*. He is also a frequent literary commentator on American culture and literature for BBC Radio. Gioia has published three books of poems: *Daily Horoscope* (Graywolf Press, 1986), *The Gods of Winter* (Graywolf, 1991), and *Interrogations at Noon* (2001), which won the American Book Award. He has edited several anthologies, including college literature textbooks coedited with X. J. Kennedy. Gioia's critical collection, *Can Poetry Matter? Essays on Poetry and American Culture* (Graywolf, 1992), was chosen by *Publishers Weekly* as one of the Best Books of 1992. His most recent critical volume is *Barrier of a Common Language: An American Looks at Contemporary British Poetry* (Michigan, 2003). Gioia was appointed by President George W. Bush to be chairman of the National Endowment for the Arts. When he is not in Washington, he lives in Santa Rosa, California, with his wife and two sons.

Elton Glaser

Elton Glaser, a native of New Orleans, is Distinguished Professor of English Emeritus at the University of Akron and former Director of the University of Akron Press. He graduated from the University of New Orleans (BA, 1967; MA, 1969) and the University of California, Irvine (MFA, 1972). Nearly five hundred of his poems and translations have appeared in literary magazines and anthologies such as *Poetry*, the *Georgia Review*, and *The Pittsburgh Book of Contemporary American Poetry*. He has published four full-length collections of poems: *Relics* (Wesleyan, 1984), *Tropical Depressions* (Iowa, 1988), *Color Photographs of the Ruins* (Pittsburgh, 1992), and *Winter Amnesties* (Southern Illinois, 2000). Among his awards are two fellowships from the National Endowment for the Arts, three fellowships from the Ohio Arts Council, the Iowa Poetry Prize, and the Randall Jarrell Poetry Prize. In 1996, he was presented the Ohioana Poetry Award in recognition of his contributions to poetry as a teacher, publisher, and poet. His poem "Undead White European Male" was included in *The Best American Poetry 1995*. "Smoking" was reprinted in *The Best American Poetry 1997* and *Scanning the Century: The Penguin Book of the Twentieth Century in Poetry*. His critical writing has appeared in *North Dakota Quarterly*, *Mississippi Review*, *Teaching Wallace Stevens* (Tennessee, 1994), and *Temperamental Journeys: Essays on the Modern Literature of Travel* (Georgia, 1992), among others. He, his wife Helen, and family make their home in Akron, Ohio.

Louise Glück

Louise Glück teaches at Williams College. She attended Sarah Lawrence College and Columbia University. She currently serves as Poet Laureate and Consultant in Poetry to the Library of Congress. Her work has appeared in many magazines and journals, among them the *American Poetry Review*, *Ironwood*, the *Yale Review*, *Partisan Review*, and the *Virginia Quarterly Review*. She is the author of nine books of poetry: *Firstborn* (New American Library, 1968), *The House on Marshland* (Ecco, 1975), *Descending Figure* (Ecco, 1980), *The Triumph of Achilles* (Ecco, 1985), *Ararat* (Ecco, 1990), *The Wild Iris* (Ecco, 1992), *Meadowlands* (Ecco, 1996), *Vita Nova* (Ecco, 1999), and *The Seven Ages* (Ecco, 2001). Her critical essays are collected in *Proofs and Theories: Essays on*

Poetry (Ecco, 1994). Glück won the Pulitzer Prize for *The Wild Iris* in 1993. She has also received the National Book Critics Circle Award for poetry, the William Carlos Williams Award, and the PEN/Martha Albrand Award for Nonfiction. She lives in Cambridge, Massachusetts.

Emily Grosholz

Emily Grosholz is professor of philosophy and African American studies and a fellow of the Institute for the Arts and Humanities Studies at Pennsylvania State University. She is also an advisory editor for the *Hudson Review*. Grosholz took her BA at the University of Chicago (1972) and her PhD at Yale University (1978). Recipient of a Guggenheim Fellowship for poetry, she is the author of four books of poems: *The River Painter* (Illinois, 1984), *Shores and Headlands* (Princeton, 1988), *Eden* (Johns Hopkins, 1992), and *The Abacus of Years* (Godine, 2001). She also edited *Telling the Barn Swallow: Poets on the Poetry of Maxine Kumin* (New England, 1997), and has written numerous essays and reviews. Her philosophical works include books on Descartes, Leibniz, and *The Growth of Mathematical Knowledge* (2000). Born and raised in Philadelphia, she now lives with her husband Robert R. Edwards and their four children in State College, Pennsylvania.

Rachel Hadas

Rachel Hadas is professor of English at the Newark campus of Rutgers University, and has also taught at Columbia University and Princeton University, as well as at the Sewanee Writers Conference. She earned her BA at Harvard University (1969), her MA at Johns Hopkins University (1977), and her PhD at Princeton University (1982). She is the author of numerous books of poetry: *Slow Transparency* (Wesleyan, 1983), *A Son from Sleep* (Wesleyan, 1987), *Pass It On* (Princeton, 1989), *Mirrors of Astonishment* (Rutgers, 1992), *The Empty Bed* (Wesleyan, 1995), *Halfway Down the Hall* (Wesleyan, 1998), and *Indelible* (Wesleyan, 2001). Her scholarly and critical volumes include *Form, Cycle, Infinity: Landscape Imagery in the Poetry of Robert Frost and George Seferis* (Bucknell, 1985), *Living in Time* (Rutgers, 1990), *The Double Legacy* (Faber & Faber, 1995), and *Merrill, Cavafy, Poems and Dreams* (Michigan, 2000). She has also translated Seneca's tragedy

Oedipus the King and Euripedes' tragedy *Helen*. Hadas divides her time between Danville, Vermont, and New York City.

Robert Hass

Robert Hass currently teaches at the University of California, Berkeley. He was educated at St. Mary's College of California (BA, 1963) and Stanford University (MA, 1965; PhD, 1971). His books of poetry include *Field Guide* (Yale, 1973), *Praise* (Ecco, 1979), *Human Wishes* (Ecco, 1989), and *Sun Under Wood: New Poems* (Ecco, 1996). With Czeslaw Milosz, he has translated several collections. Of these *Road-Side Dog* (Farrar, Straus & Giroux, 1999) is the most recent. Hass is also the author or editor of several collections of essays and translations: *Twentieth Century Pleasures: Prose on Poetry* (Ecco, 1984), *The Essential Haiku: Versions of Basho, Buson, and Issa* (Ecco, 1994), and *Poet's Choice: Poems for Everyday Life* (Ecco, 1998). His poetry has appeared in many national and international publications, among them: *Poetry Wales, Partisan Review*, the *American Poetry Review, Poetry*, and *TriQuarterly*. He is the recipient of the Yale Series of Younger Poets, the American Institute and Academy of Arts and Letters, and the National Book Critics Circle awards, among others. He served as Poet Laureate of the United States from 1995 to 1997. He lives in Kensington, California.

Paul M. Hedeen

Paul M. Hedeen teaches writing, contemporary literature, and film at Wartburg College. He earned his degrees at Kent State University (BA, 1976), the University of Akron (MA, 1984), and Northwestern University (PhD, 1990). His poetry and critical writing have appeared in numerous magazines and journals, including the *North American Review, Rosebud, Philosophy and Literature*, the *Maine Scholar, Modern Fiction Studies, Language and Style*, the *Great Lakes Review, Southwest Review, Voices International*, and *Confrontation*. He received the Margaret Church Memorial Prize, best essay for the year 1985, at *Modern Fiction Studies* and teaching awards from the University of Maine at Fort Kent and Wartburg College. He was the Carnegie/CASE Iowa Professor of the Year, 1999-2000. He lives in Waverly, Iowa, with his wife Kate and two daughters, Marian and Sarah.

Jane Hirshfield

Jane Hirshfield has taught at the University of California, Berkeley, and the University of San Francisco. She is currently on the core faculty of the Bennington MFA Writing Seminars. Hirshfield attended Princeton University where she earned her AB (1973). She is the author of five books of poetry: *Alaya* (Quarterly Review of Literature Poetry Series, 1982), *Of Gravity & Angels* (Wesleyan, 1988), *The October Palace* (Harper Collins, 1994), *The Lives of the Heart* (Harper Collins, 1997), and *Given Sugar, Given Salt* (Harper Collins, 2001). She has collected her essays in *Nine Gates: Entering the Mind of Poetry* (Harper Collins, 1997). She has received fellowships from the Guggenheim and Rockefeller Foundations, and her work has received the Bay Area Book Reviewers Award, the Poetry Center Book Award, and other honors. Her poems have appeared in the *Atlantic Monthly*, the *New Yorker*, the *New Republic*, the *Nation*, and many literary periodicals. Hirshfield lives in Mill Valley, California.

Mark Jarman

Mark Jarman is professor of English at Vanderbilt University. A graduate of the University of California, Santa Cruz (BA, 1974) and the University of Iowa (MFA, 1976), he is the author of seven books of poetry: *North Sea* (Cleveland State, 1978), *The Rote Walker* (Carnegie-Mellon, 1981), *Far and Away* (Carnegie-Mellon, 1985), *The Black Riviera* (Wesleyan, 1990), *Iris* (Story Line, 1992), *Questions for Ecclesiastes* (Story Line, 1997), and *Unholy Sonnets* (Story Line, 2000). With David Mason, he has edited *Rebel Angels: 25 Poets of the New Formalism* (Story Line, 1996). Jarman's awards include a Joseph Henry Jackson Award for his poetry in 1974, three NEA grants in poetry in 1977, 1983, and 1992, and a fellowship in poetry from the John Simon Guggenheim Memorial Foundation for 1991-1992. His book *The Black Riviera* won the 1991 Poets' Prize. *Questions for Ecclesiastes* was a finalist for the 1997 National Book Critics Circle Award in poetry and won the 1998 Lenore Marshall Poetry Prize from the Academy of American Poets and the *Nation* magazine. His poetry and essays have been published widely in such periodicals and journals as the *American Poetry Review*, the *Gettysburg Review*, the *Hudson Review*, the *New Yorker*, and *Poetry*. Jarman has published two recent collections of essays: *The Secret of Poetry* (Story Line, 2001), and *Body and Soul* (Michigan, 2002). He lives in Nashville with his wife Amy and two daughters.

Mary Kinzie

Mary Kinzie teaches at Northwestern University and serves as head of the undergraduate writing major. She served as executive editor of *TriQuarterly* magazine from 1975 to 1978 and for six years as editor of Elpenor Books. She graduated from Northwestern University (BA, 1967) and did graduate work at the Free University of Berlin and John Hopkins University (PhD, 1970). More than 150 of her poems have appeared in various magazines and national journals. *The Threshold of the Year* (Missouri, 1982) won the 1982 Devins Award for a first volume of verse. Among the volumes that have followed are *Summers of Vietnam* (Sheep Meadow, 1990), *Autumn Eros and Other Poems* (Knopf, 1991), and *Ghost Ship* (Knopf, 1996), and *Drift* (Knopf, 2003). Kinzie has also won numerous awards from the Illinois Arts Council, the *Southwest Review*, and the Poetry Society of America, and grants from the Illinois Arts Council and the Guggenheim Foundation, among others. Much of her critical work has been collected in *The Cure of Poetry in an Age of Prose: Moral Essays on the Poet's Calling* (Chicago, 1993), *The Judge Is Fury: Dislocation and Form in Poetry* (Michigan, 1994), and *A Poet's Guide to Poetry* (Chicago, 1999). She makes her home in Evanston, Illinois.

David Mason

David Mason teaches at Colorado College. He earned his BA there in 1978 and his PhD at the University of Rochester (1989). Mason has written two prize-winning books of poems: *The Buried Houses* (Story Line, 1991) and *The Country I Remember* (Story Line, 1996). With Mark Jarman, he is coeditor of *Rebel Angels: 25 Poets of the New Formalism* (Story Line, 1996) and with John Frederick Nims the fourth edition of *Western Wind: An Introduction to Poetry* (McGraw-Hill, 1999). Mason's essays are collected in *The Poetry of Life* (Story Line, 1999). He has written for many periodicals, including the *Hudson Review, Poetry, Mondo Greco*, the *Georgia Review*, the *New Criterion*, the *Southern Review*, and the *Irish Times*. He lives in Woodland Park, Colorado.

Robert McDowell

Robert McDowell—poet, critic, fiction writer, and screenwriter—is the publisher and editor of Story Line Press. He has also taught literature and writing at the University of Southern Indiana and at the University of California, Santa Cruz. He took his BA at Santa Cruz (1974) and his MFA at Columbia University (1976). His books of poems include *At the House of the Tin Man* (Chowder, 1980), *Quiet Money* (Holt, 1987), and *On Foot, In Flames* (Pittsburgh, 2002). Other writings have appeared in many publications, including the *Hudson Review*, the *American Scholar*, *London Magazine*, and *Poetry*. He works and makes his home in Ashland, Oregon.

D. G. Myers

D. G. Myers is associate professor of English and religious studies at Texas A&M University. He was educated at the University of California, Santa Cruz (BA, 1974), Washington University (AM, 1977), and Northwestern University (PhD, 1989), where he held the *TriQuarterly* Fellowship. Author of *The Elephants Teach: Creative Writing Since 1880* (Prentice Hall, 1996), he is now writing a book on the cultural reception of the Holocaust. His scholarship and criticism have appeared in *Comparative Literature*, *American Literary History*, *Commentary*, the *Weekly Standard*, the *AWP Chronicle*, the *Sewanee Review*, and elsewhere. He makes his home in Houston with wife Naomi and twin sons Dov and Saul.

Robert Pinsky

Robert Pinsky is the thirty-ninth Poet Laureate of the United States. He teaches in the graduate writing program at Boston University. He earned his BA from Rutgers University (1962) and both his MA (1965) and PhD (1966) from Stanford University. Among his numerous books of poetry are *Sadness and Happiness* (Princeton, 1975), *An Explanation of America* (Princeton, 1980), which was awarded the Saxifrage Prize, *History of My Heart* (Ecco, 1985), which was chosen for the 1985 William Carlos Williams Prize of the Poetry Society of America, *The Want Bone* (Harper Collins, 1991), and *The Figured Wheel: New and Collected Poems 1965-1995* (Farrar, Straus & Giroux , 1996), which was nominated for the Pulitzer Prize in poetry and also received the Lenore

Marshall Award and the Ambassador Book Award of the English Speaking Union. *Jersey Rain* (Farrar, Straus & Giroux , 2000) is a recent poetry collection. Pinsky's books of criticism include *Landor's Poetry* (Chicago, 1968), *The Situation of Poetry* (Princeton, 1977), and his collection of essays, *Poetry and the World* (Ecco, 1988), which was nominated for the National Book Critics Circle award in criticism. He is also co-translator of *The Separate Notebooks, by Czeslaw Milosz* (Ecco, 1988). His book *The Inferno of Dante* (Farrar, Straus and Giroux, 1995), a new verse translation, was awarded the *Los Angeles Times* Book Award in poetry and the Howard Morton Landon Prize for translation. Of late, he has published *The Sounds of Poetry: A Brief Guide* (Farrar, Straus & Giroux, 1998) and *The Handbook of Heartbreak* (Morrow, 1998), an anthology. Pinsky's work has appeared in many journals and anthologies, including *Antaeus*, the *New Yorker*, the *Paris Review*, and *The Norton Anthology of Modern Poetry*. He lives in Newton, Massachusetts.

Rosanna Warren

Rosanna Warren teaches at Boston University. She took her BA (1976) at Yale University and her MA (1980) at John Hopkins University. She also studied at the New York Studio School, Paris Program (1975); the Skowhegan School of Painting and Sculpture (1974); and the Accademia delle Belle Arti, Rome (1971-1972). Among her awards are a Yaddo Fellowship, June–July 1980; an Ingram Merrill Grant for Poetry, 1983; the Lavan Younger Poets Prize, Academy of American Poets, 1992; Lamont Poetry Prize, Academy of American Poets, 1993; and the May Sarton Prize, New England Poetry Club, 1995. Her books of poems include *Snow Day* (Palaemon, 1981), *Each Leaf Shines Separate* (Norton, 1984), and *Stained Glass*, (Norton, 1993). She has edited a number of collections, among them: William Arrowsmith's translation of Eugenio Montale's *Satura* (Norton, 1998), *In Time: Women's Poetry from Prison* (with Teresa Iverson, Boston, 1995), and *Springshine: Poetry from Prison* (with Meg Tyler, Boston 1998). She lives in Roslindale, Massachusetts.

A

Musée des Beaux Arts, 39; prosodic facility, 116; rejection of lyric, 122–24; *September 1, 1939*, 111; Spender and, 274; syllabic verse and, 116–17, 121; turn from politics, 125

audience: academic, 283; appropriate for, 102; community and, 193; dedicated, 294; demands upon, 189; diverse, 290; enlarging poetry's, 298, 301–02; imaginary, 304–06; independence of, 210; new, 188; poetry's lost, 191, 291, 295–97; poetry's specialist, 13, 282, 286, 299; shaking up an, 35; specific, 87, 307; success with, 69; Whitman on, 291

Austen, Jane, 256

authority, 38, 39, 44, 48, 112, 117, 238, 255, 295, 303

autonomy, artistic, 210

AWP Chronicle, 284, 286

B

Barth, John, 266, 283

Barthelme, Donald: on beginnings, 36

Barthes, Roland, 229

Basho: *The Royal Road to the North*, 256

Bawer, Bruce, 14; on poetic value, 288–89

Beardsley, Monroe, 229

Beat Generation, 265

Beethoven, Ludwig von, 262

Bell, Marvin: on beginnings, 37, 42; on titles, 30

Bellow, Saul, 271

Belushi, John, 157

Bennett, Arnold, 272

Beowulf, 109

Berry, Wendell: on contemporary poetry, 265

Berryman, John, 292, 295; *Dream Songs*, 40; *Love and Fame*, 70–71; on Auden, 39; on Stephen Crane, 15–16

Bible, 80, 139, 149, 153

Bidart, Frank, 223

Bishop, Elizabeth, 40, 104, 285, 295, 314; *Crusoe in England*, 213; interviewed, 273

Blackmur, R. P., 11, 14, 62; career, 294–95

Blake, William, 100

Bly, Robert, 37, 51, 290; *American Poetry*, 287

Ellington, Duke, 320
Ellison, Ralph, 150
Emerson, Ralph Waldo, 63
energy, 45, 105, 122, 166, 170, 228, 282, 295, 302, 309, 314
enjambment, 124, 164, 166, 314
Epstein, Joseph, 290; *Who Killed Poetry?*, 284–85
Eros, 62
Eurydice, 231
evaluation, 18–20, 33, 55, 62, 75, 188–89, 227, 258, 287
exile, 82, 91, 116, 118–19, 122, 125, 140, 145, 155, 157; in
    Walcott, 197, 201–02
explication, 169, 171

F
feminism, 275, 290
Fenton, James, 188
Fiedler, Leslie, 284
finish, 41, 44–45, 47, 54, 56, 165. *See also* closure
Fitzgerald, Robert: interviewed, 269
Ford, Ford Madox: on titles, 29
form, poetic: advantage of, 67; consolations of, 230; criticism
    and, 11, 19; defying, 319; demands of, 306; elegy, 182–83,
    224; established, 228; finish in, 165; freely emerging, 227;
    grammatical, 100; haiku, 54; in Lowell, 178; in Tennyson,
    236; in Walcott, 145, 197, 199; inclusive, 312; Kumin on,
    46; literacy and, 110; lyric, 104, 111, 191, 218, 220, 284,
    291, 305; Mackenzie on, 54; new, 227; not mechanical, 219;
    ode, 34, 115–17, 119, 121, 181; opening lines and, 43; par-
    allel, 49; public, 291; repetition and, 99–100, 156; resource-
    ful, 313; restoration of, 35; Roethke on, 228; sonnet, 64–65,
    100; stereotyping of, 211; surprise and, 315; symbolic, 230;
    titles and, 34; traditional, 113
Forster, E. M., 263; *A Passage to India*, 215; *Howards End*, 239
Fortune, 294
Foucault, Michel: on the author, 228–29
free verse, 48, 110, 117, 199, 219–20, 312
Freud, Sigmund: as truth-teller, 124; death of, 115; effect on
    Auden, 122; effect on future, 123; exile, 119; on coitus, 176;
    on commerce, 218; triumph, 123

Hass, Robert: *Meditation at Lagunitas*, 43

Havelock, Eric A.: *Preface to Plato*, 102–03

Hayden, Robert: career, 294

Hecht, Anthony, 200, 290

Hemingway, Ernest, 263, 270

Herbert, George, 164; *The Altar*, 110

Hesiod, 97

Hirsch, Jr., E. D.: *Cultural Literacy*, 261

history, 74–78, 110, 134, 162, 172, 181, 192, 225–26, 284; of
art, 302; of poetry, 176

Hitler, Adolph, 115

Hollander, John, 124, 255

Holocaust, 157, 259

Homer, 97, 101–04; *Hymn to Hermes*, 111; *Iliad*, 241–42, 306;
Odyssey, 80, 159, 269–70

honesty: aesthetic, 218; distinguished from truth, 61; evaluation
of, 62; in anthologies, 301; in criticism, 291, 295; in lan-
guage, 299; sounding like, 69; writers of, 258

Hope, A. D., 225, 231–32, 285; on discursive poetry, 219–20

Hopkins, Gerard Manley, 311; *God's Grandeur*, 45

Horace, 116–18

Hound & Horn, 294

Howard, Richard, 188

Howe, Susan, 110

Hudson Review, 265, 267, 286

Hughes, Langston, 295

Hugo, Richard, 13, 38; on beginnings, 39

Hunt, William: *The Last Hour*, 231

I

Ignatow, David, 283

imagery: arriving upon, 267; as evidence, 169; breathtaking, 146;
closure and, 47, 50–51; deep, 112; energy and, 122; fierce,
148–49, 171; generalization and, 195; gnomic, 30; Homeric,
306; in Ashbery, 192; in titles, 31; in Walcott, 199, 201;
leaps of, 191; meaning and, 189; memorable, 111; orgasmic,
46; precise, 54; profuse, 220; recycled, 159; religious,
167–73; sauntering, 133; sexual, 175; subliminal power of,
168; surprising, 37; surrealistic, 134, 168; tension of, 41

imagination, 103–04, 147, 162, 174, 178, 195–96, 219, 222, 224, 232, 247, 313

imitation, 140, 145, 156, 178, 198–99, 224, 240, 314

Inge, William, 270

interpretation, 33–34, 74, 76–79, 93, 107, 214, 247, 258

intertextuality, 248

Interview (magazine), 275

interviews, 14–15, 44, 45; accuracy of, 270–71; as oral biography, 277–78; critical standards and, 267; form of, 262; fun of, 279; good interviewers and, 275–76; para-critical, 268–69; personality and, 271–74; popularity of, 262–63; reverent, 287; self-promotion and, 274–75; vérités, 264–65

Ionesco, Eugene, 266

Iowa Writers' Workshop, 18

Iowa, University of, 293

irony: in Ashbery, 224; in Justice, 181–86; in Larkin, 53; in Levine, 314; in Lowell, 172, 177; in Walcott, 137, 153; in Wright, 305

Issa, 54

J

Jacoby, Russell: *The Last Intellectuals*, 282

Jakobson, Roman: *Subliminal Verbal Patterning*, 100

James, Henry: on George Sand, 239

Jarman, Mark, 12

Jarrell, Randall, 12, 14, 40, 285; critical writing, 268, 294–95

Jeffers, Robinson, 163, 285, 293–94, 296

Jefferson, Thomas, 307

Jet, 142

Jones, Chuck: *Daffy Duck in Hollywood*, 193

Jones, Rodney: *Transparent Gestures*, 283

Jonson, Ben, 11, 199–200

Joyce, James, 199

Justice, Donald, 13, 39, 42, 49, 186, 290; elegies, 183, 185; minimalism, 182; neglect, 181; *Ode to a Dressmaker's Dummy*, 34; *Poem*, 182–83; *The Telephone Number of the Muse*, 186; *Unflushed Urinals*, 184–85

S